THE FULFILLMENT OF THE SCRIPTURES

THE FULFILLMENT OF THE SCRIPTURES: ABRAHAM, MOSES, AND PIERS ℂ *By Ruth M. Ames*

NORTHWESTERN UNIVERSITY PRESS

EVANSTON 1970

Ruth M. Ames is Assistant Professor of English at Queensborough Community College of the City University of New York.

Contents

List of Abbreviations

Ante-Nicene Library

Translations of the Writings of the Fathers down to A.D. *325.* Ante-Nicene Christian Library. Edited by Alexander Roberts and James Donaldson. Edinburgh, 1867.

Nicene and Post-Nicene Fathers

A Select Library of Nicene and Post-Nicene Fathers of the Christian Church. Edited by Philip Schaff. New York, 1890–1908. 2d ser. Edited by Philip Schaff and Henry Wace. New York, 1890–1900.

PL

Patrologiae Cursus Completus— Series Latina. Edited by J. P. Migne.

THE FULFILLMENT OF THE SCRIPTURES

Chapter I

THE SIGNIFICANCE OF THE FULFILLMENT OF THE

SCRIPTURES ⟪Medieval literature is filled with Biblical stories that are familiar even to those who do not read the Bible. It is saturated, too, with seemingly strange efforts to teach Christian doctrine through Old Testament stories. In the great cycles of plays, for example, we all recognize the plot and the cast. We are less easy, however, when the Old Testament patriarchs and prophets teach the Trinity and the Incarnation, when the Creator identifies himself in the play on Genesis by quoting from Revelation, and when speech and dress are modern-medieval. Not only do past, present, and future mingle on the middle stage called earth, but heaven and hell are viewed concurrently on the upper and lower stages.

It is this looking up and down and back and forth that seems most peculiar to later readers. In part, the strangeness is due simply to a change in theatrical technique; but the fact that we use only the middle stage means something in the history of ideas as well as in the history of the drama. Whether or not we share the doctrine, we are more comfortable with the devices and time machinery that have survived not only because they have survived, but because they represent our way of looking at the universe. In a modern work, whether the characters go on foot, ship, or plane, whether their destination be Canterbury, the moon, or hell, the action moves, as it were, on the middle stage. A medieval writer in the tradition of the mysteries would be more likely to place his hero on a ramp, with a bridge tower overhead and a tunnel below, with traffic moving back and forth, and ready communications up and down.

The dreamer in *Piers Plowman* does, in fact, see a field full of folk, set between a tower of truth and a pit of falsehood. The machinery does not creak as in the plays, but it is obviously the same machinery, and it serves the same purpose. The purpose is made clear in the first canto in which Holy Church descends from the tower

3

to teach the dreamer in the field how to avoid the pit. In the course of the poem, Abraham, Moses, Jesus, and the dreamer all meet on the field, and all are equally informed on fourteenth-century social problems and Christian doctrine. This meeting of men and ideas is no accident; what we separate as Old and New Testament, as politics and religion, as past and present, Langland brings together. In this framework of the eternal and the temporal, all the characters move freely in both time and space. When we learn to move freely in it, we see that Langland's "present" means the twentieth century as well as the fourteenth. The dreamer's questions about the meaning of salvation, the place in that salvation of the Jews and the righteous heathen, and the justice and mercy of God are still asked. And the answers of Langland's Abraham, Moses, and Jesus are still worth listening to.

The leaps of imagination that make time seem to touch eternity in *Piers* are not readily found elsewhere. But the theological view implicit in the poem was commonplace enough in the Middle Ages. The same way of looking at the world and the Scriptures and of teaching Christian doctrine through the Old Testament appears in apologetics, homilies, and devotions, in romances and legends and versified histories of the world. Although there is no one formula which neatly decodes all these Scriptural references and allegories, there is, I believe, one theme that underlies and runs through a great many of them—the fulfillment of the Scriptures.

The Doctrine of Fulfillment

The fulfillment of the law and the prophets is one of the basic tenets of Christianity; it is the main theme of the Gospels, the Acts, and the Epistles. Christians still hold that Jesus, by his life, death, and Resurrection, fulfilled all the Old Testament promises of redemption —that he was the promised Messias, the Incarnate Word who fulfilled the law and through whom the word of God was carried to the Gentiles. But while the outline has not changed, the old way of filling it in has gone out of fashion. Chronology has triumphed: Abraham and Moses have been put back into the Old Testament, the old proofs are not related to contemporary affairs, and Revelation is only the last book of the New Testament. One might almost say that the doctrine itself has passed out of the general consciousness. True, it appears in works of theology and textbooks on religion; but it no longer has much impact on religious argument or experience. If one may judge by its absence from religious fiction, the fulfillment of the Scriptures neither convinces men of the truth of Christianity nor justifies the manner of Revelation.

For many centuries, it was strikingly otherwise. Church fathers and medieval poets alike were enamored of the doctrine and of the way of presenting it. They used it not only to support the claims of Jesus but also to show how God transcends time and history and how Revelation is unfolded by each generation. The same texts served to argue with the Jews, to convert the Gentiles, and to edify and refresh the faithful. Even those who slept through the sermon had only to open their eyes to see the symbols of the argument portrayed on the church windows and walls. At about the time of the Renaissance, however, the figurative, prophetic interpretation of the Old Testament was supplanted by the literal view; the old arguments and allegories finally lost their hold and were then gradually forgotten.

They are worth recalling, I believe, as something more than a closed chapter in the history of ideas. The doctrine of fulfillment and the way of proving it are part of the Judaeo-Christian heritage, and a study of that heritage helps us to understand not only the basic ideas and attitudes of authors we still read but also our own cultural and religious history. Formulated by the first Jewish-Christians in their attempts to convert their fellow Jews, the doctrine of the fulfillment of the Scriptures stressed the Judaism of Christianity. The apostolic method of "proving" the fulfillment of the Trinity, of the Messianic promises, and of the law out of the Old Testament was enlarged on by the Fathers and became an enormously influential convention among Christians at large, without ever quite losing the impress of the controversy with the Jews. At the same time, the exegetical methods of the tradition continued to propagate an essentially Judaic and Scriptural view of Christianity and of the history of the world. And since both form and substance were assimilated in the literature in Old and Middle English, a study of that tradition throws light on a number of points in that literature—on obscure Scriptural allusions, on apparent anachronisms, on remarks about the Jews and Judaism, and on the Judaic emphasis of so much Christian thinking.

5

THE IMPACT OF THE DOCTRINE ON EARLY CHRISTIAN THOUGHT

Our principal concern is with the influence of the doctrine on the mainstream of Christian thought, especially on *Piers Plowman*, which was written for Christians, not Jews. But there is no escaping the controversial background, for the fact that the Jews had rejected and continued to reject Christianity continued to influence life and thought throughout the Middle Ages. It seems as though Christians, in order to prove that they were right, had to keep proving that the Jews were wrong, even if there were no Jews present. And the points that were developed in argument with the Jews became part of the standard proof of the doctrine. The same proofs appear in Bede and Cynewulf and Aelfric; in the Anglo-Norman debates with the Jews; in medieval homilies, legends, plays, and allegories. In fiction, the point is sometimes lost and the proofs are often cryptic because an author not really interested in the controversy with the Jews was nonetheless drawing on a familiar exegetical tradition. The meaning of the Scriptural references in such works is likely to escape us because the tradition has been forgotten.

Langland, for example, often seems difficult even when he is not, simply because he did not feel it necessary to explain what was obvious to him and to his contemporaries. A surprising number of Scriptural texts and arguments had appeared in similar contexts from the earliest days of the Church through the Middle Ages, in popular as well as in learned works. The same Messianic prophecies, the same arguments on the Trinity and the law, the same mystical and allegorical interpretations of Scripture, the same Old Testament heroes appear not only in *Piers* but in dozens of other medieval works. Langland had no reason to suspect that his work would ever need a learned gloss. Many of his contemporaries might miss his aesthetic subtleties, but they would surely catch his Scriptural references, most of which were taught from pulpit, paintings, and stage. But Langland was not a theologian writing a tract, or a hack excerpting a sermon, but a poet seeing a vision. Even in his most prosaic discussions, instead of explaining, he freely alludes and digresses. Though some of the allegories may be lost on the modern reader, they are actually derived directly from old material—the episode of the Good Samaritan, for

6

example, is a poetic transformation of a well-known allegory of the fulfillment of the law.

Furthermore, the ideas underlying the proofs of the doctrine help to explain why, to the modern reader, the history in many medieval works seems so curiously muddled and anachronistic. The popularity of Old Testament prophecies and prefigurations accounts for some of the foreknowledge of the Scriptural figures portrayed, for authors and readers alike were familiar with the texts which foretold events not only in the life of Jesus but in the history of the Church; prefigured in Scripture, for example, were the sacraments of the Church and the supplanting of the Synagogue by the Church. But besides quoting prophecies, Old Testament figures enunciate Christian dogma in detail; and in the medieval histories of the world, in the mysteries, and in the many allegories—past, present, and future are run together in a scene or a sentence.

Of course many of these authors seem to have been writing by rote, and one would be slow to credit them with either insight or profundity. Still, they were probably as aware as the rest of us of the straight line of history—1066 and all that. But they also inherited what Erich Auerbach has called, in a most perceptive essay, the "figural" interpretation of Scripture and history, which he traces to the "phenomenal prophecy" of the Fathers.

> Figural prophecy implies the interpretation of one worldly event through another. The first signifies the second, the second fulfills the first. Both remain historical events; yet both, looked at in this way, have something provisional and incomplete about them; they point to one another and both point to something in the future. . . .[1]

Auerbach believes that this combination of prophecy and historicity helps to explain the "mixture of spirituality and the sense of reality which characterize the European Middle Ages and which seems so baffling to us." This "historicity both of the sign and what it signifies" distinguishes *figura* from abstract allegory. Auerbach traces this difference to the fact that figural prophecy grew out of the Christian break with Judaism and then served a historical function in the Christian mission to the Gentiles.

---

1. Erich Auerbach, "Figura," trans. Ralph Manheim, in *Scenes from the Drama of European Literature* (New York, 1959), pp. 54, 61.

When this application of the figural to history became a convention, as it did in the early centuries of the Church, texts and events were often juxtaposed with little or no explanation. But thoughtful men were not simply juggling texts to prove a point. They assumed, even if they did not always articulate, both the unity and continuity of Revelation that were set forth by St. Paul and the Fathers and medieval theologians like Grosseteste.

From the earliest days of the Church, the unity of Abraham, Moses, and Jesus had been taught: unity in faith as well as in morals. God does not change and, if the doctrines of the Church are true, they must have been always true. The first Christians believed precisely this: that their teaching was not new but the fulfillment and clarification of the old. The whole New Testament, it was said, was foreshadowed in the Old, and the meaning of the Old Testament was unveiled in the New. That is not to say that Revelation has no history. While God is the same from the beginning, the knowledge of God has only gradually been revealed; for though the saints of the Old Testament understood some of it, it was opened to all men by Jesus. This kind of interpretation was not only a way of looking at the Bible but a way of looking at the universe and at the history of mankind. Dwelling on the unity of the Old and New Testaments, the Fathers not only "proved" the truth of Christianity but saw the same Truth throughout Scripture and the working out of the providence of God in history. Even second-rate authors saw past, present, and future, heaven, earth, and hell all related and interrelated under God, both in time and in eternity. The three stages of the mysteries, on which heaven, earth, and hell are all viewed at once, are but a graphic symbol of this theological view of the universe.

Langland's Artistry

As *Piers* surpasses these plays in artistry and insight, so it transcends all the other works we shall glance at. In these other works we pause only to note the repetition of points and texts and variations in tone and manner. In *Piers*, it is often a joy to analyze the way in which the common material was transformed into a unique work of art. While the details of the tradition illuminate many passages in the poem, the vision of the poet amplifies the meaning of the tradition itself.

That is not to say, however, that in his use of the traditional material Langland always rose above the prejudices of his time. Applying the Messianic prophecies to the fate of the Jews, he argues that it was because of their rejection of the Messias that they were rejected by God and were therefore deprived of country and citizenship. At the same time, however, he was deeply troubled by the irony that it *was* the Jews who had crucified Jesus, for the same tradition stressed the Jewishness of the Messias. And when Langland urges the clergy to convert the Jews, he keeps reminding them to begin with the common ground of Jews and Christians—belief in the same God the Father and the same Scriptures.

The disbelief and the conversion of the Jews, however, are only of minor importance in *Piers;* it is the Scriptures that really count. It was in order to convince and convert Christians that Langland used the old exegetical methods and then went beyond them to realize the deepest implications of the Scriptural argument.

Like other medieval authors, Langland cites chapter and verse to prove that the Trinity appeared to Abraham. He goes further than most of his contemporaries in portraying Abraham as the chief expositor of the Trinity and in running texts and times and Testaments together with no regard for chronology. But underlying this apparently gross anachronism is a view of God and man that is far from naïve. Like the Fathers, Langland sees that if the doctrine of the Trinity is true, it was always true; and that if the same God appears in both Testaments, the God of the Old Testament must have been Trinitarian. Further, since the triune God was always charity, it follows for Langland that wherever and whenever men practice love, they begin to know the Trinity. It was because of his great goodness and faith that Abraham was able to recognize and adore the Trinity and then to become the teacher of the doctrine for all time.

As Langland loved the unquestioning faith of Abraham, so he reverenced the law of Moses. Throughout the poem, he discusses and allegorizes the law. In the episodes of the Good Samaritan, the dinner party, the pardon of Piers, and the debate between Christ and Satan, his familiarity with the old arguments on Christ's fulfillment of the law is apparent. But Langland does not discuss such practical matters as the changes in the eating habits of Jews and Christians, or even the fulfillment of circumcision in baptism, as did most writers.

Indeed, he surpasses even the theologians in his understanding of the law as an aspect of the Truth that is beyond time. Always he stresses the unity of the two Testaments; always he insists that as Christ fulfilled the law in his life, so the Scriptures must be fulfilled by every man.

In brief, he used the tradition, as he used everything else that came to hand, to call men back to the great truths of religion. Langland was anything but the "blind traditionalist" who defends unquestioningly the *status quo;* in fact he was always doing battle against religious practices which, he considered, had become traditional for the wrong reasons. Comfortably pious persons get short shrift from him, for he doubts that they can save their souls by fasting and churchgoing if they do not have charity for the poor. The popular ways of gaining indulgences he condemns almost entirely. The traditional pilgrim with staff and scrip is, for him, a figure for satire. And the miracles that fill medieval story are rather surprisingly absent from his book of visions. The dreamer finds himself in odd places, but he is not carried there by rudderless boats.

The miracles described in *Piers* are the great miracles of Scripture. Scripture (understood literally and figuratively) is the standard by which all else is measured. The basis of Langland's attack on the corrupt practice of indulgences is that it bypasses the law. On Judgment Day, he thunders, a man will be safe with the Ten Commandments, not with bought pardons. The professional pilgrim is condemned because he does not seek first the Truth taught by the Scriptures; Langland's pilgrims must follow Abraham, Moses, and Jesus. And the Jews are condemned because they reject the Messias taught by their own Scriptures. Whatever else Langland questions, he accepts with his whole mind and heart the authority of Scripture and its continuing relevance to both the affairs of men and the doctrines of the Church.

Actually, Langland does not separate doctrine from practical affairs as most men do. He had no patience with the philosophers and dialecticians who tended, then as now, to make theology a subject in the university curriculum, and he rebuked those priests who preached over the heads of the congregation in the language of the schools. His Trinity is no philosophical abstraction but the God of Israel, whose justice and mercy can be understood only insofar as they are practiced. Like the prophets, Langland believed that true religion consists in caring for the poor, the fatherless, the widowed, and the stranger. This is his "Truth of Trinity," and this is the law that the Second Person fulfilled in his life and death. It was the same God of Love who created the heavens and man, appeared to Abraham, gave the Law to Moses, and spoke through the prophets, the same who became man. Entirely confident that the same Truth is taught in both Testaments, Langland quotes parallel passages, whether he is raging against the complacency of the clergy, or sorrowing over the miserable, or allegorizing the Trinity and the law.

I do not mean to suggest that the doctrine of the fulfillment of the Scriptures is the only key to the meaning of *Piers*. *Piers* was the product of a lifetime of study, prayer, and creation. Just as Langland looked at God and men in a multitude of aspects, many ways are required to look fully at his masterpiece. In their introduction to a new edition of *Piers*, Professors Salter and Pearsall remark that Auerbach's description of figural interpretation makes it "easier to understand the whole complex relationship between the real, the literal, the dramatic and the spiritual in *Piers Plowman*."[2] Similarly, I believe, a study of the traditional teaching on the fulfillment of the Trinity, the Messianic promises, and the law helps us to understand Langland's Scriptural references, his choice of heroes and their significance in his allegory, and, indeed, his basic theology. His use of the tradition also opens one corner of his mind and art. He did not simply borrow scraps of argument and piece them together as so many lesser writers did. Partly because the material was so deeply rooted in tradition, he was free to use it as a springboard. He frequently reinterprets the old material in a way that reveals great independence of mind as well as hard thought. In discussing the Trinity, for example, Langland starts with the old proofs, many of which are no longer considered valid exegesis, and then raises questions modern enough to be debated by Christians of our own day, questions on the nature of Truth, the Church, and salvation. The quality of his art is revealed by the way he selects and rejects, assimilates and allegorizes the old material, transforming the conventions of others into a work of art uniquely his own. What is often

2. Elizabeth Salter and Derek Pearsall, eds., *Piers Plowman* (Evanston, Ill., 1967), p 24.

rather dry apologetic in other hands is touched in his by prophetic fire and a passion for God and for souls. The ancient doctrine of the fulfillment of the Scriptures, so often stereotyped in the hands of his contemporaries, became in his hands a vision of God and man filled with new and profound insights.

Chapter II

THE HISTORY OF THE DOCTRINE IN THE APOSTOLIC AND PATRISTIC PERIODS

¶ It is sometimes assumed by professors of literature that in its Christological reading of the Old Testament, the medieval Church strayed far from primitive Christianity. Actually, the searching of the Scriptures to prove their fulfillment in Christ and the Church is as old as Christianity itself. All the characteristics of the medieval tradition—the listing of Messianic prophecies, the proofs of the Trinity, the prefigurations of the Church, the contrasting of the Old and the New Laws, and the mystical and allegorical interpretations of texts—can be traced back through the Fathers to the apostolic Church. Some of these interpretations may seem fantastic to twentieth-century readers of medieval literature, but they were the commonplaces of first-century Jews and Christians, who used them in discussing and arguing the Faith.

THE GOSPELS

The first Christians, of course, were themselves Jews, and converted and unconverted alike shared the same exegesis. Indeed, the historic Jesus was himself a Jew who was brought up in and claimed the Judaic tradition. It was Jesus himself who insisted that he did all things so that the Scriptures might be fulfilled, and that he came not to abrogate but to fulfill the law and the prophets. In the last chapter of St. Luke, we find both his blanket endorsement of Christological interpretations of the Old Testament and a hint of how necessary such interpretations were for the peace of mind of the first Jewish-Christians. St. Luke tells us that, when the downcast disciples met the Master on the road to Emmaus, they did not recognize him, and they spoke only of the empty sepulcher. Jesus reproached them for their lack of faith, and "beginning at Moses and all the prophets, he expounded to them in all the Scriptures the things that were concerning him" (24:27).[1] Again in Jerusalem, he explained "that all things must need be fulfilled which are written in the law of Moses and in the prophets and in the psalms, concerning me." And "he opened their understanding, that they might understand the scriptures" (24:44–45). Only when the Master had confirmed the Crucifixion and the Resurrection from the Old Testament (24:46) were their troubled hearts set at rest.

That the Scriptures were to be opened in the mystical and allegorical way so popular among medieval writers is suggested by several other passages. For example, Jesus identified himself with the "stone" of Psalm 117 and of Isaias. In both Matthew (21:33–46) and Mark (12:1–11), Jesus tells the parable of the husbandmen who slew the only son of the owner of the vineyard and who were therefore driven away, with the vineyard then let out to other husbandmen. Jesus said to them, "Have you never read in the Scriptures: 'The Stone which the builders rejected, the same is become the head of the corner? By the Lord this has been done; and it is wonderful in our eyes' " (Ps. 117:22–23). As the vineyard was let out to other husbandmen, as the rejected stone became the cornerstone of a new building, so the kingdom of God would be taken from the Jews and given to others. And in explaining the parable, Jesus apparently referred to Isaias 8:14–15, saying that whoever falls on "this stone" will be broken (Matt. 21:44; Acts 4:11; Rom. 9:33; 1 Pet. 2:7).

MIDRASHIC EXPOSITION

The very ease with which such references are made throughout the New Testament suggests that the exegetical method implicit in them was not new. It was, in fact, familiar in the schools of Jerusalem, where the rabbis offered literal, allegorical, homiletic, and mystical interpretations of the historical acts of the Bible. Especially applicable

1. All references to the Bible are to the Douay Version. I have used the Douay because it is a translation of the Vulgate, the Latin Bible familiar to medieval writers.

to the method most popular among Christians was what was called a "midrash." The term "designates an exegesis which, going more deeply than the mere literal sense, attempts to penetrate into the spirit of the Scriptures, to examine the text from all sides, and thereby to derive interpretations which are not immediately obvious."[2]

This rabbinical method embodies a philosophy of Revelation that was most congenial to the Christians. In this finding of new meanings in Scripture, the rabbis presumably were not adding anything to Revelation. They believed the Word of God to be so rich and full that each generation might, in pious meditation, find meanings that had remained hidden from earlier scholars. As in the Catholic theory of the development of doctrine, the basic assumption of this interpretation is that God transcends time and history. Because God is eternal and immutable, his Word is valid for all time. But since man is mortal and changeable, he can only gradually understand the Scriptures. The meaning of events of the Biblical past may thus be clarified by contemporary affairs; and contemporary events may be tested against the message recorded long ago.

"The Talmud compares this kind of midrashic exposition to a hammer which awakens the slumbering sparks in the rock."[3] The basic truths, Jews and Christians agreed, were contained in the rock of Scripture. If, then, the Christian message was true, it could be hammered out of the Old Testament. The whole New Testament is in the Old, the Christians said, and the whole meaning of the Old is revealed in the New. The Trinity, the Incarnation, the Virgin Birth, the Crucifixion, the Resurrection, the calling of the Gentiles, the end of circumcision and sacrifice—all are taught in the Old Testament. Of course, all of these things were not clear before the advent of Christ; but all of the hidden meanings were unveiled by his life and teaching. The good men whose lives and words are recorded in Scripture were capable of perceiving part of God's meaning, and each one saw a little

2. *Jewish Encyclopedia,* s.v. "Midrash"; *Midrash Rabbah,* trans. H. Freedman and M. Simon (London: Soncino Press, 1961).

3. *Jewish Encyclopedia,* s.v. "Midrash"; *Hammer on the Rock: A Short Midrash Reader,* ed. Nahum N. Glatzer (New York, 1962), p. 7.

of the wisdom and the way of God. Finally, Wisdom himself came and opened the Way for all men.

St. Paul

That this was the meaning and method of the apostolic preaching is abundantly clear in the Acts and the Epistles. In both the opening and the conclusion of the Epistle to the Romans, Paul says that he has preached Christ to the Jews from Moses and the prophets. His gospel is but the "revelation of the mystery which was kept secret from eternity," and "now is made manifest by the scriptures of the prophets" (16:25–26). Before King Agrippa, he insists that there is nothing in his message which goes beyond what the prophets and Moses spoke of as things to come: a suffering Christ, and one who would show light to his people and to the Gentiles by being the first to rise from the dead (Acts 26:22–23). And in Berea, the Jews received such words "with all eagerness, daily searching the Scriptures, whether these things were so" (Acts 7:11).

In searching the Scriptures, the Jewish-Christians found parallels and prefigurations and allegories for the present in the past. St. Stephen, for example, compared the present with the past incredulity of the Jews. When Moses was sent by God to the Hebrews, instead of receiving him with joy, they asked, "Who has appointed you prince and judge over us?" Even after Moses had received the law and brought them out of Egypt and performed signs and wonders, they would not yield obedience but offered sacrifice to an idol. As they would not hear Moses, so they will not hear Jesus, the prophet promised by Moses. As they persecuted the prophets, so now they persecute the Christians (Acts 6:8 ff.).

Using a similar method of interpretation, St. Paul draws on the same history for a moral lesson. He writes to the Corinthians that they can learn from the sins of the Israelites to beware of counting too much on the favor of Christ. For while "our fathers" all passed through the Red Sea and were fed manna and drank water from the rock ("and the rock was Christ"), God was not pleased with most of them. "Now these things were done in a figure of us so that we should not covet evil things, as they also coveted." For "all these things" are "written for our correction" (1 Cor. 10).

"For it is written. . . ." Whatever the lesson, Paul supports it by quotations. When, for example, he tells the Romans that the Gentiles also were to glorify God, he quotes from Kings, two Psalms, and Isaias, the only connective being "and again," repeated three times. It may not be fair to blame St. Paul for the medieval failure to write smoothly; but he certainly set a style of stringing texts together without benefit of transition.

Even the allegorical form, so dear to the medieval writer, is found fully grown in St. Paul. Most famous was his interpretation of Isaac and Ishmael as the two Testaments and the two peoples. "For it is written," he writes to the Galatians, "that Abraham had two sons, the one by a bond woman and the other by a free woman." The son of the bond woman

was born according to the flesh; but he of the free woman was by promise. Which things are said by an allegory. For these are two testaments, the one from Mt. Sina engendering unto bondage, which is Agar. For Sina is a mountain in Arabia, which has affinity to that Jerusalem which now is; and is in bondage with her children. But that Jerusalem which is above is free: which is our mother. . . . Now we, brethren, as Isaac was, are the children of promise. But as then he that was born according to the flesh persecuted him that was after the spirit: so also it is now. But what say the Scriptures? Cast out the bondwoman and her son: for the son of the bondwoman shall not be heir with the son of the free woman (4:21–30).

The family image is peculiarly useful in describing the relations between the two peoples. The Galatians to whom Paul's allegory was addressed were Gentile converts who were so enamored of the mother religion as they had learned it from the Christians that they wanted to be Jewish-Christians, to be circumcised and to observe the law. At the same time, the Christians could not understand how the Jews, brothers of Jesus according to the flesh, could reject him who fulfilled the promises of their own prophets. For their part, the Jews had especial hatred for Paul because he who was so entirely Jewish, a Hebrew of the Hebrews, and a Pharisee learned in the law, taught Jews and Gentiles alike that the time had come to end circumcision, and with it the separateness of the Jewish nation. On both sides, the very closeness of the relationship easily turned what should have been brotherly love into fratricidal strife.

As all the elements of the early relationship, even to Judaizing,

continued through the centuries, so allegories similar to Paul's delighted the Christian world for the next fifteen hundred years. Any
Old Testament conflict of two sons over the inheritance of the father,
or of two wives over the favor of the husband, represented the
conflicting claims of Church and Synagogue to the kingdom of God.
The Synagogue is the elder, displaced by the younger Church; or the
Synagogue is the first wife, unloved but prolific, while the Church is
the long-barren beloved one, who finally bears the true heir.

THE CHURCH FATHERS

The continuing argument with the Jews probably had something to
do also with the medieval habit of ascribing authority to the Old
Testament, an attitude which goes considerably beyond what modern
Christians consider reverence. Such an attitude was inevitable in the
apostolic period, when both Jews and Jewish-Christians appealed to
the Bible as the only authority recognized by both sides. By the
second century, however, the Christian was usually a Gentile convert
(like the famous Justin Martyr); but he agreed at the outset of a
debate to refer all his points to the Old Testament. Strictly speaking,
he could not appeal to reason; nor was it within his province to
describe the beauty of Christ's parables or the emotional impact of the
Crucifixion. The acts of Jesus could be cited only insofar as they
fulfilled Messianic prophecies, the doctrines of the Church only as
they fulfilled the Scriptures.

It is harder to understand at first why the same method was
extended to the pagans, even to the apparent slighting of the Gospels.
But the fact is that in tract after tract addressed to both pagans and
Christians, the Fathers "prove" Christianity not out of the New
Testament but out of the Old—an extraordinary procedure to use with
pagans. In order to prove, for example, the possibility of Christ's
Resurrection after three days in the sepulcher, the Fathers point to
Jonas' emergence after three days in the whale. The parallel might
be meaningful to a Jew who accepted literally the story of Jonas, but
not, we would think, to a pagan. And when a fourth-century Gentile
convert, writing for pagans, says "we accept the Christ" and "en-
deavor prayerfully to tread in the steps of his teaching, for so we do

what Moses himself would approve,"[4] we are tempted to ask, "What's Moses to him or he to Moses?"

The approval of Moses is a recurrent theme in patristic apologetic primarily because the Fathers are often, explicitly or implicitly, answering the Jewish objection that Christianity departs from Moses. Again and again they insist that Jesus did not abrogate but fulfilled the Mosaic law. The permanent meaning of God's law is moral, they say, not ceremonial or national. In the old days, they explain, Jewish separatism was right, for the Jews believed in God while the heathen worshipped idols. But it is wrong now that the Gentiles worship the one God. It is, indeed, according to the promise of the patriarchs and the prophets that the Gentiles worship the God of the Jews and have reformed their lives in accordance with that worship. Adoration of the Son is not idol-worship: Moses himself stated the doctrine of the Trinity, and the prophets awaited the coming of God. Over and over again, the Fathers insist on the concordance of the two Testaments, on the unity of Abraham and Moses and Jesus. The same spirit of God, they say, is in both Testaments; the same Holy Spirit enlightened the hearts of David and Amos, of Peter and Paul; the same God who worked miracles for the Jews now works similar ones for the Christians. If, therefore, the Jews really followed Moses (as they say), they would follow Christ, as did Peter and Paul. For the Christians are the true Jews, the spiritual Israel; and the Church of the Nations is the true Synagogue of God.[5]

While Moses was thus a mouthpiece for an argument, he was also a great deal more to the pagan converts. They gladly accepted the authority of the Old Testament, and they desired to belong to the family of God. Gentile converts never denied the pagan charge that they had deserted their ancestral religion for the law of the Jews. On the contrary, a good part of antipagan polemic began with a defense of Judaism as a preliminary to a defense of Christianity. In *The*

---

4. Eusebius *Demonstratio Evangelica* (trans. W. J. Ferrar) I. 7.

5. See, for example, Justin Martyr *Dialogue with Trypho;* Tertullian *An Answer to the Jews;* Irenaeus *The Demonstration of the Apostolic Preaching* (trans. J. Armitage Robinson); Lactantius *The Divine Institutes* IV. 18; Cyprian *Three Books of Testimonies against the Jews* II. 7; Cyril of Jerusalem *Catechetical Lectures.*

Preparation for the Gospel, for example, Eusebius, in the fourth century, relates the history of the Jews, their doctrines, their heroes, and "their mode of life, so as to teach you that it is not without sober reasoning that we have preferred their philosophy to that of the Greeks," and then goes on to compare at length the divine oracles of the Jews with the foul tales of the gods of the Greeks.[6]

Eusebius' emphasis on the Judaic basis of Christian morality is typical of the Fathers. When they appeal to the conscience of the pagans against ritual murder and sex orgy, against the exposure of infants and aged, and against social injustice, they point out that all of these evils were denounced by the Jewish prophets of the God of Righteousness.

And even the ceremonial law, no longer practiced by Christians, was defended by them to the pagans. St. Augustine had no patience with the pagan argument that idols were, like circumcision, not to be understood literally, but as signs. For, he says, the Jews were under bondage to useful signs, which taught them to worship the one God, while the bondage of the Gentiles was useless. "What difference does it make to me," he asks, "that the image of Neptune is not itself to be considered as God, but only as representing the wide ocean? . . . Any statue you like to take is as much god to me as the ocean. . . ."[7]

Having praised the religion of the Jews so highly, Augustine (and Eusebius *et al.*) had perforce to explain to pagans as well as to Jews why Christians no longer practiced the observances of the Jews. The explanation was, in brief, that Christ had fulfilled the sacrifices of the law for all men for all time and that the Church was the fulfillment of the Synagogue. Christians do keep the Old Law, Augustine insists, in a way deeper than the carnal way of the Jews; and the Old Testament belongs more to the Christians than to the Jews.[8]

Augustine himself offers the clearest proof of the strength of the Judaic Scriptural tradition. A student of philosophy and literature, he is insistent that he has chosen Moses over Plato and Homer. In all his works, in *On The Spirit and the Letter,* in *On the Trinity,* in *The City of God,* in *The Tract against the Jews,* he stresses the closeness of Christianity to Judaism through Christological interpretations of

6. (Trans. E. H. Gifford) IX. 1.
7. *On Christian Doctrine* (ed. Rev. Marcus Dods) III. 5–7.
8. *Tractatus adversus Judaeos, PL.* 42, col. 64.

the Scriptures. It is an essential part of his teaching that "all divine Scripture" was written in the view of "presignifying the Lord's Advent;" that the Old Testament is the "veiling of the New," the New Testament the "revealing of the Old." [9]

"PSEUDO-AUGUSTINE"

Even more interesting from the literary view are two works falsely ascribed to Augustine, one a debate between the Church and the Synagogue, the other a tract addressed to the Jews. They not only had an enormous influence on later works, including *Piers*, but they were also the forerunners of the numerous works which combined learned matter with popular manner. And their history reveals most graphically the way in which apologetics, liturgy, art, allegory, and drama were linked.

The fifth-century pseudo-Augustinian *De Altercatione Ecclesiae et Synagogae* stepped into the world of literary scholarship through the door of art, for it served first as a key to some of the forgotten meanings of medieval iconography. After some puzzling, nineteenth-century students of art observed that two ladies who appeared frequently in painting, in glass, and in stone, from the fifth century to the Renaissance, were personifications of the Church and the Synagogue. A number of French pioneers in this research remarked next that the same two figures were found in liturgical poetry and in the drama, and it was thought that the symbols originated in the liturgical hymns of Bernard of Clairvaux and Adam of St. Victor. It was some years later that a German scholar traced the imagery to the fifth-century *De Altercatione*, and another showed in a detailed study its influence in later works of literature, including the drama.[10]

It might be argued that the basic notion of allegorizing the two churches ought to be traced to St. Paul, who, as we have seen, identified them with Isaac and Ishmael. In some patristic works they are even two ladies, Leia being a type of the Synagogue, Rachel a

9. *On Catechising* (ed. Dods) IV. 8.

10. *De Altercatione Ecclesiae et Synagogae, PL.* 42, cols. 1131–40; Fr. Charles Cahier and Fr. Arthur Martin, *Monographie de la cathédrale de Bourges.* Part 1: *Vitraux du XIII*ᵉ (Paris, 1841–44); Paul Weber, *Geistliches Schauspiel und kirchliche Kunst* (Stuttgart, 1894); Hiram Pflaum, *Der allegorische Streit zwischen Synagoge und Kirche* (Geneva, 1935).

type of the Church. Still, it was a stroke of genius on the part of pseudo-Augustine to personify the Church and the Synagogue as two mothers and to portray them in lively debate over their rights to the kingdom of God before the Roman censors. Under the guise of a witty legal allegory, they argue according to the Scriptures, the Synagogue saying that the Church has departed from Moses and abrogated the law, while the Church contends that Christ fulfilled the Scriptures and that she has supplanted her rival in the affections of the Father. The tone is impudent, but the texts and arguments are those of the most solemn Fathers.

The other pseudo-Augustinian work is a brief tract with a long history. Part of a larger treatise against Jews, heathen, and Arians, the section addressed to the Jews begins "Vos inquam," for Augustine "calls" on the prophets to give their testimony to Christ. Isaias, Jeremias, Moses, David, Habacuc, and Daniel respond in turn by reading their prophecies in order to refute the unbelief of the Jews.[11] Like the *De Altercatione*, the manner is not Augustine's, but the matter is; and this work was even more influential than the other. As was pointed out by M. Sépét about a hundred years ago, this tract was one of the germs of the European theater.[12] Read as a lesson in many churches on a Sunday in Advent or on Christmas Eve, it was versified as a trope in the monastery of St. Martial de Limoges in the eleventh century, and soon after it was turned into a real if simple play, the *Procession of the Prophets*. The *Procession*, in turn, was the germ of other Old Testament plays. For example, the popular Daniel plays, which are echoed (as we shall see) in *Piers*, developed from what was originally an amplification of the prophecy of Daniel as it appeared in the *Vos Inquam*.

APOCRYPHAL GOSPELS

Probably even more influential as source books were the Apocryphal Gospels—a conglomeration of story, discourse, and debate. In many

11. *Contra Judaeos, Paganos, et Arianos: Sermo de Symbolo, PL.* 42, cols. 1115–30.

12. Marius Sépét, "Les Prophètes du Christ," *Bibliothèque de l'école des Chartes*, XXVIII (1867), 1–27, 211–64; XXIX (1868), 105–39, 261–93; XXXVIII (1877), 397–443. Later students of the drama have confirmed Sépét's principal points; cf. Karl Young, *The Drama of the Mediaeval Church* (Oxford, 1933), II, 304 ff.

instances, they teach the same doctrine of the fulfillment of the Scriptures that we have been looking at, but they do so in a spirit much further removed from Augustine's than the *Vos Inquam* or the *De Altercatione*. For these works are often popular in the worst sense of the word, and they reflect the controversy between Jews and Christians on its lowest level. We need not go into the complex history of the apocrypha, but it is apparent from even a cursory reading of, say, the *Avenging of the Savior* and the *Gospel of Nicodemus* that they include violence and slander that are a far cry from polite disputation.[13] As we might guess, and as Jewish and pagan as well as Christian sources confirm, relations between the two peoples always did include these elements. Especially at home and in anti-Christian propaganda among the pagans, the Jews spread parodies of the Gospels, like the *Toledoth Jesu*, according to which Jesus was a liar, a magician, and an evildoer.[14] As for violence, it is enough to say that in early history, as at the time of the Jewish uprising against Rome in A.D. 70, Christians were singled out for annihilation, and, of course, later history is scarred by Christian massacres of Jews.

The apocrypha willy-nilly spread knowledge of the slanders in their very attempt to refute them. The Gospels were supplemented with spectacular miracles, over-much protesting by Jesus and the apostles, and conclusive testimony of eyewitnesses. Both defenders and attackers are Jewish in these works, for, as on a higher level, Jewish witness is all-important to the Christian cause.

The stories are also interspersed with debates in which both sides appeal to Scripture, debates which include the same texts used by St. Paul and the Fathers. But while the words may agree, the cast of mind is different. Often enough, the arguments of the Jews are presented not to be answered but to show how wicked the Jews are to say such things. All their arguments are to be taken as proof of their stubbornness and willful blindness. The Christian of the polite debate makes almost the same point: Justin Martyr, for example, cites Old

13. *Apocryphal Gospels, Acts, and Revelations,* Ante-Nicene Library, vol. XVI (1870); *Apocryphal Acts of the Apostles,* ed. and trans. W. Wright (London, 1871).

14. Origen *Against Celsus* X, XXIII (especially Books 1, 2); S. Krauss, "The Jews in the Works of the Church Fathers," *Jewish Quarterly Review,* V (1893), 143; R. Travers Herford, *Christianity in Talmud and Midrash* (London, 1903); M. R. James, *The Apocryphal New Testament* (Oxford, 1924).

Testament predictions of the blindness of the Jews to explain the Jewish rejection of Jesus. But in the debates, the argument remains textual and impersonal. In the legends, the Old Testament argument is often only a prologue to the opening of the eyes of the Jews by a miracle—or the violent (usually supernaturally induced) deaths of those who refuse to see. In brief, some apocrypha are often on the same intellectual and spiritual level as the Jewish parodies they attempt to refute.

It would be going too far to blame later hostility to the Jews on these sensational stories, for they only reflect a historical situation which was itself repeated. They do seem, however, to be the forerunners of what might be called the mixed tradition of so many later popular works, including parts of *Piers*. Characteristic of that tradition is the seemingly unconscious juxtaposition of two extreme attitudes towards Judaism and the Jews—veneration for the law and contempt for its followers.

It must be observed, finally, that these varied works are important not only because of their influence on later literature but because of their own continued popularity. The legends, the pseudo-Augustinian tracts, the patristic commentaries and debates were, like the New Testament itself, transmitted in their entirety and widely disseminated in an unbroken tradition throughout the Old English and later medieval period.

Chapter III

THE HISTORY OF THE DOCTRINE IN ANGLO-SAXON AND LATER MEDIEVAL ENGLAND

⚏ In the same sixth century in which the *Vos Inquam* was written, Pope Gregory sent another Augustine as a missionary to the Anglo-Saxons. What thrilled Gregory about these Angles was not so much that they looked like angels, but that they were the Gentiles whose conversion would fulfill the prophecies. When they were converted, they rejoiced to apply the prophecies to themselves. Their hearts were kindled by the thought that they were those very Gentiles from "the ends of the world" who had been called, as Isaias had prophesied, from the darkness of idolatry to the light of the God of Israel.[1]

COMMENTARY AND HOMILY

And like the converted pagans of earlier centuries, the English fell in love with the Scriptures and with the patristic manner of interpreting them. So constant is the tradition that it is necessary to say only that the Latin commentaries of Bede and Alcuin are laden with Old Testament "testimonies" which prove that Christ fulfilled the Scriptures. The mystical and allegorical interpretations are carried further than ever, and nobody ever delighted more than Bede in finding prefigurations of Christ and the Church in the Old Testament. What seems even more significant to the student of literature and social history is the pervasiveness of patristic apologetic, its influence on preachers and poets being truly extraordinary.

The best example of the pulpit is that good priest, Aelfric. Aelfric did not simply translate Jerome or Augustine; in his earnest way he

---

1. Bede The *Ecclesiastical History of the English Nation* (trans. John Stevens, rev. Lionel C. Jane) III. 29.

adapted his own learning to the needs of the unlettered. For example, in the sermon he preached on the Feast of the Circumcision, we can see how he anticipated the questions of simple Englishmen. "It is probable," he remarked reasonably, "that some of you know not what circumcision is." In his explanation, typical of Christian thinking both before and after his time, Aelfric dwelt on the virtue of the patriarch Abraham and then explained why Christians celebrate the circumcision of Jesus but do not practice it themselves.[2]

Aelfric's concern with Judaism, like Langland's, runs very deep in his thinking. He understood Christianity to be wholly Judaic—in theology, in practical morality, in history. The revelation of God in the Old Testament was easily as important to him as that in the New. Indeed, he never questioned that it was one harmonious revelation, that the saints of the Old and New dispensations are members of the same communion. And while he follows the Fathers (including Bede) in his allegorical expositions of Scripture, he goes further than most of them in his reverence for the Old Law. He is awed by the great teaching of Moses and the prophets; and he never belittles the observances and customs of the Jews, who, he believed, refrained from pork and practiced circumcision as acts of piety and obedience to God. These were their sacraments, well-pleasing to Christ, who instructed Moses in them. While the Gentiles, his forebears according to the flesh, lived in bestiality, the Israelites, his ancestors according to the spirit, walked in the way of the Lord.[3]

Less erudite clerics than Aelfric absorbed the same way of looking at the Scriptures and the Jews from the services of the Church. The Psalms, for example, which formed such a large part of the office and the liturgy and were read daily in the Psalter, were interpreted Christologically, as they had been since the days of the earliest Jewish-Christians, who sang them to Christ. There were traditional patterns of interpretation, one of which was to see in them the prefiguration of the supplanting of the Synagogue by the Church. The rubrics of the Old English translation known as the *Paris Psalter* were taken verbatim from the pages of a commentary on the Psalms,

2. Aelfric, *The Sermones Catholici* or *Homilies,* with English version by Benjamin Thorpe, 2 vols. (London, 1844, 1846), I, 91 ff.; hereafter cited as *Homilies.*
3. *Homilies, passim.* See also *Lives of Saints* (ed. W. W. Skeat), vol. I, EETS 76, 82; vol. II, EETS 92, 114.

part of which was in this tradition. Indeed, many of them read much like the early Cyprian's *Testimonies against the Jews*.[4]

Old Testament testimonies proving that Jesus was the promised Messias appear in the old argumentative way in a lesson read in the Sarum use on the fourth Sunday of Advent. Indeed, the text of the lesson was nothing more nor less than part of the pseudo-Augustinian *Sermon against the Jews*, the *Vos Inquam* that we have already looked at. Occurring on the last Sunday before Christmas, this flourish of argument with the Jews is an act in the larger drama of Advent. Throughout the liturgical season, the Christian relives the history of the centuries preceding the birth of Christ. On the one hand, he awaits with the Jews of old the coming of the Messias and sings the prophecies of the Incarnation and the Virgin Birth. At the same time, the Christian identifies himself with the Gentiles waiting in the darkness of sin for the Savior; so he sings the prophecies of the calling of the Gentiles and the rejection of the Jews. Finally, the Christian turns to the Jews themselves; half angrily, half defensively, he asks them once again to listen to the testimony of their own prophets.

LYRICS AND LEGENDS

These same themes were dramatically versified by the poets. The Old English *Advent Lyrics*, for example, include all the prophecies used in the Advent services.[5] Paraphrases of the Old Testament are freely interpolated with Christological passages gleaned from the liturgy and the Fathers. Apocryphal gospels and saints' legends include commentaries and debates. All are translated not only into the vernacular but also into the native rhythms; in many, the new Judaeo-Christian doctrine is naturalized in the swinging rhetoric of the old pagan epics.

4. Pierre Batiffol, *History of the Roman Breviary*, trans. Atwell M. Y. Bayley (London, 1898); Gregory of Tours *Les Livres des miracles* (ed. H. L. Bordier) III. 402; J. Douglas Bruce, "Immediate and Ultimate Source of the Rubrics and Introductions to the Psalms in the *Paris Psalter*," *MLN*, VIII (1893), 72–82; Bruce, "The Anglo-Saxon Version of the Book of Psalms Commonly Known as the *Paris Psalter*," *PMLA*, IX (1894), 43–164.

5. Jackson J. Campbell, *The Advent Lyrics of the Exeter Book* (Princeton, N.J., 1959).

Most interesting is the way in which all the characters are portrayed in contemporary terms, a style that anticipated Langland's handling of Biblical personalities. In Cynewulf's *Elene,* for example, the story of the finding of the Cross by the mother of Constantine is transformed into an English epic. Good and bad Jews alike all seem to be English. Jewish sages and Christian queen are equally heroic and dignified. Yet, for all the warlike imagery, it is exclusively Judaeo-Christianity that is preached. In one spectacular scene, the missionary queen, who will argue only with Jews learned in the law and the prophets, confronts a thousand of the most wise with the ancient testimonies transposed into Saxon style. "Hear ye," she begins, "O men of knowledge, holy runes, word and wisdom. Lo! ye have known the lore of the prophets. . . ." Quoting Scripture, she tells them that Moses sang of the Messias, and King David, the ancient sage, the prince of warriors, chanted of him. So Elene, speaking, it is said, in Hebrew, claims the authority not of her famous son but of the forefathers of the seemingly helpless Jews she is addressing. For she, too, preaches the fulfillment of the Scriptures and the unity of the two Testaments.[6]

THE ANGLO-JEWISH SETTLEMENT

Soon after 1066, argument with the Jews became more than a literary tradition, for in 1070 William the Conqueror sent across the channel for the Jews, and in a very few years there was a considerable settlement in England. For the next two hundred years, until the expulsion of the Jews by Edward I in 1290, the Jewish question was a lively one. The clergy attempted to convert the Jews and feared that Christians might be converted by them; kings and commoners borrowed from them at high rates of interest and preferred not to repay; the populace alternately fraternized with them and murdered them.[7]

6. *The Poems of Cynewulf,* trans. W. Kennedy (London, 1910; reprint ed., New York, 1949).

7. For much of the material on the Jewish settlement, I am indebted to Albert M. Hyamson, *A History of the Jews in England* (London, 1928); among other works consulted are Michael Adler, *The Jews of Medieval England* (London, 1939); Joseph Jacobs, *The Jews of Angevin England: Documents and Records* (London, 1893); John Elijah Blunt, *A History of the Jews in England* (London, 1830); Cecil Roth, *A History of the Jews in England* (Oxford, 1941).

And as the new situation repeated the old, the new Latin debates and tracts apparently copied the old.

Langland, who was born some twenty-five years after their expulsion, makes no direct reference to English Jews or to the works written about them. Because his writing reflects so little change in the traditional arguments and attitudes, it is often hard to tell whether he derived his notions from St. Paul and St. Augustine or from the writers who flourished shortly before his own time in his own country. In his treatment of the fulfillment of the Scriptures in the Trinity and the law, Langland follows the highest patristic tradition, which was continued in the Anglo-Norman debates. On the fulfillment of the Messianic prophecies, he was apparently influenced in part by the Fathers and in part by the apocryphal tradition, which was likewise unchanged. His attitude towards the Jews and contemporary Judaism, which varied from zeal for their conversion to hostility towards a race of usurers, was no doubt influenced by their role in the recent history of England.

It should be made clear at the outset that these aspects of Langland's treatment of the Jewish question are not equally important. While the doctrine of the fulfillment of the Scriptures is basic to *Piers*, the references to contemporary Jews might be expurgated without damaging the fabric of the poem. In the interest of logic and clarity, it would be tempting to leave them out of this discussion and thereby leave out the often painful history of the relations between Jews and Christians. But the Jews do come into the poem, and, if we would understand Langland's ambiguous attitude towards them, we have to consider history as well as Scripture, at the risk of spending a disproportionate number of words on the history.

DEBATES AND TRACTS

Some economy can be practiced by looking at history and doctrine together as they are reflected in various debates and tracts. There is a surprisingly large number of these works, and it is equally surprising that so little mention of them is found in histories of literature. Even the dullest of them reflect the social history of the times at least as much, say, as chronicles and sermons. For while their content closely follows earlier works, they also mirror contemporary attitudes and situations, from friendly discussions in monastery gardens to angry denunciations of evil influence in the market place. And the fact that some of them continued to be best-sellers reflects both literary and theological tastes.

Once famous and now all but forgotten is a debate written soon after the Jews came to England by a Norman named Gilbert Crispin (his noble family was called Crispinus because their hair stood on end). Trained at the abbey of Bec, he was a favorite pupil of both Lanfranc and Anselm and was called to England in 1079 by Lanfranc, then Archbishop of Canterbury. When he died as Abbot of Westminster many years later, the epitaph on his tombstone addressed him "Mitis eras justus prudens fortis moderatus"; and truly, the gentleness and fairness of the man are apparent in his writing.

The letter to Anselm which prefaces his *Disputatio Judaei cum Christiano de Fide Christiana* (ca. 1098) describes in most civil tones the setting of the *Disputation*. Gilbert says that a certain Jew, whose name he is withholding to spare him embarrassment, often visited the abbey, sometimes on business, sometimes just to talk. Whatever the occasion, we are told, they discussed religion in a friendly way. The Jew, who was learned in Christian writings as well as in the Old Testament, brought forth points against the faith out of his law, and Gilbert tried to answer. The *"Judaeus"* of the discussion was not convinced, but, Gilbert is happy to tell Anselm, another Jew present was, by the mercy of God, converted; he asked for baptism "among us all and remained with us as a monk." [8]

Although the preface is charming, the debate that follows is likely to disappoint the reader unfamiliar with the tradition. An excellent scholar of the romances, interested in the debates because of the literary influence of the allegory of the Church and the Synagogue, observes that the "method most frequently used is the simplest kind of appeal to authority, combined with a mystical and allegorical interpretation of Scripture carried to fantastic lengths." She adds that "it must appear that the arguments make little attempt to establish a common ground between the disputants." [9] But as we have seen, it is exactly the appeal to Scripture and the mystical and allegorical inter-

8. *Disputatio Judaei cum Christiano de Fide Christiana*, PL. 159, col. 1005.
9. Margaret Schlauch, "Allegory of Church and Synagogue," *Speculum*, XIV (1939), 464.

pretation that *were* the common ground of Jews and Christians. Furthermore, Gilbert's was the very model of a dialogue. A Jewish scholar comments that the Jew speaks as only a Jew would have, and he is astonished to find in an eleventh-century monk such scrupulous presentation of the real objections of Jews to Christianity.[10] To judge from the wide circulation of the book (MSS. exist in the British Museum, and in libraries at St. Alban's, Oxford, Paris, Troyes, Rouen, Munich, etc.), Christians were more than satisfied with Gilbert's method of justifying the faith.[11]

There are more dialogues than one would think which, like Gilbert's, reveal sincere attempts at mutual understanding and are set against a background of informal cordiality. There must also have been plenty of free discussion and many a midnight conversation in the universities, where scholars met on an equal footing. By 1075, the Jews had a settlement at Oxford, and later the Jewish students had their own halls there. The rabbis instructed Christians as well as Jews in Hebrew language and literature, which, it seems, the Christians were most eager to learn.

There was always the danger that they would learn more than they were supposed to. As early as 1073, monks were sent to Cambridge to neutralize the efforts of the Jews to propagate their faith— presumably with good reason. One wonders about the story behind the story of the two Cistercian monks who, not long before 1200, fled the convent and became Jews. We need not tell in detail the fantastic story of how, at the time that Anselm and Gilbert were trying to bring Jews to Christianity, King William Rufus was threatening to become a Jew and was forcing converts back to Judaism at the instigation, and for the pay, of influential Jews.

For their part, the Jews had to listen to more Christian preaching than most of them cared for. When the Dominicans came to England in 1221, thirteen of them went immediately to Oxford and took a house in "Jewry, to the end that they might begin first with the conversion of the Jews." The Franciscans were equally zealous. Jewish historians are nonetheless grateful to the preachers, for it was they

10. Israel Lévi, "Controverse entre un juif et un chrétien au XIe siècle," *Révue des études juives,* V (1882), 238–45.

11. J. Armitage Robinson, *Gilbert Crispin, Abbot of Westminster* (Cambridge, Eng., 1911), p. 62.

31

who defended the Jews against the populace and intervened on their behalf with the authorities. In time of trouble, the Jews turned also to the bishops and sometimes took refuge in their houses.

Somewhere midway between the friends of the Jews at one extreme and the murderous mobs at the other were the churchmen who formulated policy. The church in England maintained the papal position asserted centuries earlier and frequently repeated, that Jews were not to be baptized against their will or deprived of their property or molested in their religion. On the other hand, Christians were forbidden to attend the synagogue or eat with Jews. Jewish prohibitions against eating or drinking or mingling with the Christians were both specific and stringent. When they first came to England, the Jews lived in Jewries by choice, because of differences in food, in worship, in the day of worship, even in burial; later the separation of the two groups was made law. But as the frequent repetition of the warnings by rabbis and priests testifies, the Jews never stayed in and the Christians never kept out.

Assuming that encounters outside university and clerical circles led to religious discussions, we wonder what was discussed. To some extent, at least, it appears that the less learned followed their betters, albeit in a rough manner. Among a number of extant works written to help Christians win arguments with Jews, the most comprehensive was written by Peter of Blois, Archdeacon of Bath and London. The opening words of the *Contra Perfidiam Judaeorum* (probably before 1200) are addressed to an unnamed correspondent who has complained to Peter that he is surrounded by Jews and heretics, is continually attacked by them, and has no "authoritative statements of Holy Writ ready to hand" with which to rebut them. Both request and reply take us back to the earliest days of the Church. The disturbed Christian evidently wants not a copy of the Bible but a convenient selection of Old Testament passages. Peter obliged with a treatise consisting of thirty-eight chapters of "testimonies" on the Trinity, the Incarnation, the fulfillment of the Messianic prophecies, the calling of the Gentiles, and the Old Testament promises of the New Law and the sacraments. He also quotes from the apocrypha, citing as evidence the spurious letter of Pilate to the Emperor Tiberius, in which Pilate presumably reported the true story of the Crucifixion and the Resurrection and warned the emperor not to believe the false reports of the Jews.[12]

Mob Violence

The "false reports" lead us to the crudest version of the Judaeo-Christian debate, in which libel substituted for argument and even led to murder. In view of the enormity of Christian retaliation, it seems mean-spirited to mention Jewish provocation, real and imaginary. I do not believe myself that religious zeal, however misplaced, was the driving force behind the massacres of Jews in England. It is clear, however, that the mobs responsible for the atrocities considered the Jews "enemies of Christ," not solely because of the Crucifixion but because of their continued hostility and derision. It is hard to tell how well known were the scurrilous accounts of Jesus and his mother. But everybody knew of the cases in which Jews were arrested for beating or attempting to murder converts to Christianity and for publicly ridiculing Christian customs. Many professed to know, too, of cases of Jewish ritual murder of Christian children. In brief, some of the hostility between the two peoples was due to religious conceptions and misconceptions, and no doubt, whatever the social and economic situation, there would have been "incidents."

What turned the incidents into massacres, however, was the social and economic position of the Jews. In every way, the Jews were inevitably outsiders, for in feudal society, every civic, legal, and military tie was made binding under a Christian oath which, of course, they could not take. They were never citizens in Norman England; they gave no military service, and they were not even responsible to ordinary courts of justice. They were simply the personal property of the kings, who used them as a sponge "by which they soaked up the wealth of their subjects, and then squeezed it out for their own use." A prudent king would cheerfully watch the Jewish usurers grow rich and then levy a tax on them. Under Henry II, for example, the richest man in the kingdom was a Jew, Aaron of Lincoln, and he kept Henry almost solvent. In 1187, the Jews were reckoned to have one-fourth of the movable wealth of the kingdom,

12. *Contra Perfidiam Judaeorum, PL.* 207, cols. 825–70.

THE FULFILLMENT OF THE SCRIPTURES

and theirs were the only stone houses, besides the king's, in the realm. Inevitably, Christian debtors considered the wealth of the creditors to be built on their misery. And however a riot started, it ended in the robbing of the houses of the moneylenders—and the burning of the records of indebtedness.

The chroniclers are agreed that whatever reasons were advanced by the leaders of the mobs, the real reason for the massacres was greed. As William of Newburgh satirically remarks, the crusaders (in the third Crusade) "were indignant that the enemies of the cross of Christ . . . should possess so much while they had not enough for the expenses of so great a journey." Considering, therefore, "that they could be doing honour to Christ if they attacked his enemies, whose goods they were longing for," they broke into their houses, seized their money, and slew all in their way. Even if the death of the Jews checked the "insolence of that perfidious people" and their blasphemous tongues, the rioters were "bold and greedy men" who pretended to be doing an act pleasing to God, while they "carried out the work of their own cupidity with savage joy, and without any, or only the slightest, scruple of conscience, God's justice, indeed, by no means approving such deeds." [13]

ROBERT GROSSETESTE

The greatest spokesman for the justice of God, and the best-known protector of the Jews, was the bishop of Lincoln, Robert Grosseteste. Lee M. Friedman says that, when in the middle of the thirteenth century tension between the two groups was severe, it was principally Grosseteste's influence that protected the Jews of Lincoln. Immediately after Grosseteste's death in 1255, there was violence in Lincoln, as the result of an accusation of ritual murder. Ninety-two Jews were imprisoned, and eighteen were executed because they refused trial by an all-Christian jury. Through the intervention of the Franciscans, who denied the truth of the charge, the rest were released. Adam Marsh, the Franciscan who defended them to king and people alike, was Grosseteste's beloved disciple.[14]

13. Quoted in Jacobs, *Jews of Angevin England*, pp. 113 ff.
14. Lee M. Friedman, *Robert Grosseteste and the Jews* (Cambridge, Mass., 1934), pp. 23 f.; see also the *Lanercost Chronicle,* quoted in Andrew G. Little, *The Grey Friars in Oxford* (Oxford, 1892), p. 24.

Grosseteste was not only a sincere Christian but a serious scholar and a great churchman. The righteous administrator of the See of Lincoln, he might well qualify for Langland's rating of Do Best. Like Langland's ideal prelate (in Passus XV), Grosseteste was a missionary bishop who fed his flock with both bodily and spiritual food, and who went out to preach to Christians and to convert Jews. Since the Hebrews "know the first clause of our creed, *Credo in unum Deum*," Langland advises prelates to teach them "little by little" to believe also "in *Jesum Christum filium*" and "in *Spiritum Sanctum*." Grosseteste was a prelate well equipped to begin a discussion with the common beliefs of Jews and Christians. In his student days at Oxford, he had studied Hebrew with a rabbi, and when he later became chancellor of the University, he encouraged similar studies by the Franciscans there. In his lifelong efforts to convert the Jews, he patiently developed, little by little, the theme of the growth of the Church from the Synagogue.

It was because he hoped it would conclusively answer Jewish Scriptural objections to Christianity that he was overjoyed with the discovery of the Greek text of the *Testaments of the Twelve Patriarchs*. He did not realize that, far from being actual utterances of the patriarchs, the *Testaments* was an apocryphal Jewish work of the second century B.C. and that some (not all) of the Christian-sounding passages were really Christian interpolations. As far as he knew, these were genuine prophecies which gave even clearer proof than David or Isaias that, for example, the Jews expected the coming of God himself rather than a merely human Messias. With the help of a Greek clerk at St. Alban's, he therefore translated the work in the hope of converting the Jews.[15]

Also directed to the Jews was his own *De Cessatione Legalium*. While the main thesis is that the law was not abrogated but fulfilled by Jesus, this lengthy work includes all the prophecies and all the arguments, not in the brusque testimony method of Peter of Blois but in the full manner of Augustine. Actually, Grosseteste's chief source was not Augustine's *Tract against the Jews*, but his *On the Trinity*, and the work is, it seems to me, in the great tradition of patristic

15. R. H. Charles, ed. and trans., *The Testaments of the Twelve Patriarchs*, in *Apocrypha and Pseudepigrapha of the Old Testament*, vol. II (Oxford, 1913); Matthew Paris, *Chronica Majora*, ed. H. R. Luard (London, 1872), IV, 232–33.

apologetic. Enormously popular and influential among medieval Christians, the work is unfortunately not available in a modern printed edition.[16]

While the conversion of the Jews was thus one of Grosseteste's dreams, Jewish usurers were a practical problem of the administration of his diocese. Applying the Scriptures equally to Jews and Christians, kings and commoners, he censured both the Jews who robbed the people and the kings who robbed the Jews. God will turn away from those kings, he writes, for their "hands are full of blood" (Isa. 1:15). Considering that the misfortunes of the Jews had been brought upon them by their sin of rejecting Christ, he did not actually believe in equal rights, but he did suggest that the Jews be put to other work and usury outlawed.[17]

In 1275, Edward I tried to work out Grosseteste's suggestion, even though, as he put it, the Jews had been profitable to him and to his predecessors. He forbade all usury, that is, all taking of interest, and "because Holy Church wills it," he took the Jews into his protection, commanding his sheriffs to guard and defend them. They were allowed to take farms and purchase houses for ten years and to "practice merchandise or live by their labour, and for those purposes, freely converse with Christians." But the change was too sudden, and the Jews were financially distressed at once. Recognizing the fact, Edward finally permitted usury but established fixed rates. This act was really an acknowledgement of failure, and in the following ten years, great pressure was put on Edward from all sides to expel the foreigners. He did so in 1290, after Parliament sent him a petition, accompanied by a large gift. Edward tried to ease their going with a number of humane measures, but the populace and the sailors shamefully robbed and murdered them.

THE TRADITION IN LATER MEDIEVAL LITERATURE

The departure of the Jews from England does not signal their disappearance from the written or spoken word. The faith continued

16. *De Cessatione Legalium, Parts 1 and 2. A Critical Edition from the Extant MSS,* ed. Arthur M. Lee, Ph.D. dissertation, University of Colorado (1942), New York Public Library microfilm.

17. *Epistolae,* ed. H. R. Luard (London, 1861), vol. XXV, *Chronicles and Memorials of Great Britain and Ireland during the Middle Ages,* pp. 33 ff.

to be taught *contra Judaeos*, and many a late sermon and stanza are punctuated by a direct appeal to the Jews to hearken. So often does this happen in the recorded homilies of John Bromyard (fl. ca. 1400) that a modern editor of medieval sermons reasonably assumes that he was attempting to convert the Jews, forgetting that there were no Jews in England when the famous Dominican preached. Of course, the Jews were just across the channel, and Continental Latin debates and tracts written there were read in England, while earlier ones continued to be copied. The debates continued to be popular because medieval Englishmen remained interested in the Jews and always enjoyed disputation.

Furthermore, the methods used in the apologia to convert Jews were the same as those used in homilies to catechize Christians. Langland himself drew on other methods of proof—on nature, reason, and philosophy. But with Langland, as with most of the homilists and commentators, the old way of exegetical proofs held sway. It seems inevitable that discussions of the Trinity cite the Old Testament texts in much the same sequence as the early tracts. And the preachers are never tired of pointing out that Christians, not Jews, are the true Israel, that the sacraments of the Church were prefigured in the sacraments of the Synagogue, that it was the Jewish prophets who foretold every act of Christ's—as well as the rejection of him by the Jews and their subsequent rejection by God. In brief, ordinary medieval Christian teaching seems as much concerned as was the early Church with the relation of Christianity to Judaism.

Like St. Paul, these later Christians seek authority for the New Testament in the Old. Writing for other Christians, Richard of St. Victor sounds rather like the *Judaeus* of the debates in his insistence that even the personal appearance of Christ is insufficient without the warrant of Moses. Warning other mystics against delusions, the twelfth-century mystic writes:

> Even if you think that you have been taken up into that high mountain apart, even if you think that you see Christ transfigured, do not be too ready to believe anything you see in Him or hear from Him, unless Moses and Elias run to meet Him. I hold all truth in suspicion which the authority of the Scriptures does not confirm, nor do I receive Christ in His clarification unless Moses and Elias are talking with him.[18]

18. *A Treatise Named Benjamin* in *The Cell of Self-Knowledge,* ed. Edmond G. Gardner (London, 1910), p. xv.

Of course, Richard was not really questioning the primacy of Christ. But so basic in his view of religion and history was the doctrine of the fulfillment of the Scriptures in Christ that the presence of Moses served as a touchstone of truth.

Many medieval Christians besides Langland applied the Scriptures to current events. When Grosseteste wanted to prove his right of visitation in his diocese, he turned to Moses. In an epistle to the dean and chapter of Lincoln, he explained that Moses is the type of Christian prelates: the pope in the Church and the bishop in the diocese correspond to Moses and his assistants. He added that Moses and the prophets had made it clear that the sins of the assistants and the people would be held against neglectful prelates. Numerous examples of good and bad shepherds were then duly cited as proof of the bishop's duty to examine the lives and works of his subordinates. Most amusing is the extension of the figure to Adam and Eve. Long considered figures of Christ and the Church, here Adam is bishop, Eve his assistant (Gen. 3:16). And everybody knows the evil that happened when that bishop neglected for a moment to watch that assistant.[19]

Even those who disagreed with him would not deem comical the bishop's assumption that the dean, chapter, and bishop of Lincoln were all prefigured in the Old Testament. The Old Testament was not a dead historical record to them but a perennially fresh source of truth, in which, could we but read it aright, is the whole of history, the middle and the end, as well as the beginning. The prefigurations of Christ and the texts that proved the fulfillment of the prophecies did not seem to them to be word-juggling, as they often seem to us, but were indeed the clearest part of the story.

Popular Literature

It is a story that is further told, in whole or in part, in the most diverse popular works. Literary genre has little force here, for works with the framework of a debate are likely to be weak in doctrine, while theological notions may be successfully argued in such unlikely works as the romances. There is, for example, a fourteenth-century poem called a *Disputison by-twene a cristenmon and a Jew* that seems

19. *Epistolae* CXXVII. 357 ff.

at first to be a versified rendering of Gilbert Crispin's *Disputation.*[20] For here are two "clerks" of divinity, a Jew and an Englishman, both learned and upright; and the Jew is a man "muchel of his miht," who holds to his "truth," true as a tree, and is not convinced by argument. But we are only *told* that they dispute all the day; the arguments are not given. The real interest of the author is in a magic-miracle contest, and it is the miracle which converts the Jew—to the great joy of the pope. There are many similar stories of the apocryphal type, in which argument is subordinated to miracle and which reflect with equal casualness intimate friendships between Jews and Christians, Jewish contempt for Christian beliefs, and Christian belief in Jewish ritual murder. The old Apocryphal Gospels themselves were, of course, extremely popular; the influence of the harrowing of hell, for example, is plain in *Piers,* in the mysteries, and in the versified lives of Christ.

These versified religious histories, such as the *Ormulum* (ca. 1200), the *Cursor Mundi* (ca. 1300), the *Stanzaic Life of Christ* (fourteenth century), and the *Miroure of Mans Salvacionne* (a fifteenth-century translation of the popular *Speculum*), have much the same scope as *Piers* and the play cycles. They freely mingle lore from the apocrypha with arguments from the preachers; and they share the same doctrines, proofs, and general outlook. Written by comparatively unsophisticated authors, the history taught in these ambitious works often seems naïve, and from our view, unhistorical. The world presented in them is entirely Christological; Christ is the alpha and omega, the beginning and the end. The history of the Jews is, of course, related from this point of view: it includes the prophecies and prefigurations of Jesus, Mary, and the Church, the pre-existent Christ's role as creator of the world and leader of the Israelites, his choice of the Hebrews, their rejection of him, and their subsequent misfortunes.

From the Creation to the Last Judgment, the mysteries dramatize the same material. While, for the most part, the plays simply paraphrase Old and New Testament stories, many episodes are interpreted in accordance with the prevailing commentaries. Others draw freely on the apocrypha and other popular works. The story of Christ and

20. In *The Minor Poems of the Vernon MS,* ed. F. J. Furnivall, vol. II, EETS 117, pp. 484–93.

the Doctors, for example, is told in much the same way in all four cycles and in a thirteenth-century poem entitled "A Disputison betwene child Jhesu & Maistres of the Law of Jewus."[21] The title is apt, for all versions change the New Testament story into a debate, in which the Child argues the Trinity with the Jewish doctors, albeit he is not well versed in the texts.

The prophets, in the processions, the Nativities, and in individual plays, are better equipped, because they came to the dramatists text in hand. As we have seen, the processions were derived from the pseudo-Augustinian *Sermon against the Jews*, and many plays were elaborations of individual prophets. By and large, however, the controversial tone is lost on the English stage. In the Chester *Balaam and Balak*, for example, the Expositor who, I would guess, is descended from the Augustine who appeared in the Continental plays, explains how the birth of Jesus fulfilled the prophecies, without mentioning the Jews. In other Nativity plays, there is a certain amount of discussion among the prophets, but it is far removed from the *Sermon*, or even from the twelfth-century *Adam*, in which a representative of the Synagogue appears to dispute the meaning of his prophecy with Isaias.

The doctrine of the fulfillment of the Scriptures is taught most explicitly, in the course of the plays, by Abraham, Moses, and Jesus. As in the lives of Christ, in the liturgy, and in *Piers*, Abraham is the expositor of the Trinity and of the substitution of baptism for circumcision. In the plays of the Last Supper, Christ himself teaches the fulfillment of the law and the sacrifices in the Passion and in the sacraments of the Church. And when the cycles approach an end, the fulfillment of the Messianic prophecies is finally proved to the Jews, who were expected to be converted at the end of the world.

Allegories in Art and Literature

Accustomed to the perpetual contrasting of Church and Synagogue from pulpit and play, the medieval man was not puzzled, as are his descendants, by the allegories in art and literature. The symbols stained on the windows had been described from the pulpit, and a child might have recognized the meaning that has baffled later scholars. The child William Langland may well have heard from the

21. *Ibid.,* pp. 479–83.

pulpit the allegory of the Good Samaritan which he made use of in his own vision.

The richness of Langland's presentation is in part due to the fact that he had heard and seen the law allegorized in many ways. For in one form or another, the fulfillment of the law had lent itself to allegory from the earliest times. In St. Paul's allegory of Isaac and Ishmael, in the Scriptural interpretations of the Fathers, in early and later medieval commentaries and homilies, the two laws had been personified disputing over the kingdom of God. A medieval Latin debate modeled on the pseudo-Augustinian *Altercation,* called the *Disputatio Ecclesiae et Synagogae* (and falsely ascribed to Gilbert Crispin), is particularly interesting because of its exceedingly close connection with the plastic arts. It is remarkable how often the symbols described in the debate occur in stone, in glass, in ivory, in sermon, play, and romance.[22]

The most attractive example in sculpture appears in the thirteenth-century Cathedral of Strassburg. A strikingly beautiful pair of statues there personifies the two religions as two ladies, and their relation to each other is portrayed in familiar symbols. She who is the triumphant Church wears a crown; in her right hand, she holds the cross erect, while in her left she carries a chalice. She who is the rejected Synagogue wears a blindfold; in her right hand is a broken lance, while from her left fall the tables of the law. What seems most extraordinary is the basic similarity of the two statues. Both have the same lovely face and form, the same hair and hands and dress; indeed, they can be told apart only by their attributes. And why not? The ladies look alike in sculpture because in argument and poem and play the Church is called the true Synagogue, the spiritual Israel. It was the traditional teaching of the Church that the same Holy Spirit gave beauty to both, and that the beauty of the Synagogue was marred only by blindness, the blindness which kept her from being one with the Church.

So familiar was the allegory that Gower could reverse its meaning in order to satirize the vices of Christians. In the *Vox Clamantis,* he says that the Church has lost her virtue and the Synagogue has

22. *Disputatio Ecclesiae et Synagogae,* in Edmond Martène and Ursin Durand, *Thesaurus Anecdotum* (1717), vol. V, cols. 1497–1506; Hiram Pflaum, *Der allegorische Streit zwischen Synagoge und Kirche* (Geneva, 1935), p. 60.

become the spouse of Christ. Paul is reconverted into Saul. Bad friars are ministers of the Synagogue rather than of the Church, children of Hagar not of Sarah—and they are even dispersed over the world like the Jews! [23]

As Gower could count on his readers' recognition of his allusion to Hagar and Sarah, so other writers could be sure that their variations on the allegory would not be lost on their audience. In the legends of the Cross and the Grail, especially in the closely related stories of Solomon, the well-known prefigurations of the Church explain part of the complex meaning of the building of the temple and the ship. In Malory's *Quest*, in the adventures of both Perceval and Bors, there are even two ladies called the New and the Old Laws, whose description is clearly influenced by the allegory of the Church and the Synagogue, the elder complaining, like the mother in the *Disputatio*, that she who was the richest gentlewoman in the world has been disinherited.[24] In Lydgate's *Pilgrimage of the Life of Man* (a translation of Deguilleville's *Pélérinage*), there is no hint of conflict between the two laws. Indeed, the two are one to the point of confusion, "Moses" representing both the Jewish prophet and any Christian bishop administering confirmation.

Piers Plowman

Nobody knows, of course, whether or not William Langland read "background" works such as these. The chances are that as we read them, so did he. Actually, the same material is found in so many places that a few omissions or additions to the list make little difference in the general pattern, and it is the pattern, rather than specific sources, that concerns us. As we shall see in the following chapters, Langland's treatment of the Trinity, of the Messianic prophecies, and of the law reveals the characteristics of that tradition—the same reverence for authority, the same interpretation of texts, the same arguments against the Jews, even the same images and allegories.[25]

23. *Vox Clamantis* (ed. G. C. Macaulay) IV. 22–23; VI. 19.

24. Sir Thomas Malory, *The Quest of the Holy Grail,* ed. Eugène Vinaver (Oxford, 1947), II, 912 ff.

25. William Langland, *The Vision of William concerning Piers the Plowman,* in Three Parallel Texts, ed. Walter W. Skeat (London, 1968); unless otherwise

One might easily draw lists of parallel passages between *Piers* and the works we have been glancing at from the days of the early Church through the early and later medieval periods.

At the same time, the reader is always aware of similarities and differences that go deeper than the question of sources and analogues. While Langland must certainly have been acquainted with contemporary mysteries and lives of Christ, he seems closer in feeling and attitude to Grosseteste, St. Augustine, and St. Paul, even to Aelfric and Cynewulf. It is, perhaps, largely a matter of intelligence: first-rate minds working on the same material will be close kin even if a few centuries separate them. Langland's understanding of the relation of the Old to the New Law is so close to Grosseteste's that part of *Piers* might almost be a poetic transformation of parts of the *De Cessatione Legalium*—which he may not have read. The difference between the two is also instructive: the allegory of *Piers* is rich in creative insights that the great bishop was powerless to communicate.

More creative than the theologians, Langland is far more searching than his fellow poets. In reading the bulk of medieval fiction, with its uniformity of doctrine and phraseology, one wonders if the authors ever examined their beliefs. With Langland, one suspects that he had gone through a spiritual crisis and struggled with all the still-agonizing questions, before coming back finally to the faith of his fathers.

For all his fierce criticism of the clergy, it is abundantly clear that Langland considered the Church the only guardian of the deposit of the faith. It is just as clear that he does not adhere easily to a party line. On more than one subject, he tells us that while clerks carp one way, he thinks *contra*. In one rather amusing passage, of no importance in itself but typical in its tone, he even prefers the psychology of the Old Testament to the charity of the New and goes out of his way to make his disagreement explicit. Having described the flood as a punishment put upon the descendants of Cain, he notes that the Gospel denies that the sins of the fathers are visited upon their children. From his own experience, however, he has observed that if

noted, subsequent references are to the B text. The translations which follow passages of four or more lines are taken from *The Vision of Piers Plowman,* trans. Henry W. Wells (New York, 1945).

43

THE FULFILLMENT OF THE SCRIPTURES

the father is "false and a shrewe," the son has some of his faults (IX.142 ff.).

While smart alecks and frivolous snipers at the faith earn only scorn at Langland's hands, his dreamer is all too familiar with them. Dame Study reminds him rather testily that the seeker after truth must study with humility and not copy those who, sitting at table, glibly ask why our Savior suffered the snake to beguile Eve. Why should we suffer for their sin? "Resoun wolde it neuere" (X.101 ff.). In the same false spirit, unlearned men question why Adam did not cover his mouth first, since it was with his mouth that he ate the apple! The dreamer himself is rebuked for his presumption when he asks Reason why he does not make men as sensible as the birds and the beasts (XI.363 ff.).

That is not to say that the Christian must believe blindly. The Good Samaritan stops, at some cost to the movement of the poem, to provide answers against the heretics. And the quite orthodox pilgrim is always asking hard questions which deserve an answer from Dame Study or Wit or Holy Church. What is God? How am I to understand the union of body and soul? What is necessary for salvation? Can good pagans be saved? What about the Jews and the Saracens? If these can be saved, what need was there for Christ? These and other questions are pondered throughout the poem. For the most part, the answers are taken from the Scriptures, interpreted in the old way, and then assimilated in the poet's way.

Pagans and Jews

In Passus XI, for example, Scripture preaches on the text concerning the many summoned to the feast, summarized pithily as the porter plucked in some "and lete the remenaunt go rowme!" (XI.109). Now Will trembles at the implications of the parable and "disputes" with himself whether or not he is among the chosen. He decides that Christ called us all—Saracens, schismatics, and Jews. As the pagan Trajan was saved by love and loyalty, so, if mercy prevails, all can be saved. Now it was conventional (compare Bede, for example) to interpret this parable as a representation of the calling of the Gentiles. But it is something else again to portray a Christian finding hope for himself in the example of Trajan.

In the following passus, Langland turns to the theme again. Hav-

44

ing rebuked unlearned men for asking foolish questions, he chides the clerics for giving narrow answers. No cleric knows, he asserts, whether that great clerk Aristotle be saved or not—or Socrates either. But God is good; and since they taught us, we are beholden to pray for them. Further on in the same passus, he complains that clerks say that neither Saracens nor Jews can be saved. "Contra," says Imaginative; if they live according to the best they know, God will judge accordingly.

While Langland is thus very much aware of his shared humanity with them, the good pagans were only of minor concern, probably because paganism was, after all, of little moment. It was Judaism that touched him close. True, the promise of redemption was made to all men; but salvation is of the Jews. The Gentiles were redeemed not by Plato or Aristotle but by being called to the God of Israel.

The Jews were viewed by Langland, as by many other Christians, in a double light. He revered them both as the people of Abraham and as the guardians of the law of Moses. He goes further than most Christians in placing the blame for the continued Jewish rejection of Christianity on the failure of Christians to teach and live their doctrine, and, when he implores the bishops to preach to the Jews, he sounds as though their conversion might be easy. Elsewhere, however, he condemns them most bitterly for their continued disbelief. Like the pagans, they are invited to the feast; but their refusal to come is far more blameworthy. Since they have the Scriptures and the prophecies, even more since they are of the same family, their refusal is treason to their king, who has justly rejected them. The Scriptural arguments employed by Langland are the ancient ones, but there is a contemporary note in his consideration of their practice of usury as the fulfillment of the prophecies of rejection.

One cannot help wondering how much his views were influenced by the past history of the Jews in England—and by their absence from the contemporary scene. Certainly there is no hint of approval of violence against them, and he is so far from repeating stories of ritual murder (such as that told by Chaucer's Prioress), that he states firmly that they live according to the law, which they still think best. Actually, his description of them, for better and for worse, is quite conventional, probably because he had never met a live Jew any more than a live pagan. Even his quip that Jews are better than Christians because they at least take care of each other had been made before. Had he lived a century earlier, the cast of characters in *Piers* might well have included a usurer and a rabbi, rather than mere stereotypes. But while he had never discussed religion with a rabbi, as had Gilbert Crispin, Langland hated usury as much as Grosseteste did. And it may be that his Scriptural justification of their plight as despised and dispersed usurers was used in part as a vindication for their expulsion from England. In any event, when he refers to the rejection of the Jews for their rejection of the Messias, he seems to deny the Jews the freedom of conscience he grants them in the parts of the poem dealing with the Trinity and the law.

The Unity of the Two Testaments

Writing about these two supremely important subjects, Langland forgets the blindness of the Synagogue and sees only her beauty. Here he does not argue with the Jews, as almost everybody else did. We know that he was familiar with the arguments, for the old texts, often in the old sequence, are recognizable in his discussions. But he filters out the controversial tone and incorporates the material in his context in such a way that the joints do not show. The remarkable thing is that there were no joints in his thinking. Everybody *said* that the New Testament was the unveiling of the Old, that the New Law was the fulfillment of the Old, and that, as St. Paul had said, there was nothing in Christianity that went beyond what Moses and the prophets foretold. And in so saying, everybody compared Christian and Jewish beliefs and practices. Langland does very little comparing; so deeply realized is the doctrine of unity in *Piers* that Langland hardly seems to notice the differences.

His Abraham mentions the circumcision commanded by God, but he does not compare it with baptism. He is Faith itself, and his doctrine is as unchanging as the God of Israel. And since that God is and always was Triune, Abraham's faith is Trinitarian. Similarly, Moses does not compare the sacrifices of the Jews with the Eucharist of the Christians. Like the Trinity, the law, which is indeed one aspect of the truth of God, is eternal, and the patriarch and the prophet are above superficial changes in ritual. The bewilderment of the dreamer, however, shows Langland's awareness of the less enlightened view. The dreamer runs after Abraham, Moses, and Jesus

46

to demand whom he should believe, for, in his earthbound way, he sees only the superficial changes in the laws. To the Old Testament saints and heroes (and to the poet) the concordance of the Scriptures is clear and simple. So it is that as they await Christ in the course of the poem, they teach the very doctrine that he is to fulfill by his birth, his life, and his death.

Throughout the poem, various aspects of the Trinity and the law are debated, allegorized, and incorporated in the total vision with surpassing art and insight. A study of the tradition enriches our appreciation of Langland's technique and knowledge. When, for example, Piers says that the tower of truth is set above the sun, and "he" may do as he likes with the day-star (A.VI.82–84), he is alluding to the ancient Christological interpretation of the psalm, according to which the Son was with the Father at the creation of the day-star. It is not especially important if one misses the allusion, except that one may also miss the point that Truth is Christ and that Truth has always been Trinitarian. One passage sheds light on another. When Langland speaks of the Truth of Trajan, he means that the goodness of the pagan emperor stemmed also from the Trinity and was essentially the same as the faith of Abraham, the law of Moses, and the charity of Christ.

The Plan of Piers

A study of the tradition also helps us to appreciate the plan of the poem, for the history of Revelation is, I believe, one of its underlying themes. Certainly it is not the only theme, nor can Langland be tied to a classical plan. The very framework of the dream sequence allows him the latitude of the technique we call stream of consciousness. And since the "I" of the poem is both inside and outside his dreams, he is free, when asleep, to question the other characters and, when awake, to talk things over with his readers. There are few subjects he does not talk over—politics and economics, war and peace, philosophy and religion—all as they apply to all classes of society from kings to barmaids. While *Piers* is no neater than the Gothic cathedrals to which it has been compared, all its diversities are similarly unified by a single theological view. The same questions are raised more than once in various contexts, not because the poem is without a design, but because the dreamer only gradually understands the unfolding of

God's plan for himself and for all men. For the dreamer is both an individual and a member of the human race, with a place both in his own field of time and in the history of Revelation. Perhaps a brief outline will show the place in this complex plan of the traditional teaching of the fulfillment of the Scriptures.

In the prologue, the dreamer sees a field of folk, set between a tower of truth and a pit of falsehood. The first person to address him is Holy Church, who has come down from the hill to explain the ways of God to men, beginning with the beginning, that is, with the story of Creation. The story pertains to him, for it is the first story of God's love, which is the same as truth, and he realizes that in order to save his soul, he must seek the true and learn to shun the false. Throughout the rest of the poem, the dreamer attempts to follow the lady's counsel in every way, time, and place. He dreams and wakes, and, waking or dreaming, he argues and analyzes and allegorizes.

For a number of cantos, he discusses problems of government and justice and allegorizes them in the story of Lady Meed. He denounces the falseness of kings and courtiers, and the priests who pander to them, while Conscience points out the way of truth. Conscience also prophesies the final coming of the Messianic Kingdom, when Meed will no longer rule the world and when the fulfillment of Isaias' prophecy of peace will convert the Jews. From high places he moves to low, to low-life embodiments of the Seven Deadly Sins, characters who remind us of the motley crew seen in the field of folk in the prologue. As reparation for their sins, they must seek St. Truth, and although they are willing, they blunder about without a guide. It is here that Piers appears, and a simple enough plowman he seems at first—except for the fact that he alone is pure and single-minded, and somehow in sole possession of the way to Do Well. His is a hard way through the Ten Commandments, and all are not willing to work. Piers is given a pardon for the folk, but they are not ready for it, and he vanishes. This pardon of Piers is discussed later in the poem and concerns both the obligations of justice and the fulfillment of the law by Christ.

From Passus VIII on, the dreamer proceeds, alone and sad, to ask everyone he meets where he can find Do Well, Do Better, and Do Best, for he does not know how to follow the precepts he has learned. The quest becomes, if one may say so, interiorized, and in a series of discourses with such characters as Thought, Wit, Study, Clergy, and Imagination, the dreamer probes ever more deeply into the meaning of salvation. At the same time, the scope of his exterior vision broadens to include not only the life of his own time but the history of the world, and the place in it of Jews, Moslems, pagans, and Christians.

He meets Trajan, the pagan emperor who was saved without Christian learning or Masses, and ponders the salvation of the heathen. He attends an allegorical dinner party with Conscience and Patience and hears a hard riddle which is really a prophecy of Christ's fulfillment of the law of love. He meets Haukyn, the Active Man, who seems better than the learned crowd, until he is viewed closely. An extraordinary creature called Anima discourses at great length on the meaning of charity and ascribes the Christian failure to convert the Jews and the Saracens to the lack of charity of proud priests. He prepares the pilgrim for the coming meeting with Christ by describing the law of Moses, which taught the love of God and neighbor, until the coming of the Messias. Then to the dreamer's great delight, Piers reappears and shows him the Tree of Charity and begins the story of the life of Christ. He joins Faith-Abraham and Hope-Moses, both seeking Christ. Together they meet the Samaritan (Charity) riding to Jerusalem to the Crucifixion. Then follow the Passion, the debate between the four daughters of God on justice and mercy, and the harrowing of hell, which includes a debate between Christ and Satan on the fulfillment of the Old Law. The dreamer awakes to find it Easter Sunday, and he goes to Mass. Asleep again, he hears Conscience explain that Christ is the king of the Jews, who rejected him and are now punished for their treason. The history moves on to the founding of the Church on Pentecost and finally to the last indefinite age of the world, with the prolonged struggle against Antichrist, in which most Christians are on the wrong side. At the end, Conscience sets out once again to seek Piers.

In the plan of the poem, the dreamer is not only a fourteenth-century pilgrim, but everyman, from the beginning, seeking salvation. While the dreamer travels in time, the truth he seeks is eternal. It follows that, throughout the poem, passages of moral and theological teaching are cited from the Old and New Testaments with equal authority. Obviously, what Solomon or Matthew preached, say, about covetousness, was equally true in the fourteenth century, for covetousness is as old and as persistent as man. Equally obvious to Langland was the unchangeable nature of God, and the belief that the same God is taught in both Testaments.

While God is thus always the same, the knowledge of God has only gradually been revealed to men. Truth is present at the very beginning of the poem, and Christ is referred to because he was always the Second Person of the Trinity. But it is rather as though Christ is present in the first part of the poem in the hidden way in which he is present in the Old Testament, and the pilgrim is not ready to perceive him. Actually, Christ does not appear until late in the poem, and when Holy Church describes the Creation, she only hints at the Incarnation. When we finally reach the Tree of Charity, we see that the same love that came from from heaven to unite matter with spirit in the Creation took flesh in the Incarnation; the Word of God in Genesis is the same Word made flesh according to St. John. On the branches of the tree are the patriarchs and the prophets; on the top is Christ. Continuing his pilgrimage to Jerusalem, the dreamer meets Abraham and Moses, and they go on together to meet Christ. For the faith of Abraham and the law of Moses were not abrogated but fulfilled by the charity of Jesus.

As Langland points out more than once, although love is the teaching of the Old Testament as well as of the New, the greatest revelation of love was the Incarnation and the Crucifixion. In the poet's image, Christ thirsts, and love is his drink. Prophesied from the beginning, the Incarnation happened at a particular moment in history, and it was with the advent of Christ that those things known only to a chosen few were unveiled to all, that the promises made to the Jews were fulfilled. For Jesus was the Messianic king of the Jews through whom the God of Israel was made known to the Gentiles. The same prophets predicted that the Jews would reject the kingdom of Christ until the Second Coming at the end of the world, when all will believe. Then the Jews will see that the apostles stood on the shoulders of the prophets, that the Church fulfilled the Synagogue, and that the New Law fulfilled the Old. At the end of the poem, having gone through the history of the race, the dreamer is any fourteenth-century Christian. He sees plainly the wickedness and corruption in the world and in the Church, but he is also equipped to seek the salvation whose meaning has been gradually unfolded to him. He understands that the Scriptures must be fulfilled in him, and in every man, until the end of the world.

Piers himself is a mythical figure whose poetic ambiguities cannot be translated satisfactorily into prose. We are meant to understand many things about him, however, and one of them is his role in instructing mankind. While his teaching becomes richer and deeper, he does not stumble along the path of learning like the dreamer. He is always enlightened by the knowledge of God and is apparently free from sin. Throughout the poem he represents human nature at its best, perhaps as it would be had there been no Fall to deform the image of God in men. But since the Fall, he must wait on history. He understands the "Infinity" of Christ's love, but he cannot pass on the pardon of God until after the Passion. In the early cantos, in what is the time of the Old Law in the history of the world, he teaches the way of the Ten Commandments. Later, his is the "human nature" taken by Christ, the "armor" worn by the Good Samaritan. Through him, the pope has the power to pardon, and he builds the Barn of the Church and plows the field of Truth with two harrows, the Old and the New Testaments. Certainly Piers's disappearance in the last age portrayed in the poem is an indictment of the Church in Langland's day, but it means something more. It means that men must always seek Piers, who will always be hard to find. At the end of the poem, Piers is not priest, pope, or Messias but Christ's steward, who must see to it that men give and forgive before they are given to and are forgiven. In order to win this pardon, men must follow Piers on the road of the Commandments, the road to Jerusalem, and the road to heaven.

It is in the nature of the poem and the poet that the same ideas are both discussed and allegorized, for Langland was as talky as Shaw and as apocalyptic as St. John. He was also a highly articulate theological poet, who understood better than most theologians the deepest meaning of the Scriptural tradition. A student of tradition and the Bible, he saw through dogma with the eyes of a poet. Believing that the doctrine of the Church can be traced back to Genesis and that the Church is the interpreter of Scripture, he sees Holy Church as a beautiful woman, coming from the mountain of God at the very beginning (of the poem, of time) to explain to the dreamer the meaning of Creation. In debate, in narrative, in allegory, he hammers the doctrine of the fulfillment of the Scriptures out of the rock of Scripture, from the "Giant Genesis" through the Old and the New Testament, through the Church and the Fathers to his own time and to the end of time. Langland sees the unfolding of the law and the prophets as a continuous and living tradition, in which *Piers*, too, has a place.

Chapter IV

THE OLD TESTAMENT TRINITY: FROM THE APOSTOLIC AGE THROUGH THE MIDDLE AGES

⊄The concordance of the Testaments on the subject of the Trinity was neatly summarized by St. Jerome when he said that "Whatever we read in the Old Testament we find also in the Gospel; and what we read in the Gospel is deduced from the Old Testament. There is no discord between them, no disagreement. In both Testaments, the Trinity is preached." [1]

Now this is the prose behind the Trinitarian poetry of *Piers Plowman* and much of Old English and later medieval literature. Not only the outline but also many of the details of this teaching appear in literature, sometimes submerged, sometimes on the surface. And more often than not, the concept of the fulfillment of the Scriptures bears the impress of the early environment in which it was first formulated.

Word and Wisdom

For example, it was assumed by the poets, in common with the rest of the Christian world, that the "Word" and the "Wisdom" of Genesis, the Psalms, and the sapiential literature referred to Jesus. Sometimes the poets explain the identifications, but even their lightest allusions have a Trinitarian meaning that goes back to the earliest days of the Church. For these are not primarily poetic metaphors, but the first step in an ancient exegetical argument.

No doubt the early importance of the identifications was due to the fact that the first Christians were Jews who were attempting to persuade other Jews that Jesus was not a new god, but the Son of God from the beginning. Jesus had said, "Before Abraham was, I

1. *Letters and Select Works* VI. 22.

53

am" (John 8:58). But his words could not be quoted to the Jews, who might well have replied that it was for just such blasphemy that Jesus was crucified. If the Christian contention was true, it could be, and had to be, proved from the Old Testament. Reading the Scriptures in the light of their belief in Christ, the Jewish-Christians believed that Jesus was the Word of God who created the heavens and man, who spoke with the patriarchs and prophets, and who finally (in the words of the Psalmist) came down from heaven and dwelt among men.

To some, this interpretation must have seemed the final step towards which their study of the texts had been leading. For there was an established pre-Christian pattern of Jewish exegesis in which Wisdom was personified as an "intermediate being between God and the world . . . a personality existing alongside of God, but separate from Him." [2] In popular Jewish apocalypses like 4(2) Esdras (as well as in Proverbs), God was thought to have created the world by means of his Word or his Wisdom. In his Targum (i.e., paraphrase), the Jewish Onkelos substituted "Word" for "God" throughout. The prevalence of the idea in Jewish circles is borne out by the Jewish-Christian debates, in which the Jewish disputant often accepts the existence of an intermediate person, even if he does not agree that that person was Jesus.[3]

To the earliest Jewish-Christians nothing was more obvious than that this Old Testament Word and Wisdom was Christ. The familiarity of the doctrine, no doubt formulated before the Gospels were written down, probably explains the difference in wording of two parallel passages in Matthew and Luke. While according to Matthew (23:34), Jesus said, "*I send* to you prophets and wise men," according to Luke (11:49), Jesus said, "*the wisdom of God said: I will send* to them prophets and apostles." The meaning is identical in both, and the Evangelists would not have considered the interchange of words and tenses a "discrepancy." The most eloquent summary of the doctrine occurs in the opening verses of the Fourth Gospel. St.

2. W. O. E. Oesterley, *The Books of the Apocrypha* (London, 1916), pp. 235, 237.

3. B. F. Westcott, *Introduction to the Study of the Gospels* (London, 1895), pp. 151, 152. See also "Dialogue of Athanasius and Zacchaeus," trans. F. C. Conybeare, *Expositor*, V (1897), 302.

John was not indulging in rhetoric, but carefully paraphrasing the opening verses of Genesis in the light of Christ when he wrote: "In the beginning was the Word: and the Word was with God: and the Word was God. The same was in the beginning with God. All things were made by him: and without him was made nothing that was made."

Gentile converts later attempted rational explanations of the doctrine, but never to the exclusion of the Scriptures. In attempting to explain the separateness of the preexistent Word from the Father, second-century Justin Martyr asks if this is not what we see in ourselves. For, he says in an oft-repeated argument, "When we utter a word we beget it, but not by division, so as to lessen the word that is in us," but as one fire is kindled from another without diminishing the first. Then, like the Jewish-Christians, Justin simply quotes the Scriptural passages as self-evident. This Word of God spoke thus by Solomon: "When He did prepare the heavens, I was by Him" (Prov. 21:36). Christ was the "first-born," "from the beginning and before the world" of Ecclesiasticus (24:5,14). Indeed, Christ was Creator, for he was the "word of the Lord by which the heavens were established" (Ps. 32:6). Wisdom 9:1 is even clearer: "O God of my fathers and Lord of mercy who has made all things by thy Word and by thy Wisdom didst form man." In the same manner were interpreted Proverbs 1:1–6, Isaias 10:23, and dozens of psalms, favorites being 2, 44, 106, and 109. Origen, Clement of Alexandria, Irenaeus, Lactantius, Augustine—all cite the same texts, the phrases of which echo through later literature.[4]

OLD TESTAMENT APPEARANCES OF THE SECOND PERSON

For many centuries, Christians believed also that a careful reading of Genesis indicated that the Second Person is mentioned in the story of the Creation. Please observe, they said to Jews and heretics, the extraordinary mixture of singular and plural verbs and pronouns: "And *God* said 'Let *Us* make man in *Our Image*'" (Gen. 1:26). God

4. Justin *Dialogue* 61; Origen *Commentary on John* I. 22, 23, 34; Clement of Alexandria, *Stromateis,* in Montague Rhodes James, *The Apocryphal New Testament* (Oxford, 1924), p. 486; Irenaeus *Against Heresies* III. 22; Lactantius *The Divine Institutes* IV; Augustine *On Faith and the Creed* II. 3.

must have spoken here to one different in number, but not in will, from himself. So, they added, in Genesis 3:22, "God said, 'Behold, Adam is become as *one of Us,* to know good and evil.' " [5]

Remote as this exposition of the divine grammar may seem to us, it seemed most convincing to generations of Christians (Langland's among them); and it was not dismissed lightly by the rabbis, either. While Philo had said that "Let Us make" shows an "assumption of other beings to himself as assistants," most Jewish teachers taught that in this verse God was talking to himself. In a witty Talmudic story, Moses himself is disturbed by the Christian argument. According to the story, when God was dictating the Torah to Moses, Moses foresaw the Trinitarian use that the Christians would make of plural pronouns in Scripture. When, therefore, Moses came to the verse, "God said, 'Let Us make man,' " he protested. "Lord of the world," he said, "how thou art giving a chance to the Minim [i.e., heretics, Christians]! I am astonished!" God replied, "Write, and he who will err, let him err." [6]

Who, indeed, dictated the law to Moses and spoke with Abraham? The Jews said "God" or "angels." The Christians said "Christ": it was the Son rather than the Father, the Word who spoke with the patriarchs and the prophets. And again, it was an examination of grammar that proved the point.

So popular for over a thousand years was the appearance of the Trinity to Abraham that the same phrase summarized it in the Fathers, the breviary, the commentaries, and the poets. "*Tres vidit et unum adoravit*"; he saw three and worshiped one. The gist of the argument may be given most quickly by excerpting Justin Martyr's analysis of chapters 18 and 19 of Genesis. As Abraham was sitting at his tent door, "*God* appeared unto him." And he looked, "And lo, *three* men stood over him." When he saw "*them*," he bowed to the ground and said "*Lord*." Justin asks if God was one of those whom the Holy Ghost terms men. No, replies the Jewish Trypho in Justin's *Dialogue,* Abraham saw God before he saw them; they were angels.

5. Ignatius, "Epistle to the Antiochians" [spurious], *The Apostolic Fathers,* Ante-Nicene Library, I (1870), 462; Justin *Dialogue* 61; "Dialogue of Athanasius and Zacchaeus," p. 303; Eusebius *Ecclesiastical History* (trans. Hugh Lawlor and John Oulton) I. 2, 4.

6. Philo *On Creation* (trans. C. D. Yonge) I. 21; R. Travers Herford, *Christianity in Talmud and Midrash* (London, 1903), p. 301.

How then, demands Justin, is one of them later called God? One of the three, both sides agree, promised Sarah a son and also promised to return. When he did return after the birth of Isaac, he was called God. "Hear the plain words of Moses," says Justin, " 'And *God* said unto Abraham . . .' "

From the earliest days of Christianity, the Christians delighted in finding similar proofs. As a matter of fact, according to Matthew (22: 40–46), Jesus himself claimed the famous Psalm 109. When he asked the Pharisees whose son is the Christ, they answered, "David's." How then, he replied, did David "in spirit call him Lord, saying 'The Lord said to my Lord, sit thou at my right hand, until I make thy enemies thy footstool?' " Who is the second Lord here, the Epistle to the Hebrews (1:13) asks, and "to which of the angels" did God ever speak so? The commentators point out that when the "Lord rained upon Sodom brimstone and fire from the Lord out of heaven" (Gen. 19:24), the first "Lord" must be "another," other "in number, not in will." Similarly, Josue saw a "Man" and then fell on his face and called him "Lord." [7]

St. Augustine warns that we "may not rashly affirm which person of the Trinity appeared to this or that of the fathers . . . unless when the context attaches to the narrative some probable intimations on the subject." Actually, most contexts did give him probable intimations, and he stops only just short of the many learned and popular writers who freely attributed the whole Old Testament to the Son. In the *Apocryphal Acts of Philip*, for example, the converted Jew declares:

> I believe in the Messiah thy God, that He is I am that I am, El Shaddai, Adonai, the Lord [of] Sabaoth, the Glorious in His holiness, who made heaven and earth by His word; and made Adam in His image and likeness; and He accepted the offering of Abel, and He rejected the offering of Cain the murderer; and He removed Enoch without his tasting death; and He delivered Noah from the flood; and He spake with Abraham His friend; and He preserved Isaac from the knife; and He revealed Himself to Jacob at Beth-El; and He expounded His secrets to Joseph; and He led Israel out of Egypt; and He spake with Moses in the thorn-bush; and He divided

7. Justin *Dialogue* 56, 58, 59; Hilary of Poitiers *On the Trinity* IV. 23–25; Ambrose *Of the Holy Spirit* II. 4; Evagrius *Altercatio Legis inter Simoneum Iudaeum et Theophilum Christianum,* in *Corpus Scriptorum Ecclesiasticorum Latinorum* (ed. E. Bratke) II. 1.

the sea before the people; and He sent down the manna from heaven; and He brought up the quails from the sea; . . . He delivered Joshua . . . He destroyed Goliath . . . He took Jonah out of the fish; and He brought Daniel out of the pit; and He extinguished the fire of Ananias . . . and He rescued the wronged Susanna; and this is Emmanuel, the mighty God.

As St. Irenaeus said, to the "truly spiritual" man it will be clear that the whole revelation is the work of the Son of God, always the Word of God, although only recently manifested, and always the same Spirit of God from the Creation of the world.[8]

THE INCARNATION

It was only a step, albeit a long one, to conclude that this same Second Person bowed down the heavens and came as a man to visit men. To St. Cyril of Jerusalem, as to many other Christians, the Incarnation followed the Old Testament appearances in an obvious logical progression. Instructing fourth-century catechumens, he said: "If the Jews still disbelieve, let us hold this forth to them: What strange thing do we announce in saying that God was made Man, when yourselves say that Abraham received the Lord as a guest? . . . The Lord, who ate with Abraham, ate also with us." [9]

By and large, Christians were likely to argue that the appearance of God in the New Testament was no more "strange" than in the Old —that if you can believe the one, you can believe the other. Just as the nature of God is a mystery in Judaism, so the Incarnation is the central mystery of Christianity. We understand something of it when we say that God created man in his Image, every man being spirit united with matter. In the Incarnation, God did not change, for he is unchangeable: while he became man according to the flesh, he was God according to the spirit.

Furthermore, the Christians insisted that God himself, not a mere human Messias, was predicted by the prophets. "Lord, bow down thy heavens and descend," cried the Psalmist (Ps. 143). "He bowed the heavens and came down" (Ps. 17). "For a child is born to us, and a

---

8. Augustine *On the Trinity* II. 13, 18; *Apocryphal Acts of the Apostles,* ed. and trans. W. Wright, II, 73 f.; Irenaeus *Against Heresies* IV. 33.

9. *Catechetical Lectures* XII. 16.

son is given to us," wrote Isaias (9:6), "and his name shall be called Wonderful, Counsellor, God the Mighty, the Father of the world to come, the Prince of peace." It was on the basis of verses like these that pre-Christian Jews, like the author of the apocryphal Book of Enoch (second century B.C.), hoped for the coming of the Lord. In a passage that rather reminds us of the mountain and the field of folk in *Piers*, Michael tells Enoch that the summit of a particular mountain is like the one on which the "Holy One, Lord of Glory, Eternal King will sit, when He shall come down to visit the earth with goodness" (1 En. 25:3). There are similar phrases in the *Testaments of the Twelve Patriarchs*, written, as we have seen, during the same period, to the effect that God himself would come down from heaven to save men.

Numerous other prophecies seemed to Christians to specify the incarnation of the Second Person. The Psalmist said that "He sent his *word* and healed them" (Ps. 106). And Baruch foretold also the New Testament appearance of Wisdom: "This is our God. There shall not be reckoned beside Him any other. He found out all the ways of wisdom, and gave it to Jacob his servant, and to Israel his beloved. Afterwards He was seen upon earth and conversed with men" (3: 36–38). When St. John wrote that "the Word was made flesh and dwelt among us," he was echoing the phrases of these prophecies, beloved by early and medieval Christians alike.

THE OLD ENGLISH PERIOD

The doctrine as it has been sketched here appears in much fuller form, with texts and examples multiplied, in the works of the Fathers. The tradition remains constant in Anglo-Saxon and later medieval England, not only in Latin and English homilies but in poems and plays. Apparently the argument or assumption that the Trinity was preached in the Old Testament was very widespread; and the Wisdom and Word, the "Let Us make" texts, the Old Testament appearances of the Trinity, and the prophecies of the Incarnation are frequently cited.

It would be hard to overestimate the importance of the whole argument in Christian thinking throughout the Middle Ages. It is not just that it appears in a formidable number of works; it has an intensity that is surprising to modern readers who find a good part of it quaint. There has been a real shift on this subject—not indeed in the doctrine of the Trinity but in the way of presenting it. So marked has been the decline in importance of the old way since the Renaissance that literary critics have often passed over or misinterpreted passages derived from it.

For one thing, the old method of examining Scriptural grammar has long been discredited by Biblical scholars. Further, the identification of Christ with Old Testament Word and Wisdom has been forgotten, and the concept of Christ as Creator has been blurred. The phrases remain in the liturgy, but their significance is not generally realized. The reason may be that modern Christians learn the doctrine of the Trinity from the catechism, in which it is defined in abstract and philosophical terms. That may also be why the Trinity now seems the least exciting part of Christian doctrine and is left largely to professional theologians.

It was far otherwise with Anglo-Saxon and later medieval Christians. Liturgy and literature from the eighth century to the sixteenth were filled with poetic devotion to the Trinity, couched in the same Scriptural phrases, in an apparently unbroken tradition. And the well-known arguments of the preexistence of Christ underlie not only the whole concept of the history of the world but the popular allegories, such as *Piers,* as well.

Commentary and Liturgy

Some of the lyricism was inherent in the Old Testament phrases of the argument. Bede's sapiential commentary on the Creation and the Incarnation, for example, could easily be turned into a poem. He interprets "The Lord by Wisdom hath founded the earth" as "God the Father made all through the Son." It follows that "Wisdom hath built herself a house" is a description of the way in which Christ assumed humanity; [10] it is also, if one may say so without scandal, a charming metaphor for the Incarnation.

At Christmas, Aelfric told his congregation how the shepherds went to Bethlehem, "saying" let us go "see the Word." And we can see in his writings how easily the same theology slipped into prayer:

10. *Opera Omnia,* ed. J. A. Giles (London, 1844), IX, 72, 90.

"O thou Almighty God, thou who through thy coeternal Wisdom didst create man . . ."[11]

A common beginning for many prayers was "My God and my Maker and my Savior." The full meaning of the phrase is clear in a Kyrie in the missal, which follows the very order of the theological argument: "O Christ, the brightness of God, the strength and Wisdom of the Father, have mercy upon us. Thou, the maker of the image of man, and the restorer of him when fallen, have mercy upon us." The gradual of the Christmas Mass is the verse from Psalm 109 that had been used as a proof text from the earliest days of the Church: "The Lord said unto my Lord: Sit thou on my right hand. . . ." In the same Mass, two clerks chant in alternate sentences the ninth chapter of Isaias, with a number of "farcings." These additions include appellations long familiar as titles of the Second Person:

> And his name shall be called,
> Messiah, Sother, Emmanuel, Sabaoth, Adonai,
> Wonderful,
> The Root of David,
> Counsellor,
> Of God the Father,
> God,
> Who created all things,
> Mighty,
>   .   .   .   .
> He shall sit upon the throne of David
>   and upon his kingdom.[12]

This concept of Christ as Creator probably explains what has been considered a curious translation of King Alfred's. Turning the Latin into English, Alfred always translated "Dominus" by "Dryhten"—except once when he translated it as "Crist": "Crist geworhte heofonas . . ." According to a later editor of his, this cannot be a mistake of the scribe but must be Alfred's rendering. Well, why not? St. Ambrose had said that it was "indifferent" whether you said "God made the heavens and earth in the beginning (i.e., in the Son), or that God the Son made them, or that God made them through the

---

11. *Homilies* I. 41; II. 599.

12. *The Sarum Missal* (trans. Frederick E. Warren) I. 96–98. While the Sarum Missal is later than Bede and Aelfric, the liturgy described in this chapter is very old and was probably known in Anglo-Saxon England.

Son." The good king may not have realized that he was taking liberties with his text when he wrote that Christ made the heavens.[13]

Poetry and Story

In many instances in Old English poetry, it is not clear whether "Lord" means the *Father* or the *Son*, but it seems to me that many allusions that are taken by literary critics to mean *Father* were certainly meant to be *Son*. The modern reader simply assumes that any reference to the Creator is to the *Father*, unless it is specifically labeled "Christ." The medieval reader was, like Alfred, more likely to make the opposite assumption. In early times, nobody seems to have questioned the identification of the incarnate Christ with the preexistent Word which created the world; in our time, the identification has been so largely forgotten that "Wisdom" and "Word" are understood purely as poetic images.

Earlier Christians were very much alive to both the poetry and the theology. Indeed, in the Advent poems in the Exeter Book, poetry and theology are so closely united that they cannot well be separated.[14] Like Langland centuries later, the poet approached the mystery of the Trinity not by defining it but by marveling over its manifestation in history. To early and medieval Christians, that manifestation was preeminently through the Second Person, who was the preexistent Word from the beginning, and who will be the Judge at the end. As this view of Christ transcends time, so the *Advent Lyrics* bring together past, present, and future "awaiters"—Jews and Gentiles before the Incarnation, patriarchs and prophets in limbo, and later Christians who await not merely the feast of the Nativity, but the coming of the Judge.

This whole Christological view of the universe is expressed most beautifully in Poem VIII. There is no doubt here that the Creator

13. Milton Haight Turk, *The Legal Code of Alfred the Great* (Halle, 1893), p. 34; Ambrose *On the Holy Spirit* II. 86, 87 and *On the Faith* V. 197, quoted in F. H. Dudden, *The Life and Times of St. Ambrose* (Oxford, 1935), II, 581.

14. Often printed as the first part of the *Christ* these poems have been edited separately by Jackson J. Campbell, *The Advent Lyrics of the Exeter Book* (Princeton, N.J., 1959). Subsequent references to these poems give the poem number in Campbell and the line numbers in the *Christ* in *The Poems of Cynewulf,* trans. Charles W. Kennedy (London, 1910; reprint ed., New York, 1949). On the antiphons, see also Albert S. Cook, ed., *The Christ of Cynewulf* (Boston, 1900), introd. and notes.

and the Judge are as much Christ as the Incarnate Jesus. Both ideas and language follow the Wisdom argument. As the apologists paraphrased the opening phrases of Genesis and then went on to the Incarnation, so the poet begins with the Old Testament phrases and marvels at the inexplicable origin of the Son:

> O true and pacific
> King of all Kings, Almighty Christ,
> you existed before all
> the glories of the world, by your wondrous Father
> begotten a child by his power and might!
> There is not now any man under the skies,
> any clever-thinking man so deeply wise
> that he may to mortals say,
> explain aright how the Guardian of the Heavens
> at the beginning took you as his noble Son.
>
> . . . .
>
> You are the Wisdom which shaped fully
> This wide creation with the Ruling Father
> (Poem VIII, ll. 1–10, 26–27; *Christ*, ll. 213 ff.)

To later readers, it may seem that there is little connection between this doctrine and the petition section of the poem in which Christ is asked to come to save men from evil. Contemporaries of the poet, however, would have felt the sequence of ideas to be entirely appropriate. The crucial point is that it was the same God who created man, redeemed him from the consequences of the sin of Adam, and who continues to save him. According to the Fathers, the Psalmist called not to a mere human Messias but to God himself to bow down the heavens and come to earth. Here the poet calls the "High Lord of Heaven" to come now and visit the earth, to open the "golden gates" of heaven, and finally to save men from the power of hell.

As Cook pointed out long ago, certain lines in the poems recall Aelfric's homilies. They also recall St. Augustine and Langland and a host of others, at the same time that they bear the stamp of the poet who wrote them. Unique as a work of art, the lyrics reflect a dramatic way of thinking about the Second Person of the Trinity that was shared by the whole Christian world.

Through liturgy and literature, everybody knew, too, about the Old Testament appearances of Christ. Again, it is not always clear in the poetry, especially in the versified episodes from the Bible, whether the Father or the Son is intended. I rather think that in the Old English *Exodus,* for example, the "Lord" who is the "Leader" of Moses was supposed to suggest the preexistent Second Person rather than the Father. The allusions are subtle here, because the poet was sensitive to nuances, aesthetic as well as theological. Still, the Old Testament phrases used to describe the Lord are those used in the ancient "proofs" of Christ's appearances to Josue and Moses. That it was Christ who appeared is assumed in the second O antiphon of Advent, with which the poet was certainly familiar. Begging Christ to come and redeem us, the antiphon calls him "Adonai" and "leader of the house of Israel," who "did appear to Moses in the flame of the burning bush, and didst give unto him the law on Sinai." In the poem, the leader of Moses has something of the spirit of the young hero Jesus, the leader of the apostles in the Old English *Andreas,* and is called the "Prince of Glory" and the "Lord of Life." Moses tells the Israelites not to fear Pharaoh because the God of Abraham, "the Lord of Angels," the "Strong Captain," the "great leader" is with them.[15]

Another reason for assuming that these are prefigurations of Christ is that this is not a straightforward paraphrase of Exodus. If it were, why would so seemingly competent a craftsman pause for a hundred and fifty lines, with the Israelites on the very banks of the Red Sea, to tell a little about Noe and Abraham? Probably, we would think, for some of the same reasons that Langland pauses before the Crucifixion in *Piers* to present Abraham and Moses. There is a complex of symbols behind these Old Testament heroes, for their stories were considered "prophecies" in a number of ways. For one, the Passing of the Red Sea was itself considered a type of the Resurrection, and the Passover of the Jews was a figure of the paschal or Easter service.

Actually, as Professor Bright pointed out many years ago, the structure of the *Exodus* is closely related to the Easter liturgy, to the "prophecies" read in the Mass for Holy Saturday.[16] These were readings from the Old Testament, and they included the two patriarchs as well as Moses and others. The three stories, as they appear in

15. *Exodus,* in *The Caedmon Poems,* trans. Charles W. Kennedy (London, 1916; reprint ed., Gloucester, Mass., 1965), ll. 22, 23, 93–97, 273 ff.

16. James W. Bright, "The Relation of the Caedmonian *Exodus* to the Liturgy," *MLN,* XXVII (1912), 97–103.

the readings and in the poem, are deliverances: Noe from the flood, Isaac from the knife, the Israelites from the Egyptians. All prefigured the ultimate deliverance by Christ. While the Old Testament texts were read without comment on Holy Saturday, their Christological interpretation had been given explicitly in the liturgy of the previous day, Good Friday. During the service of the Adoration of the Cross, the "reproaches" of Christ to his people were sung. In these, Christ cites his deliverances of the Israelites. It was he who led them out of the land of Egypt, led them through the desert, led them over the Red Sea, went before them in a pillar of cloud, and gave them water of salvation from the rock. Since these are exactly the episodes which are related in the *Exodus*, it may well be that the "great leader" of Moses in the poem is the same Christ as in the liturgy.

As even the barest summary of Old English works indicates, there is no doubt at all that it was Christ who appeared to Abraham. The breviary for Quinquagesima relates the story of Abraham substantially as it appears in the Bible. But a "response," breaking the narrative to make the Trinitarian point, says that Abraham at Mambre saw three men: "He saw three and adored one." Bede and Aelfric discuss the point at greater length, Aelfric calling the three "angels." [17] In the *Exodus*, he who gave the promise to Abraham is called the "lord of angels." In the *Andreas*, in which the action takes place A.D. rather than B.C., a supernatural voice reproaches the Jews for not recognizing Christ as their creator and helper in days past, for he is the "same all-ruling God whom in days of old" their fathers knew; "to Abraham, to Isaac, and to Jacob he granted grace, decked them with wealth." Unconvinced by the voice, the Jews believe only when Abraham himself arises from the grave to bear witness that he knew Christ of old. In the Old English *Daniel*, based, perhaps, on the twelfth prophecy read on Holy Saturday, we are told that it was the "Savior of men" who made a covenant with Abraham, Isaac, and Jacob.[18]

17. *Breviarium ad Usum Insignis Ecclesiae Sarum,* ed. Francis Procter and Christopher Wordsworth (Cambridge, Eng., 1879–86), vol. 1: *Kalendarium et Temporale,* pp. 541, 546; Bede, *Opera Omnia, PL.* 91, col. 238; Aelfric *Homilies* II. 235.

18. *Andreas* may be found in *The Poems of Cynewulf; Daniel* in *The Caedmon Poems.*

In this same *Daniel,* the three children in the fiery furnace bless the Father, the Son, and the Holy Ghost. The "angel" who sheltered the youths from the fire was popularly considered to be Christ. Aelfric was only quoting the Fathers when he preached on Christmas day of the way in which Nebuchadnezzar looked into the furnace and saw four figures, the fourth "like unto the child of God." Thus, adds Aelfric, "the heathen king saw the Son of the Living God,—he knew him through God's revelation." The heathen king is, indeed, one of the "prophets" taken to witness in the pseudo-Augustinian *Sermon* read during Advent. "Speak, Nebuchadnezzar!" cries the Doctor; "Tell what was revealed." [19] Curiously enough, the *Daniel* poet apparently did not care for this interpretation. While his three children know the Trinity, he seems to go out of his way to imply that the angel was only an angel, who went back to heaven with the other angels when his errand was done.

The Later Medieval Period

Literary forms and language changed enormously in the next few centuries, but the old style of teaching the Trinity held its own. Wherever we turn in the great popular school of the drama, for example, we find the old proofs of the divinity of Christ. The contexts vary, but the phrases are the same: Christ, the Word, the Wisdom of God, the Creator of the world and of man in his image, who took flesh to redeem man and will come again to judge—always one and the same God.

The Drama

There is no denying that some of the anachronisms in the plays are the result of ignorance and artlessness. On the other hand, a certain share of naïvete, not to say ignorance, seems to have been bequeathed to later readers who see only a painfully physical concept of God in the old plays. It seems to me that the Creation scenes, for all their awkwardness, reflect not so much an anthropomorphic God as a theological argument that at best would be difficult to dramatize. Just as in many examples of medieval art Christ is portrayed as Creator,

19. Aelfric *Homilies* II. 21; Pseudo-Augustine *Contra Judaeos, Paganos, et Arianos: Sermo de Symbolo, PL.* 42, col. 1126.

so, in many plays, it is the Son, the preexistent Word, who is the speaker.

In the highly liturgical twelfth century *Adam*, for example, instead of reading "God," the rubric reads "The Figure." M. Sépét suggested that "Figure" represented the "Word, later to become incarnate in Jesus Christ," and he pointed out that the same divine personage is once called "Salvator" in the rubrics.[20] All of the later cycles open with the announcement by Deus: "Ego sum alpha et omega." The rest of the line varies: "Vita via, Veritas primus et novissimus" (York); "primus et ultimus . . . primus et nobillissimus" (Chester). As everybody knew, this is not the way Genesis opens; the phrases are, of course, from the Apocalypse of St. John, the Revelation of Jesus Christ. So spoke Christ to St. John, thought the medieval man. The Father is not forgotten in the Creation. The initial announcement is followed in all by the ancient explanation of the Trinity: in whom is no beginning or end, one God in persons three, through whom all things were made. "Make we heaven and earth," says Deus (Towneley), using the plural pronoun that for so long had been taken to prove that there was more than one person at the beginning. Perhaps the Word is speaker? [21]

At least there is no doubt that Christ is the speaker in the Last Judgment plays, and it seems more than a coincidence that the Chester *Judgment* begins with exactly the same words as the *Creation:* "Deus: Ego sum Alpha et O, Primus et Novissimus." Then, after explaining the Trinity exactly as at the opening of the cycle, Christ shows cross, thorns, and spear. Angelus Primus then addresses him as the Lord who made heaven and earth.

There are frequent reminders throughout the Crucifixion, Resurrection, and Judgment scenes that the same Christ created the earth and man and then died for him. There is something of a pattern here that suggests that the anachronisms are at least in part deliberate. The "good" Jews in the plays regard Jesus as the Creator; they are familiar with his title of *Sapientia*, and they pray in the temple to the

20. Cited by Edward Noble Stone, ed. and trans., "Le Mystère d'Adam," University of Washington Publications, IV (1936), 159 n.

21. *Chester Plays,* ed. Hermann Deimling, vol. I, EETS (Extra Series) 62 (1893); vol. II, EETS (Extra Series) 115 (1916); *The Towneley Plays,* ed. Alfred W. Pollard, EETS (Extra Series) 71 (1897); *The York Plays,* ed. Lucy Toulmin Smith (Oxford, 1885).

Trinity. The villains, however, refuse to recognize him, and neutral characters are uncertain, usually for purposes of instruction. In the Weavers' *Prophet Play*, for example, Prophet I wonders, quite out of character, if the Incarnation is possible. Why, retorts Prophet II, did not Malachias say, and did not Isaias foresee . . .?

As in many Old English poems, many of the Old Testament plays originated not in the Bible stories but in the lessons and responses of Advent and Lent. Many of the references to Christ's appearances to Old Testament saints are loose enough, but a large number of them retain the context of the old theological argument. For a commentary on the Towneley play of *Jacob*, for instance, we might turn to Justin Martyr, or St. Augustine, or Alcuin. Actually, the play is composed exclusively of the Christological episodes in the life of the patriarch. Jacob opens the play with a prayer, "Help me lord, adonay," and then lies down to sleep with his head on a stone (the stone, according to Augustine, being Christ). Skipping the intervening parts in the Bible, the play next presents Jacob wrestling with an angel. This episode is referred to in several parts of the Old Testament with some variations. Genesis 32:34 says "a man" wrestled with him until morning, and in verse 28 "he" said to Jacob, "thou hast been strong against God." Osee (12:4) identified the wrestler with an angel (the Fathers identified him with Christ). Furthermore, in Genesis, when Jacob asks the wrestler his name, he answers only, "Why dost thou ask my name?" In the play, the wrestler is called "Deus" throughout, and when Jacob asks his name, Deus replies, "whi askis thou it 'wonderfull,' if thou wyt" (ll.98, 99). "Wonderful" (from Isaias) was, of course, a popular appellation for Christ in the liturgy and in the commentaries.

Christ and the Doctors

Now this may not be high drama or inspired religion, but it has a certain dignity and fitness. As much cannot be said for the attempts to teach the Trinity in the numerous dramatic and nondramatic versions of the story of Christ and the Doctors, a story which was very popular in medieval England. The slight Scriptural source is to be found in Luke 2:42–47, in which, it will be recalled, the Child who stayed behind in Jerusalem was found "in the temple, sitting in the midst of the doctors, hearing them and asking them questions. And all that heard him were astonished at his wisdom and his answers." The embroideries on this theme, from the earliest Apocryphal Gospel to the latest miracle play, transform this pleasant picture into a debate, in which the principal subject is the Trinity, and in which the Child stresses his preexistence.

In most of the versions, the Jewish doctors of the law are more expert at distributing blows than texts. In the *Disputison be-twene child Jhesu & Maistres of the law of Jewus,* one of them at least knows enough to object that Jesus did not get this Trinity nonsense from Moses and that it is wrong to say that God is one and three. And in the *Cursor Mundi,* when the doctors question the child's wisdom, he tells them by way of argument that it was he who saw and spoke with Abraham.[22] The Chester play (part of the *Purification*) is rather interesting because the child is called "Deus" in the rubrics and also because one of the doctors is almost subtle in suspecting the fulfillment of the prophecies. Actually, the stupidity of the doctors in all of the versions is, like the dullness of the dreamer in *Piers,* a teaching device. In the most pleasant and theological play, the Hegge play, the doctors ask questions and listen patiently, with the audience, to the explanations of the Trinity. The child explains to them how all things were made by three persons, one of whom has taken incarnation.[23]

The History of the Holy Grail

A much fuller use of the Old Testament appears in what seems at first glance a less likely source than the Christ and the Doctors stories— that is, in Lovelich's *History of the Holy Grail.* Still, who ought to know the doctrine better than Joseph of Arimathea? In the romance, it is the task of this famous Jewish-Christian to convert a pagan (Sarrasin), King Evalach. Before the king, and in debate with learned men called by the king, Joseph sums up the Trinity competently enough. He explains that God is called Christ's Father, that he

22. *Disputison, Vernon MS,* pt. II, p. 479, ll. 5–7. *Cursor Mundi,* ed. Richard Morris, vol. I, EETS 57, 99, 101; vol. II, EETS 59, 62; vol. III, EETS 66, 68 (1874–93), ll. 12, 153 ff.

23. *Hegge Plays,* ed. K. J. Block (under title *Ludus Coventriae*), EETS (Extra Series) 120 (1922).

begat him before the angels, not carnally but spiritually; that the Holy Ghost made the prophets speak, that the three persons are One God, and that when, at the creation, God said "Let Us make man in Our Image," he was speaking to the Son.

Not only is Evalach not convinced by this Scriptural argument, but he objects, as a pagan ought, by saying that Joseph's arguments are neither true nor reasonable. In a debate called the following day, a smart heathen "clerk" objects further that if all three are one, then each cannot be fully God Himself. Now Joseph is no Thomas Aquinas, and he does not really know how to answer; he can only repeat his former "proofs." Is it possible that the author was displaying historical imagination in this selection of arguments voiced by his characters? There is some basis for thinking so: Joseph's arguments are those of a Jewish-Christian, and in fact they do not satisfy the Gentile king. On the other hand, the reason Joseph speaks so well only "out of the Scriptures" is probably that the habit of appeal to the Old Testament was so strong that the author, like his character, knew no other way to "prove" the Trinity.

But what he lacked in philosophy, Joseph made up in faith, faith that the same God who had miraculously delivered the Jews of old would now miraculously convert the heathen to Christianity. Earlier in the poem, Jesus himself had told Joseph of his great deeds for the Jews. It was he who had brought Joseph's fathers out of the land of Pharaoh, through the Red Sea, and through the desert. Now this is an echo of the Good Friday "reproaches" of the Jews, the influence of which we have seen both in Old English works and in a number of later medieval works (for example, in the *Stanzaic Life of Christ*, in the *Miroure of Mans Salvacionne*, and in the mysteries). What is interesting in this Grail romance of Lovelich's is that when Joseph loses the debate with the pagan counselors of King Evalach, he prays for a miracle in the same Old Testament terms used by Jesus to convert him. "O God of my fathers," he prays, who are the God whom they should adore, who brought them out of the bondage of Pharaoh, God, be merciful to those who worship images of wood and stone. God, by your death on the cross, by your deliverance of me from prison, by your saving David from Goliath, by your protection of Daniel in the lion's den, by your forgiveness of Mary Magdalen, by your deliverance of Susanna, God who brought Israel through the

Red Sea dryfooted, who delivered them from troubles and enemies so many times, send counsel to King Evalach.[24]

Gregory the Great and Chaucer's Man of Law

This concordance of miracles was an important theme in Christianity as far back as St. Paul, and by the time of Gregory the Great it had become curiously stylized. In Gregory's *Dialogues*, every Christian miracle is shown to be similar to an Old Testament miracle. When a skeptic wonders at this extreme parallelism, Gregory assures him that the similarity is not coincidental, nor does it suggest fabrication. What it does prove is that Christians call on the same God who helped the Jews, for it is the same Christ who gave the "sign of miracles" in both Testaments.[25]

Chaucer's Man of Law is almost as articulate on the subject of miracles as Gregory, whose outlook he obviously shares. Feeling called upon to justify the miraculous deliverances of Constance, he does so by pointing to Old Testament parallels, and he concludes that the same Christ who performed them helped also his servant Constance. Men might ask, he concedes to the skeptics, why she was not slain at the feast. In reply, he counters with an equally unlikely miracle: Who saved Daniel in the lions' den? Referring to another episode in the legend of Constance, he asks who kept her from drowning in the sea. The answer is another rhetorical question derived from the conventional concordance of miracles. Who, he asks, preserved Jonas in the fish's "mawe?" Men know, he concludes, that it was he who kept the Hebrew people from drowning in the Red Sea. Constance herself prays for a miraculous deliverance such as God had vouchsafed Susanna, whose case parallels her own.[26] The Man of Law's choice of Old Testament personages is interesting. Daniel, Jonas, and Susanna—they had been cited for centuries (in that very order, in the *Apocryphal Acts of Philip*) as proof of the preexistence of the Second Person. Christian favorites for centuries, they are

24. Henry Lovelich, *History of the Holy Grail*, ed. F. J. Furnivall, EETS (Extra Series) 20, 24, 28, 30 (1877), pp. 56–62, 94–95, 44; *A Stanzaic Life of Christ*, ll. 5501–36, ed. Frances A. Foster, EETS 166 (1925); *The Miroure of Mans Salvacionne*, ed. Alfred H. Huth (London, 1888), pp. 64, 71, 77, 78.

25. Ed. Edmond Gardner (London, 1911), pp. 67, 83.

26. "The Man of Law's Tale," *Complete Works*, ed. F. N. Robinson (Cambridge, Mass., 1933), ll. 470 ff., 639 ff.

treated as familiar friends who somehow have the appeal of contemporary folk heroes and the authority of the Old Testament.

Legends of the Rood

Something of this same free and yet reverent attitude towards the Scriptures lies behind the even less credible miracles in the legends of the rood. And even the skeptics, brought up in the old tradition, might hesitate to cavil at the Trinitarian emphasis of the miracles. At least, it would not seem inherently improbable to a medieval reader that an angel should have explained the Trinity to Seth. Nor would it surprise him that Moses should work miracles through the power of the Trinity, allegorized as three wands in one root. When David replanted them and the three became one, it was only to be expected that he would exclaim: What betokens this but Father, Son, and Holy Ghost, and all one God! [27] Indeed, the literary critics must have thought it a neat image to portray David composing the Psalter under this very tree, for it was in the Psalms that the mysteries of the Trinity were sung by David. It was, after all, the Christian contention from the beginning that the Trinity was taught in the Old Testament. Adam, Seth, Moses, David, all knew the same God, triune from the beginning.

27. *Legends of the Holy Rood,* ed. R. Morris, EETS 46 (1871); *Cursor Mundi,* ll. 6301 ff.

Chapter V

THE TRIUNE GOD OF *PIERS PLOWMAN* ℭLangland saw the whole universe
as triune; he consequently found many intimations of the Trinity in
the world around him—in nature, in history, in family life—in three
of anything. The deepest meanings, however, always come out of
Langland's study of the Scriptures. It is clear from any number of
allusions that Langland shared the exegetical approach of the Fathers,
that he was steeped in the liturgy, and that his way of looking at the
doctrine fit into an unbroken literary tradition. Yet his creative fire
transmuted the doctrine into poetry of the first order.

> Riȝte so the fader and the sone and seynt spirit the thridde
> Halt al the wyde worlde with-in hem thre,
> Bothe welkne and the wynde water and erthe,
> Heuene and helle and al that there is inne.
>
> (XVII. 158–61)

> So the Sire and the Son and *Spiritus Sanctus*
> Hold the whole wide world within them,
> Air and wind and earth and water,
> Heaven and hell and all that is within them.
>
> (XVII. 162–65)

But while he believed that the doctrine had always been true and
even manifest, Langland did not think it easy of acceptance or capable
of final proof. He says that even though St. Augustine, that great
doctor of the Trinity, wrote excellent books thereon, all the clerks
cannot explain Christ's statement, *"Ego in Patre et Pater in me est;
et, qui videt me, videt et Patrem meum."* If the unlearned would do
well, they must simply believe, for had never man "fyne wytte the
feyth to dispute, Ne man had no merite" might it all be proved (X.
230 ff.).

Nonetheless, like Augustine, Langland does try to prove the Trinity to everyone in every possible way. He explains the proper procedure to use with Jews and Mohammedans, who share belief in the

73

one God and must be led gradually to the Son and the Holy Spirit. His Good Samaritan, on the very way to the Crucifixion, provides the dreamer with arguments with which to persuade heretics. Langland's main concern, however, is with belief rather than with dissent, and his keenest desire is not to argue the doctrine but to understand and to explain it. When the dreamer raises objections with Mother Church and even with Christ himself, it is in order to probe for the deepest answers.

In looking at the Fathers and the poets, we have not been seeking sources for this or that passage in *Piers*, but sharing, as it were, in Langland's education in order to understand the ideas that helped shape his mind and attitudes. Without that background, we are likely to miss a good part of his meaning, especially because he was not a theologian setting out his points in logical order, but a poet, and a poet of a most independent turn of mind. It is clear from his allegories and parables, his dialogues and discourses that his emphasis was decidedly personal, that he thought about the Bible in his own way as well as in the way of others.

It is no anachronism that the chief expositor of the Trinity in the poem is Abraham: like most medieval Christians, Langland "deduced" the Trinity from the story of the Old Testament patriarch. And then he dramatized the concept in his own fashion. Through the role of Abraham in the action of the poem, Langland allegorized what might be called the revelation of the doctrine in history. It is part of his deepest meaning that, at the climax of the poem, it is Abraham who heralds the arrival of the Second Person become man and who joins Jesus and the pilgrim at the Crucifixion, through which the faith of Abraham was revealed to all men. Further, much of what Langland understands of the nature of the triune God comes from his understanding of the story of the Creation in the Old Testament and the story of the Incarnation in the New. Sometimes he joins parallel passages from the two Testaments; always he ponders every passage in the light of the whole revelation; always he assumes that, as the Fathers had said, there is no discord and no disagreement between the Testaments.

This assumption is likely to be confusing to many modern readers because, even if they are Christians, they do not apprehend the unity of the Trinity quite as he did. While they may define the doctrine in the same terms, they unconsciously departmentalize it in their thinking, the Father, the Son, and the Holy Spirit having different functions, as it were, in history. "God," unless otherwise specified, means the Father, and to him belongs the Old Testament. Christ is largely the God-Man of the New Testament and of subsequent miracles, while the Holy Spirit is conspicuous only in the Acts of the Apostles. In Langland there is no blurring of history, but there is no danger, either, of his thinking that the Holy Spirit was a dove.

The point so labored here did not need as much explaining to a fourteenth-century reader. The angel in *Piers* (Passus IX) who comes from heaven with a message to Seth is probably the same angel who, in the rood legend that we considered in the last chapter, is sent to teach the Trinity to Seth. The angel in *Piers* is not teaching the Trinity, but the passage makes a Trinitarian point in a characteristic way. When the command sent by "God" is disobeyed, it is observed that the sin was against the message of "owre saueoure" in heaven (IX. 126). This is not an allusion to Christ's Old Testament appearance; it is a way of stressing the unity of the Trinity, for it means that at the time of Seth, when the Savior was in heaven, God was nonetheless the Father, the Son, and the Holy Spirit.

While this was the ordinary teaching of the Church, still, more often than not, it becomes extraordinary in Langland's hands. Whoever the bearer, whatever the details, in *Piers* the message of the angels always concerns Charity. The points made in patristic and popular works on the Trinity are incorporated and carefully organized in Passus I. Old and New Testaments are linked, and the creation of the angels and man is linked with the Incarnation. But the doctrine is more than incorporated; it is illuminated by the prophetic spirit of the poet. For the Trinity that is taught in both Testaments, according to *Piers*, is unmistakably the God of the prophets. Just and compassionate, his unchanging love is manifested in the Creation, the Incarnation, and in the merciful deeds of men.

TRUTH IN TRINITY

In the opening lines of the poem, the poet promises to show first the meaning of the mountain, of the murky valley, and of the field of folk. Actually, the exposition is given by a lovely lady, later identified

75

as Holy Church, whose descent from the mountain symbolizes her role as interpreter of God to men, a reminder of his presence in the field as well as on the mountain. The meaning that emerges gradually throughout the passus is that not only has the Trinity always been true but Truth is always the Trinity. Further, the Truth that is God is the same truth that is manifested by men who refrain from lying, or who do an honest day's work. Truth is also Charity, God's love manifested in the Creation, the Incarnation, the Crucifixion, and also in the love men show each other.

Having told the dreamer that the tower on the toft is Truth's dwelling, the lady immediately makes a practical application, her style becoming appropriately colloquial. Would that you worked as his "word" teaches! she cries. He—that is, Truth—is father of faith; he formed you, gave you five wits, and also willed the world to yield you clothing, food, and drink in moderation. Beware, however, the immoderate demands of the body, for the world and the flesh are lying teachers. The dreamer professes to be delighted with this teaching but is rather overanxious to know to whom all the world's treasures *do* belong. "Treasure" becomes a key word repeated a number of times as the lady draws her pupil to the notion that of all treasures, Truth is the fairest. Indeed, it is as "derworth a drewery" as the dear God himself. For he who is true of tongue and who works with his hands with this will "is a god," and, according to St. Luke, like our Lord himself. This is a universal truth, claimed by Christian and un-Christian folk, and kings and knights should practice it in their administration of law. For he who upholds truth is the good knight, not he who fasts one Friday in five-score winters.

From the contemporary, she turns to the Old Testament, to David and to the preincarnate Christ. The order seems awkward; David ought chronologically to follow Christ the Creator, instead of preceding him as he does. An editor might be tempted to run his pencil through the lines on David, but a closer reading indicates that the Old Testament king does have a logical place in the sequence of ideas. The kings and knights of the preceding verses who were exhorted to follow truth in their rule probably suggested David, who was just such a ruler. In his turn, David, who served God in a higher way than ordinary kings, and who, everybody knew, foreshadowed Christ, suggested the King of Kings.

The whole passage of thirty-five lines reiterates the unity of the triune Truth, on earth, in heaven and in hell, in history and in eternity. David, the great Old Testament king, "dubbed kni3tes" and made them swear to serve Truth forever. Christ, the King of Kings, "knighted" the ten legions of angels, the cherubim and seraphim, and gave them might and the mirth of heaven. He taught them "bi the Trinitee treuthe to knowe," and obedience to his bidding. When Lucifer departed from Truth, he and the followers of his lies perforce fell from heaven. So men who work wrong will wend downwards, and those who work well may be sure that their souls will rise to heaven, where "treuthe is in Trinitee and troneth hem alle." So "I sey as I seide ere," when "alle tresores arne ytried, treuthe is the beste."

THE CREATION

We are treated next (l. 137) to a lively interchange between the lady and the dreamer, which is at once a bit of comic relief and a transition from the subject of the creation of the angels to that of the creation of man. The dreamer complains that he has "no kynde knowing" by "what craft" Truth comes into his body. "Thow doted daffe," she replies, "dulle arne thi wittes"; you did not learn your Latin in school. Actually, he has raised a serious problem, which a lesser writer might have chosen to ignore. What he means is that he can accept the idea of the creation of the angels, who are spirit, but he does not understand how animal man can be said to have been created in the image of God. And having got over her annoyance, Holy Church gives a thoughtful and poetic answer. It is not a categorical answer in which she says that Truth descends in this or that way but a further exploration of the penetration of the universe and man by God-Truth.

The dreamer having demanded natural knowledge, the lady supplies a certain amount. This gift of nature (conscience) is explained as the acceptance by the heart of the love of the Lord "lever than thi-selve." It is not from Nature, however, but from Revelation, from the witness of God's word that we learn how Truth operates through love. "Alle his werkes he wrou3te with loue," and taught love to "Moises for the levest thing and moste like to heuene." Suggested

77

by nature, taught by Christ to Moses, the answer to the riddle of man is now described in a lyrical passage as the descent of love into the world, of spirit into matter. This love was so heavy that heaven could not hold it

> Tyl it hadde of the erthe yeten his fylle,
>   And whan it haued of this folde flesshe and blode taken,
> Was neuere leef vpon lynde liȝter ther-after,
> And portatyf and persant as the poynt of a nedle,
> That myȝte non armure it lette ne none heiȝ walles.
>
> (I. 152–55)

> Till it had eaten heartily of the earth beneath it.
> In the flesh of the fold, in the blood of your body,
> No leaf of the linden was lighter on the branches;
> It was as piercing and poignant as the point of a needle;
> No walls nor armour withheld its passage.
>
> (I. 153–57)

This passage inevitably suggests the Incarnation. The early writers had said that the Incarnation is a great mystery, a little of which we understand when we say that man was created in the image of God. Langland uses what sounds like a description of the Incarnation (even the imagery of walls and armor was used in descriptions of the Virgin Birth) to explain the creation of man. Langland means that the way Truth descends into the body of every man is the same as the way in which Truth took flesh in the Incarnation. And he proceeds to remark that when this love became man and died for our sins, Mercy came into the world, too. When the Son died on the Cross, he wished no evil to the "wretches" who pained him.

Quite abruptly, the lady interjects a warning to the rich and commands them to have mercy on the poor. Even if you are true of tongue and true in dealing (two virtues highly recommended earlier), she says, if you do not give to the poor, you have no more merit in masses than Malkin in a maidenhood that no man desires. "Therefore," chastity without charity will be chained in hell.

This denunciation of the selfish rich is not really a digression dragged in by an irrepressible social critic. That Langland means it all to go together under God is clear not only from his "therefores" but from the matter and manner of the whole passus. Earlier we were told that Lucifer fell from heaven because lies are a departure from truth. Here, those who turn away from the poor likewise turn away from God. One idea not only follows from the other, but indeed it is essentially the same Idea: God is Truth and Charity; Lucifer is Lies and Selfishness. So, near the end of the canto, Holy Church says of avaricious curates who cannot leave covetousness, "That is no treuthe of the trinite, but treccherye of helle." Since "Loue is leche of lyf," and the gate of heaven, the key of grace is to comfort the careworn.

So unified in thought and expression is this description of Truth that had the rest of the poem been lost, Passus I would no doubt be accepted (as the whole has not been) as a finished poem. But no statement of the Truth is ever completed, and Langland never tires in his search for ways to express it. The "Treasure" motif runs through the adventures of Lady Meed (Passus II, III, IV), as does the moral that kings and commons are always choosing, whether they know it or not, between God-Truth and Devil-Falsehood. In Passus V we return to the same field full of folk "bifore tolde" (that is, in Passus I) and to another statement on the Trinity which again includes the traditional doctrinal arguments. Even more dramatically than in Passus I, the most heavenly doctrine is applied to the most earthly practice.

The Mercy of the Father through the Son

Passus V is justly famous for its portraits of the Seven Deadly Sins. In this set of dramatic monologues, the poet surpassed himself (and rivaled Chaucer and Browning) in detailing the vices and follies of men. So vivid is the action and so apt the alliteration that we are tempted to relish the satire and neglect the moral. It may be that the artist ran away with the moralist, but he did not run far. For while Langland would not have cared for literary muckraking, he did intend us to share in the humanity of his sinners. As he understood the Catholic mystery, it was for just such grafters, drunkards, swindlers, and sluts that God in his mercy became man. So it is that when Robert the Robber finishes the tale of his wickedness, Repentance has pity and asks all to kneel together to beg the Savior's mercy on all sinners.

In the thirty-four lines which follow, the traditional teaching of the Church on the Trinity is assimilated in a moving prayer which

79

begins with Genesis, moves on to the Gospels, and concludes with the fourteenth-century sinners for whom it is offered (ll. 488 ff.). The same sequence of ideas is followed here as in Passus I, but whereas there the main purpose was to explain the creation of man, in this context the stress is on the mercy of God to fallen man, indeed to these particular fallen men. "Now God," prays Repentance, who of your goodness made the world, and made man most like yourself . . . It was because of the sin of Adam that your Son was sent to earth, and through your Son you made yourself like us sinful men. This emphatic reference to the unity of the Father and the Son is followed immediately by the "Let Us make" text from Genesis, long cited to prove the divinity of the Second Person. The Old Testament text is then linked with one from the New Testament in which charity is the source of union between God and man: *"Faciamus hominem ad imaginem et similitudinem nostram;/et alibi: qui manet in caritate, in Deo manet, et Deus in eo"* (V. 495–96). Again stressing the unity of Father and Son, Langland then describes the Incarnation metaphorically as God's dying with his Son in "owre sute." Quickly, he describes the Crucifixion, the harrowing of hell, when all the blessed were blown "into the blisse of paradise," and the Resurrection, when God again walked in our garment and was seen first by the sinful Mary, "al to solace synful." Finally, he sums up the central mystery by interpreting St. John's the "Word was made flesh" in terms of medieval knighthood, saying that all four evangelists tell of the doughty deeds done in our armor. So, "owre fader and owre brother," be merciful to us and to these "ribaudes." The order of ideas is that of the doctrinal argument, the phrases are reminiscent of the prayers in the missal and in Old English poetry; and yet the whole prayer is cast in Langland's idiom and integrated into the "plot" of the poem.

God is not called Truth in this passage, but when the prayer is finished, a thousand men throng together and decide to seek "Treuthe." But none is so wise as to know the way, and they bluster about like lost beasts. Then they meet a pilgrim—not a brewer or a baker, mind you, but a professional pilgrim—and they ask if he knows anything of a Saint called Truth. Far from knowing, he replies that nobody had ever asked him such a question before! What Langland is satirizing here is not so much the bad faith of the pilgrim as his confident ignorance. He has taken on all the outward appurtenances of staff and wallet, sign and relics, all empty of meaning. His encounter with the repentant sinners is a little allegory of man's need first to be taught the meaning of the doctrine and then to be shown the way to practice it.

Prepared by doctrine and repentance, the sinners must now begin to live in accord with Truth, that is to Do Well. And here (1. 668) is where Piers the Plowman enters, both to teach and to lead them. His teaching enlarges on that of Holy Church in Passus I. An eminently practical man, he explains in detail that he digs and delves, tailors and tinkers as Truth bids. While his lecture is made up largely of advice, it is shot through with lyrical expressions of the nature of the triune Truth. In one of these, he uses the language of the Psalms applied to Christ by the early Church and the later poets, saying that "Treuthe" is above the sun, that he may do with the "day-sterre" what he likes, and that death dares not do what he forbids (A. VI. 82–84).

The *Faciamus* Text Modernized

The popular appellations for Christ and the "Let Us make" text are used again in Passus IX in a way that shows how conversant Langland was with the ancient exegetical methods. He uses them here, as they had always been used, to prove that the great God was always triune. Wit explains the nature of God. Without beginning or ending, he is the "Lorde of Lyf and of lyȝte," and man is most like him, similar in soul to God. Then, without troubling to quote "Let us make man in our image," Wit notes that "God" is singular and *"faciamus"* plural, and then he modernizes the old argument in a parable:

> For he was synguler hym-self and seyde *faciamus,*
> As who seith, "more mote here-to than my worde one;
> My myȝte mote helpe now with my speche."
> Riȝte as a lorde sholde make lettres and hym lakked
>   parchemyn,
> Though he couth write neuere so wel ȝ if he had no penne,
> The lettres for al the lordship I leue, were neuere ymaked.
>   And so it semeth bi hym as the bible telleth,
>   There he seyde, *dixit, et facta sunt;*

He moste worche with his worde and his witte shewe.
And in this manere was man made thorugh my3te of god almi3ti,
With his worde and werkemanschip and with lyf to laste.

. . . .

And that he wrou3t with werke and with worde bothe,
Thorugh my3te of the maieste man was ymaked.

(IX. 35–44; 50–51)

He was singular himself and said *faciamus*,
As one who says: more must work than my word only,
And my might must now be a help to my language.
A lord may wish to write a letter and lack parchment,
Or may be able to write, but have no pencil,
And so the letter of this Lord, I believe, will
          never be written.
Thus it seems with him, as the Bible teaches,
Saying, *dixit, et facta sunt*.
His words and wisdom must work also.
And in this manner man was made through might
          of God Almighty,
By his word and workmanship, and with life
          everlasting.

. . . .

Thus man was made by might and majesty,
And wrought with the word and work of God.

(IX. 32–42, 48–49)

The analogy of the lord who wishes to write a letter but lacks pencil and paper with the Father's need for the cooperation of the Son and the Holy Ghost in the creation of man is not a particularly happy one. But it is obvious that that is what is meant, not only from the use of the *faciamus* text but from the choice of language. "Word" and "wisdom" and "might," repeated throughout the passage, had been used in Trinitarian arguments since the earliest days of Christianity.

ALL GOODNESS THE IMAGE OF GOD

Ten lines later, Langland quotes again, "*Qui manet in caritate, in Deo manet, etc.*," which he had linked with the *faciamus* text in Passus V. Langland's repetitions are never idle, and the heart of his Trinitarian thinking is expressed in his concordance of these two texts. St. Jerome had said that "whatever we read in the Old Testament we find also in the Gospel; and what we read in the Gospel is deduced from the Old Testament." From the Old Testament "Let Us make man in Our image and likeness," Langland deduces the New Testament "*Qui manet . . . ,*" that is, "alle that lyuen good lyf aren like god almiȝti." Goodness is the image of God; the same triune Goodness who created man and then became man to show us that image is preached in both Testaments.

"All" who live good lives, Langland says in this passus on Do Well. That he did not mean simply "all Christians" is clear from a brief argument between Imagination and the dreamer in Passus XII (ll. 268 ff.). Imagination remarks that Aristotle was a great clerk, but whether he will be saved or not has not been shown to the clergy; no study in Solomon or Socrates can tell us. But God is good; and since he gave them "wittes" to show the way to us ("that wissen vs to be saued,/And the better for her bokes"), we are bound to pray that God give their souls rest. The dreamer (clearly not to be identified with Langland here!) objects that all the clerks say in their sermons that neither Saracens nor Jews "ne no creature of Cristes lyknesse" can be saved without being Christians. By the sly insertion of one phrase, Langland has made the disputant condemn his own argument. "Any creature in Christ's likeness" is an ill-timed admission of the fact that all men, not just the baptized, are created in the image of Christ. The inevitable corollary for Langland is that they forfeit this "likeness" only if they fail to do well.

Imagination's answer further relates the argument to the earlier teaching of Holy Church and Piers and Wit by its reiteration of the word "Truth." The pagan Trajan, for example, was saved without baptism because he was a "trewe knyȝte," although he was not a Christian. Furthermore,

> . . . trewth that trespassed neuere ne transuersed aȝeines
>   his lawe,
> But lyueth as his lawe techeth and leueth there be no bettere,
> And if there were, he wolde amende and in suche wille deyeth,
> Ne wolde neuere trewe god but treuth were allowed;
> And where it worth or worth nouȝt the bileue is grete
>   of treuth,
> And an hope hangyng ther-inne to haue a mede for his treuthe.
>
> (XII. 284–89)

Truth that never trespassed nor transgressed
   against his commandments,
But lives as his law teaches, and believes
   there is no better,
But if there were would amend, and with this
   will dies,—
The true God would never allow his truth
   to be dishonoured.
But whether this shall be or shall not be,
   the true man is strong,
And an hope is with him that he shall have
   meed for his truth.

(XII. 296–300)

This is something more than the pleasant platitude that there are good and bad in all faiths. This is the same Truth identified throughout the poem with the Trinity, often specifically with Christ. To exclude all the unbaptized from salvation is, therefore, to limit and dishonor the very nature of God. Good men have always lived in the likeness of Christ-Truth, whatever their time or history.

THE JEWS, THE SARACENS, AND THE TRINITY

Now this is enough for Do Well to know, but Do Better's job is to teach the fullness of Christ to those, such as Saracens and Hebrews, who do not know him. The principal reason they do not know him is, in Langland's view, that priests and bishops do *not* Do Better. Actually, the discussion of the faith of the Jews and the Saracens (in the last two hundred lines of Passus XV) develops from the main point of the passus, which is that if the clergy practiced the charity they preached, more Christians would save their souls. If clerks were kind and "curteise of crystes goodes," the unlearned would follow their example more readily than their preaching, which now seems hypocrisy to them (ll. 107 ff.). With unbelievers, too, example is ultimately more important than precept. If priesthood were more perfect, all those who despise Christendom would be converted (ll. 530–31).

Not only do the priests fail to give an example of Christian living, but they do not even attempt to follow Christ's command to preach to the whole world. It is a sign of the lack of charity in the Church that while eleven holy men once converted the world, now scholars, priests, and popes excuse themselves from their appointed task of inviting unbelievers to the feast.

Langland believed that what both Jews and Moslems needed to be taught was the doctrine of the Trinity. Both groups already worship the Father; indeed, he says that by their faith they "may be saved" (1. 383). The Jews still live according to the law of Moses which our Lord himself wrote, and they believe it to be the best. The Saracens also have something similar to our faith, for they "loue and bileue in O persone almiȝty." Both know "the firste clause of owre bileue, *Credo in Deum patrem omnipotentem.*" Since they have "a lippe" of our belief, the more lightly should men teach them "litlum and lytlum" of the Trinity, of the Son and the Holy Spirit.

In speaking of the Jews, Langland observes that they acknowledge Christ as a true prophet. His use of the phrase is interesting because it occurs so consistently in apologetic directed to the Jews, in which the Christian attempted to rebut the Jew's acknowledgement of Jesus "as a prophet" but not as God. It occurs, for example, in Gilbert Crispin's *Disputatio,* in Grosseteste's *De Cessatione Legalium,* and in Bromyard's "Fides," this last written, as we have seen, when there were no longer any Jews in England.

Actually, Langland's style throughout this Passus XV is reminiscent of innumerable medieval sermons like those of the Dominican Bromyard. Viewed in the light of what follows, this canto seems like a pause in the vision, as though the poet wanted to assure us that he knew as well as anyone what time it was and what the Jews believed —before he plunged into eternity to discuss the Trinity with Abraham. That the poet was aware that he was only preaching a sermon (a very fine one, by the way) is indicated by the significant absence of Piers. The wide-awake dreamer, having been instructed in the many excellent aspects of Charity, desires "to know him," and asks if clerks "know him." The soul explains that clerks have knowledge only "by werkes and bi wordes." But Piers the Plowman "parceyueth more depper / What is the wille and wherfore that many wyȝte suffreth" (ll. 189 ff.).

THE TREE OF CHARITY

In the following passus (XVI) the dreamer, unconscious in a long dream, begins to perceive more deeply the meaning of charity. Truly it is a fair tree on which the fruit, charity, grows through God and good men. It is Piers who explains that this tree represents the Trinity. Three props protect it from tempests, the Father, the Son (called by his ancient title of *Sapientia*), and the Holy Ghost. The fair fruit which fell from that tree and was gathered by the devil included Adam, Abraham, Isaias, Samson, Samuel, and St. John the Baptist. Leaving the image of the tree rather abruptly, the poet moves on from the forerunners to Christ himself, who came in "the fullness of time" to rescue that fruit from the devil. After hearing a brief résumé of the life of Jesus and his death on the Cross, the dreamer awakes to find Piers the Plowman gone.

This résumé is really a historical, prose preface to the poem that follows. Having described the life of Christ in the past tense, the poet takes a series of great imaginative leaps in time and history to portray the very moment of the Passion, with himself present to share in the anguish. Also present is that same Abraham, only recently portrayed in the past tense as awaiting deliverance with the other Old Testament saints.

ABRAHAM DE TRINITATE

At the opening of the grand climax of the poem, the Old Testament patriarch personifies the faith that leads men to Christ and to belief in the Trinity. Granted Langland's conception, the choice of Abraham for this role would seem almost inevitable. For the "faith of Abraham" was a medieval cliché, and faith was as readily identified in the popular mind with Abraham as was honesty, some centuries later, with "Honest Abe." Praised over and over again from the earliest days of the Church were the patriarch's unquestioning acceptance of God's unlikely promise of a son and his own hardly credible obedience to God's command to sacrifice that son. Further, it was firmly believed by all Christians that Abraham had seen and recognized the Trinity.

86

It was during Lent, as the Church relived each year the events leading up to the Crucifixion, that the account of Abraham in Genesis was read in missal and breviary, the marginal note in the breviary reading "*Abraham de Trinitate.*" That Langland was following the liturgical pattern in his recreation of the Passion is clear from the fact that the dreamer meets Abraham on mid-Lent Sunday. In the scheme of the poem, Lent represents the time in the history of the world of the long centuries of Old Testament preparation for Christ. Now on the road to Jerusalem, the dreamer is traveling in time towards the Crucifixion, which will be on Good Friday; on mid-Lent Sunday, he meets a man "as hore as an hawethorne," called Abraham.

"I am Feith," said that father, a herald of arms. He seeks a young knight he saw once, whose coat of arms was three persons in one, "*Pater, Filius,* and Holy goost." *Filius* he describes as "Wardeyne of that witte hath, was euere with-oute gynnynge" (l. 187), a phrase that echoes the Old English *Christ,* as well as the church fathers. In the long description of the Trinity which follows, Abraham seems to speak from outside time, with the authority of a friend of God. He tells how God sent forth his son for a time, as a servant,

> To occupien hym here till issue were spronge,
> That is, children of charite and holicherche the moder.
> Patriarkes and prophetes and apposteles were the chyldren,
> And Cryst and Crystendome and Crystene holycherche.
> In menynge that man moste on o god bileue,
> And there hym lyked and loued in thre persones hym shewed.
> (XVI. 195–201)

> To engage himself here till issue had arisen,
> Which were the children of Charity, and
>   Holy Church their mother.
> Patriarchs and prophets and apostles were
>   of their number,
> And Christ and Christendom and all Christian
>   people.
> Thus man must believe in One God Almighty,
> Who wheresoever he wills is witnessed in
>   three persons.
> (XVI. 245–50)

Abraham proceeds with the argument from the creation of man that was a favorite with Langland and combines with it a Trinitarian

87

analogy of Adam, Eve, and Abel that was a favorite of medieval apologetic. One God made man "semblable to hym-self er eny synne were" (C. XIX. 211–12). He is three wherever he is, and has wrought all things, this world among them. "That he is thre persones departable" is proved by mankind, "yf alle men beo of Adam." As Eve was in Adam, and Abel the offspring of both Adam and Eve, so from the Sire and the Son springs the Holy Spirit. So three encounters three "In godhede and in manhede" (C. XIX. 240).

Then the pilgrim breaks in with a question: "Hauest thow seyen this? . . . alle thre and o god?" (C. XIX. 241) In reply, Abraham tells his own story. Here we should observe, as Justin Martyr said to Trypho, the careful shifting of pronouns from singular to plural; and let us observe also the supreme freedom with which the poet's Abraham quotes the Latin commentary on himself from the breviary:

"In a somer ich seyh hym," quoth he, "as ich sat in my porche,
Where god cam goynge a-thre ryght by my gate;
   Tres vidit et unum adoravit.
Ich ros vp and reuerencede god and ryght fayre hym grette,
Wesh here feet, and wypede hem and after thei eten,
And what ich thouhte and my wyf he ous wel tolde."
(C. XIX. 239–45)

"I saw him one summer," he said, "as I sat in
    my doorway.
God came as three persons to the gate beside me.
Tres vidit et unum adoravit.
I arose and reverenced God and greeted him fairly.
And washed their feet and wiped them. They
        ate afterwards
. . . and could tell what I was thinking."
(XVI. 279–84)

This is, of course, the famous proof of the Old Testament appearance of the Trinity, used repeatedly in argument with the Jews who objected that the Christian doctrine was not taught in the Scriptures. Actually, the debate tradition, adapted, of course, to his own ends, seems to have influenced Langland's whole presentation of the argument here. When in Passus XVII the dreamer meets Spes, that is, Hope-Moses, he is disturbed by what he considers new teaching, and he argues with him. In a phrase reminiscent of the Jewish Doctors in the Christ and the Doctors stories, the dreamer objects that Spes tells naught of the Trinity in his letters (l. 33). He then argues the apparent discrepancies in Scripture with the Samaritan, when he meets him on the way to the Crucifixion. But Christ reassures him: "Sette faste thi faith" on Abraham, he says, and believe Spes, too (ll. 131–34).

Having demonstrated the concordance of the Testaments, Christ then turns to other proofs. If conscience or "kynde witte" carp against the Trinity, he says, or if heretics dispute, teach them the Trinity by the analogy of the human hand (ll. 135 ff.): the Father is the fist, the Son the fingers, the Holy Spirit the palm. When he has finished the extended metaphor of the hand, Christ compares the Trinity to a torch or a burning taper; as though "the wex and a weke were twyned" together, and then a "fyr flaumende" forth from both. (Popular in medieval apologetics, this image can be traced back to Justin Martyr who, in the second century, used as an analogy for the Trinity one fire being kindled from another without diminishing the first.)

THE INCARNATION

Then the Samaritan gallops off to Jerusalem. There, just before the Passion, the various threads of the allegory are tied together in a most meaningful way. The dreamer asks Faith what is happening, and who will joust in Jerusalem. "Jesus," is the answer; and he will fetch from the fiend the fruit of Piers Plowman. "Is Piers in this place?" asks the dreamer. Faith's eyes pried through him, and then he explained:

> "This Iesus of his gentrice wole Iuste in Piers armes,
> In his helme and in his haberioun, *humana natura;*
> That Cryst be nou3t biknowe here for *consummatus deus,*
> In Piers paltok the Plowman this priker shal ryde;
> For no dynte shal hym dere as *in deitate patris.*"
>
> (XVIII. 22–26)

> "This gentle Jesus will joust in Piers' armour,
> In his helm and harbergin, *humana natura;*
> And Christ be so concealed, for *consummatus deus.*

> This pricker is in the plate-armour of Piers
> the Plowman,
> And no dart may daunt him, *in deitate patris.*"
>
> (XVIII. 23 ff.)

This is, of course, the doctrine of the Incarnation. Jesus is not to be identified with Piers, nor has Piers developed into Christ; that would be heresy. What Faith explains by way of his juxtaposition of personalities and personifications is the twofold nature of Christ. The Fathers said that God did not change, but he took flesh. The poet says that Jesus does not change, but he puts on Piers's armor, that is, human nature. And in that armor, Christ is concealed, so that the dreamer—and the crucifiers—do not recognize his divinity. But Abraham does. As he recognized the Second Person on the plains of Mambre, so, through the eyes of faith, in Jerusalem he recognizes him again.

Again in the following canto (XIX), the dreamer asks, "Is this Jesus the Iuster" or is it Piers the Plowman? Here Conscience answers that these are Piers's ensign, coat, and armor, but "he that cometh so blody" is Christ.

Just before Christ arrives to harrow hell, the devils also ponder his identity. During his life on earth, they say, they had conjectured that he might be God or God's son because he had not fallen into sin. Now Lucifer realizes that Jesus is the same lord he knew long ago before he fell from heaven. Jesus himself says that it was he who warned Adam and Eve that they would die if they ate the apple; now he has come to claim his own creatures (XVIII. 276 ff.). As in the plays mentioned in an earlier chapter, it is clear that Jesus is the Second Person Incarnate, the Creator and the Redeemer.

THE HOLY SPIRIT

When Christ ascends to heaven, Piers remains on earth and receives the Holy Spirit at Pentecost. Christ gives him the power to bind and unbind, the Holy Spirit teaches him how to build the Church, and by God's word he has the power to celebrate the sacraments. While his grace informs the pope, he is not, however, the pope, any more than he was Christ in the previous canto. He is not set to guard the "Barn" of Unity he has established. After he sows the seeds of the virtues and harrows them with the two Testaments, Grace devises a "cart" called Christendom to carry Piers's sheaves and appoints Priesthood to care for the cart. Then Grace, or the Holy Spirit, went himself through the wide world with Piers to till Truth (XIX. 202–330).

Langland apparently means that while the Holy Spirit is, or ought to be, in the Church, the Truth of the triune God is not and never was confined to the Church. "The wide world" is a phrase he had used earlier, when he said that the "sire and the Son and *Spiritus Sanctus* hold the whole wide world within them." Piers himself is a mystical figure who also must not be limited to one meaning. But one of his meanings is that he is the channel through which Grace flows. While he is flesh and blood, he is not everyman, with faults and sins, who must learn from experience; that is the role of the dreamer. Piers is rather an idealized human nature, as it was created in the image of God, an image he never defaces by sin. His goodness is not "natural" however, in the later sense of the word; he is no noble savage but a saint and a prophet who is always in touch with God. Even when we first meet Piers as a simple plowman, he not only lives the good life but teaches it in the light of the triune Truth that was from the beginning. As the poem follows the course of history, the man partaking of the goodness of God is united with the goodness of God become man. While Piers always seems to know the whole doctrine, his revelation of it is limited by history. In the earlier part of the poem, he leads men to the Commandments. After the advent of Jesus, he is accompanied by the Holy Spirit, and he plows with the New as well as the Old Testaments. But it is the same Truth to which he leads men throughout the poem, for Christ was not a new god, but the Second Person of the Trinity, the same Person who created man, appeared to Abraham and Moses, and then became man.

In the writings of the church fathers, the separate texts and arguments taken together prove that the Trinity was taught in the Old Testament, that Christ was not a new god but the Second Person become man. In *Piers*, the same texts and arguments are woven into a poetic vision which pierces the meaning of the doctrine itself. The vision, like the doctrine, is both outside and inside time, eternally true and manifested in history. While the expository teaching is therefore the same from the first passus to the last, the action and allegory follow the history of the world according to the Christian interpretation.

Whether the speaker be Holy Church, Wit, Imagination, or Piers, the same Truth is taught throughout the poem because the Truth was always the same. Almost every discussion of the Trinity begins with the "giant Genesis," and Langland never tires of probing the meaning of the account of the creation of man. The grammatical argument derived from the "Let Us make man in Our Image" passage is basic to his thinking not so much because it "proved" that more than one person was concerned in the Creation but because the Incarnation was implicit in the Creation. What was implicit in the Old Testament became explicit in the New, and all that was veiled in the Old was revealed in the New. The light of the Incarnation illuminated the meaning of Genesis because Christ is Charity and was so at both the time of the Creation and the time of the Incarnation. That is what Langland means when he says that "Trinity" was the meaning of the tree of charity that grew in the garden of goodness. As Love bowed down the heavens to become man, so Love had come down to create man in God's image, an image that could be deformed only by sin.

While all the fruit on the tree is of one grafting (since we are all children of Adam), all are not of equal sweetness, and those on the sunny side ripen soonest. The good fruit includes all who lived well, like the good pagans, but there is a preponderance of Old Testament saints because they heard the Word of God. Abraham, David, Solomon, Moses, and Isaias all taught and lived by the Truth of Trinity.

When the Second Person became man and died for the salvation of all men, the old heroes were not left behind. Historically, Christ harrowed hell and took them to Paradise. Allegorically, Abraham and Moses join him at the Crucifixion, and Christ tells the dreamer that after the Resurrection, Faith-Abraham will be "forester here" to have the fields in keeping and to show men the way he had traveled. In other words, Abraham will always bear witness to Christ and show men the way of faith. Similarly, Do Better does not leave Do Well behind, and Do Best builds on both. Like the persons of the Trinity, the three are aspects of the same Truth. And Piers is the good man who embodies the Truth, for he always does well, better, and best, and teaches the way to others.

Chapter VI

THE MESSIAS AND THE JEWS: FROM THE APOSTOLIC AGE THROUGH THE ANGLO-SAXON PERIOD

℘ The Messianic prophecies are perhaps the best remembered part of the doctrine of the fulfillment of the Scriptures. Everyone is acquainted with the prophecies traditionally associated with Christmas, and those concerning the Crucifixion still move the hearts of the faithful. These form, however, only a very small proportion of the innumerable prophecies that once crowded the pages of both apologetic and devotional literature.

Indeed, the fulfillment of the Messianic prophecies is a prohibitively large and unwieldy subject. Since both Jews and Christians assumed that every aspect of the life of the Messias was prophesied in Scripture, prophecies were cited in controversy to prove the divinity of Christ, the Virgin Birth, the calling of the Gentiles, and the fulfillment of the law. At the same time, the specific question of whether or not Jesus was the Messias was argued as a separate issue, in which every one of his acts was matched with an Old Testament text. Pious fiction was sprinkled with prophecies which had a great devotional appeal to Christians, and with appellations taken from them, dealing with the genealogy of the Christ, his birthplace, the Virgin Birth, the miracles, the Passion, and the Resurrection.

A compilation of these prophecies would result in a Scriptural-fictional concordance which, finally, would not be altogether to our purpose. For our special interest is *Piers Plowman*, and only a small part of the Messianic material appears in the poem. Perhaps it is just as well, then, to let the part stand for the whole, and to concentrate on the aspects of the tradition which apparently influenced William Langland.

That Jesus fulfilled the promises of the prophets is, of course, assumed in *Piers*, and there are references in passing to the prophecies of the birthplace of Jesus, the Virgin Birth, and the harrowing of hell. But the prophecies do not seem to have moved the poet to devotion. In view of his extended meditation on the Passion, we would expect him to quote Isaias' much loved prophecies of the Passion or the numerous Old Testament prefigurations of the Cross that were so popular with his contemporaries. Instead, it is only when he considers the role of the Jews in the Crucifixion that he cites prophecies—those which foretold that the Jews would be rejected by God for rejecting their king. Indeed, of all the Messianic material undoubtedly familiar to him, the only aspects of the story that seem really to interest Langland deal in some way with the kingship of Christ or the rejection of the Jews—points that are not necessarily related but which do have a connection for Langland.

Indeed, at times one point or prophecy leads to the other in a stereotyped way that is rather unusual for Langland and that may reflect one of the characteristics of the whole Messianic argument. The bare listing of textual proofs was far more marked in the argument over the Messias than in that over the Trinity and the law. And while the specific points used by Langland were often discussed at some length, the supporting prophecies were likely to be interjected most abruptly.

THE EARLY CENTURIES

The reasons for this emphasis on testimonies in the Messianic controversy are not far to seek. The area of disagreement between Jews and Christians was, at least on the surface, narrower here than on any other issue. While Jews denied that certain Christian doctrines, such as the Trinity, were to be found in the Scriptures, there was no question that the Messias was there, and only there. To a pagan of ill-will, like Celsus, the whole controversy over the Messias was only a fight over the shadow of an ass.[1] And while Messianic expectations were not uniform among the Jews at the time of Jesus, all schools of thought agreed that a truly spiritual reader would find in the Scriptures specific prophecies of the deeds of the Messias, and even of the

1. Origen *Against Celsus* III. 1, 2; IV. 2.

exact time of his coming. Finally, a great many of the same texts were considered Messianic by all parties. Prophecies are naturally clearer after the event, and to a Jew who considered that the Messias had come, all the uncertainties of interpretation were over. The Jewish-Christians therefore believed that all that was necessary was to draw the old passages together in the new context, that is, to match dozens of prophecies with events in the life of Jesus. And to judge from the Acts and the Epistles, a great many of the brethren were persuaded in just this way.

In many of the prophecies, there is not much to argue about. Look, for example, at the question of the birthplace of the Messias. Jews and Christians agreed that Micheas 5:2 was a Messianic prophecy: "And thou, Bethlehem Ephrata, art a little one among the thousands of Juda: out of thee shall he come forth unto me that is to be the ruler in Israel: and his going forth is from the beginning, from the days of eternity." In debate, the Christian recited this passage and pointed to the birth of Jesus in Bethlehem. The Jew agreed that the event fulfilled the prophecy or he did not; and the debate moved on to the next prophecy.

THE CRUCIFIXION

What Micheas—and David, Isaias, Jeremias, and Daniel—meant by "ruler in Israel," however, could not be explained by yea and nay. From the beginning, controversy was especially bitter on this subject, for it touched on the very nature of the Messias and turned on the Crucifixion. It is clear from the Gospel accounts that most Jews expected an earthly king, who would sit on the throne of David and set up a great kingdom. Even Pilate asked if Jesus was the king of the Jews, and then had the royal title inscribed on the cross, to the dismay of the accusers. The crown of thorns and the purple robe were themselves a cruel mockery of the Messianic claim. And the very thieves who were crucified with him were not too low in the social scale to debate the subject. While one thief sneered at the king to come down from the cross, the other understood that his kingdom was not of this world and begged to be remembered when Jesus came into that kingdom.

It is easy to see how the controversy could become an exchange of insults, in which the Jew sneered at the notion of a king who was crucified, and the Christian jibed at the stubbornness and blindness of the Jews, the subsequent loss of their kingdom being proof that Jesus *was* finally king in heaven. Even when the argument was politely limited to an exchange of prophecies, the explosive differences of interpretation seem always ready to break forth. And no matter how remote later Christians were from the actual controversy, they seemed always aware of the galling fact that the Jews still looked for the fulfillment of the prophecies. That is why even when the exact line of argument of the debates was of no moment to writers who, like Langland, were addressing Christian audiences, the Messianic prophecies are likely to be coupled with angry references to the Jews, to the confusion of readers unfamiliar with the background.

In most of the Latin debates, the Jew says that Jesus could not have been the Messias because he died a shameful death, whereas the Messias must come "in glory, on the clouds of heaven" (Dan. 7:13) "to judge the nations" (Ps. 44:109). The Christian replies that these are prophecies of the Second Coming and that Jesus will fulfill them at the end of the world. In putting forth these objections, he contends, the Jews are deliberately ignoring other prophecies, which describe the humility and suffering of the Messias and which are equally considered Messianic by the Jews (e.g., Isa. 53). How can the Jews explain the seemingly contradictory passages in the Old Testament, those in which the Messias is described as a servant and those in which he is described as coming in glory? (As a matter of fact, some schools of Jewish thought expected two Messias, one humble and one grand; but while this belief was attacked in anti-Talmudic polemic, it does not appear to have been generally known.) Occasionally, the Jewish disputant conceded that the Christ would suffer but objected to the particular instrument of the Passion, the Cross, as being specifically cursed in Deuteronomy 21:23.[2] It was in answer to this argument that St. Paul said that Christ has "redeemed us from the curse of the law, being made a curse for us (for it is written: Cursed is every one that hangeth on a tree)" (Gal. 3:13).

However one looks at it, the subject is a touchy one. To Christians nothing could be clearer than that Jesus suffered "in order that the Scriptures might be fulfilled" (Matt. 26:27), and they found proph-

2. Justin *Dialogue* 95, 96.

ecies of the Crucifixion in Isaias, Zacharias, Amos, and numerous psalms. Furthermore, far from being a curse, the cross itself was and always had been a blessing, and the Christians of the early centuries found it prefigured in every chapter of Scripture.

Even when the Jews conceded that the prophets predicted that the Messias would suffer, they did not agree that he would suffer at their hands. They argued that if Jesus had been the Messias, they would have recognized him. It was of the greatest importance to the Christians to answer this argument, not only to the Jews, but to the pagans and to themselves. Was it possible that the Jewish Scriptures were clearer to Christian teachers than to the Jews themselves? Yes, said the Christians, for the same Scriptures foretold that the Jews would be blind and stubborn and would reject the Messias. For example, Isaias 6:9, "Hearing ye shall hear and shall not understand; seeing ye shall see and shall not perceive," was taken to mean not only that the Jews would fail to recognize Jesus but that they would not understand their own Scriptures.

The solution of one difficulty sometimes gives rise to another. If one believed that the rejection of Christ was foretold and that the Jews had to fulfill the prophecies, then it followed that the Jews did no wrong. This was not a common Jewish argument, but it troubled Christians, who never settled it to their own satisfaction. The real difficulty was not with the actual crucifiers, who were instigated by the devil and were forgiven by Jesus, but with later Jews. Justin tells Trypho: if you repent of your sins and acknowledge Christ, you will be forgiven; "but if you curse him and put his followers to death, then your laying hands on him will be required of you as unjust men." [3] The question continued to trouble later Christians, who often answered it somewhat in Justin's manner.

THE CALLING OF THE GENTILES AND THE REJECTION OF THE JEWS

The same Scriptures which foretold the blindness of the Jews also foretold the calling of the Gentiles to the God of Israel and the subsequent rejection of the Jews and the downfall of their nation. In civil debates, even this subject was presented quite politely in terms of Old Testament prophecies. But feeling ran high on the relations

3. *Dialogue 95.*

between Jews and Gentiles, and the vehemence of the argument in the early Church arose as much from contemporary conflicts as from Scriptural interpretation. Further, it is hard to judge how much of later history was influenced by the argument, and how much the argument served to explain actual relations.

As a matter of fact, the basic separation of Jews and Gentiles into two "peoples" was the result not of the Crucifixion or of the prophecies of rejection, but of the law. Everybody knows that the people of the law kept from idolatry by keeping away from the Gentiles. It was probably inevitable that this exclusiveness included contempt for the outsiders. For example, contact with a Gentile defiled a Jew, who had to perform ritual washing after a day in the market place. Rules about eating were, of course, especially strict; since eating was itself a ritual act, eating in the house of a pagan incurred the same degree of pollution as having contact with a corpse.

It is not surprising that this attitude should have colored interpretations of the Scriptural passages which referred to the calling of the Gentiles to the God of Israel by the Messias. In the first-century B.C. *Book of Jubilees*, hatred of the uncircumcised is justified as a reflection of the attitude of God, who has appointed angelic guardians over the Gentiles with the express purpose of leading them to destruction.[4] Also current among the Jews of the same period, however, was the *Testaments of the Twelve Patriarchs*. Diametrically opposed to the nationalism of *Jubilees* is the universalism of this work, which echoes the prophetic yearning for the salvation of the Gentiles and accords them a high place in the plan of redemption.

St. Peter apparently stood somewhere between the two extremes portrayed in these two works. With characteristic simplicity, he explained to the Gentile Cornelius and an assembled company: "You know how abominable it is for a man that is a Jew to keep company or to come unto one of another nation." But God had shown him a vision "to call no man common or unclean." While Peter was speaking, the Holy Ghost came upon the company, to the astonishment of the Jewish-Christians, who decided only then that the Gentiles must be baptized even as themselves (Acts 10, 15).

Unlike so many of the first Jewish-Christians, St. Paul was neither confused nor uncertain about the Messianic promises to the Gentiles.

4. *The Book of Jubilees* (trans. R. H. Charles) XV. 27, 31.

But in his own aggressive way, he was equally defensive. He had to defend his apostleship to the Gentiles, not only to the Jews and the Jewish-Christians but even to Judaizers among the Gentile Christians. It was a telling point with these Gentiles who envied Israel according to the flesh that Paul might, if he wished, "brag" about being a Jew—having been "circumcised the eighth day, of the stock of Israel, of the tribe of Benjamin, a Hebrew of the Hebrews, according to the Law, a Pharisee" (Phil. 3:5). It is rather as though he were presenting his credentials when he explains to the Judaizing Galatians that he had made progress in the Jewish religion above many of his equals, "being more abundantly zealous for the traditions" of his fathers. And "beyond measure" he had "persecuted the Church of God and wasted it." But when by the revelation of Jesus Christ, he was called to preach among the Gentiles, "immediately" he "condescended not to flesh and blood." In Jerusalem, James and John and Peter recognized the grace of God in him and gave him "the right hand of fellowship." But in Antioch, he withstood even Peter "to the face," because, when in the presence of other Jewish-Christians, Peter withdrew from eating with the Gentile Christians (Gal. 1:2). There must have been times when Paul felt himself almost alone in seeing the essential universalism of the new covenant, in recognizing that in Christ Jesus there is neither Jew nor Greek.

As he did not mince words with Peter and the elders, neither did Paul spare the feelings of Jews and Gentiles in his interpretation of the prophecies. He frequently reminds the Gentiles that they are the outsiders, who led "filthy" lives before their conversion, who lived in a spiritual desert and were "hateful" to God. Their only glory is that God has shown them mercy by calling them to the God of Israel, as was predicted in the prophecies (e.g., Ps. 17, 50, 1, 116; Isa. 10:11). All the glories of the past belong to the Jews; but as the prophets warned, they have rejected the Messias and so have rejected the favor of God. But God has not cast away his people, and Paul looks to the glorious conversion of the Jews. For if "the loss of them be the reconciliation of the world, what shall the receiving of them be, but life from the dead?" Be not wise in your own conceits, he warns the Romans. "Blindness in part happened in Israel, until the fulness of the Gentiles should come in." But finally, Israel shall be saved, as Isaias predicted of the "remnant." Paul's hope and dream is of the

THE FULFILLMENT OF THE SCRIPTURES

ultimate union of the two peoples. Writing to the Ephesians, he explains how they who had had no hope of the promise and were without God have been brought by Christ to share the heritage of the Jews. Now they are no longer "strangers and foreigners" but "fellow citizens with the saints," built in "one temple upon the foundation of the apostles and prophets, Jesus Christ himself being the chief cornerstone" (Eph. 2).

It seems not to have occurred to either side that, short of conversion or the end of the world, they might share the heritage of God. The strangers and the citizens, the ins and the outs—the heartbreaking quarrel went on for centuries. In the fourth century, Eusebius complains of the "brainless boasting" of those of the circumcision who impudently assert that "the Christ will come for them only and not for all mankind." The Hebrews "find fault with us, that being strangers and aliens we misuse their books, which do not belong to us at all, and because in impudent and shameless way, as they would say, we thrust ourselves in, and try violently to thrust out the true family and kindred from their own ancestral right." They add that if there was "a Christ divinely foretold, they were Jewish prophets who proclaimed His advent," and "announced that He would come as Redeemer and King of the Jews, and not of alien nations; or, if the Scriptures contain any more joyful tidings, it is to Jews, they say, that these also are announced." [5]

There was ample justification for the plaintive tone of the Jews that Eusebius has unwittingly reflected. It is understandable that the Christians were anxious to prove that the Messias had come for the Gentiles; and certainly it was legitimate for them to try to prove that the conditions of time and place for the fulfillment of the prophecies had passed. But the cheerfulness with which they used the destruction of Jerusalem (in A.D. 70) to prove their point must have made Jesus weep.

Given the current exegetical habits, it was probably inevitable that, in one tone of voice or another, the disaster should have been interpreted as the fulfillment of the prophecies. For Micheas (3:12) had said that "Jerusalem shall be as a heap of stones." And Isaias had said "Woe to a sinful nation," who "have forsaken the Holy One of Israel.

5. Eusebius *The Proof of the Gospel* (trans. W. J. Ferrar) II. 3.

. . . The house of our holiness and of our glory, where our fathers praised thee, is burnt with fire" (1:4; 64:11). Even more frequently quoted by Christians were the prophecies of Jacob and Daniel, for in these passages, considered Messianic by the Jews, the coming of the Messias is linked with the end of the kingdom of the Jews; and Daniel was understood to have predicted the exact time of the coming of Jesus.

Before his death, Jacob prophesied: "The sceptre shall not be taken away from Juda, nor a ruler from his thigh, till he come that is to be sent: and he shall be the expectation of nations" (Gen. 49:10). The tribe of Juda was indeed preeminent throughout the history of the Jews, and there was always a ruler "from the thigh" of Juda. But at the time of the Messias, the Jews were ruled first by Herod, a foreigner set over them by Rome, and then by the Emperor Augustus.

Daniel's "seventy weeks" and "sixty-two weeks" were the subject of much controversy but were generally understood by Christians to mean that Christ, "the Saint of Saints," was born and was "slain" at the times predicted. Afterwards, Daniel said,

> the people that shall deny him shall not be his. And a people, with their leader that shall come, shall destroy the city and the sanctuary: and the end thereof shall be waste, and after the end of the war the appointed desolation. . . . the victim and the sacrifice shall fail: and there shall be in the temple the abomination of desolation (9:24–27).

The Christians concluded that the time predicted for the Saint of Saints must have passed, because, as Daniel had foretold, both the holy city and the holy places were, in fact, demolished by the Romans under Titus in the first year of the reign of Vespasian. They concluded also that Daniel had predicted the destruction as punishment for the Jewish denial and slaying of the Christ.[6]

Sensitive men, like the author of the *Dialogue of Athanasius and*

6. These prophecies are cited, with part or all of the argument, in: Irenaeus *Against Heresies* IV. 20 and *The Apostolic Preaching* 57; Justin Martyr *1 Apology* 32; Tertullian *An Answer to the Jews* VIII; Cyprian *Testimonies* I. 21; Athanasius *On the Incarnation* (trans. Archibald Robertson) XXXIX ff.; Eusebius *Proof of the Gospel* VIII. 1; Isidore of Seville *Contra Judaeos, PL.* 83, cols. 464–65. The most detailed explanation of Daniel's chronology is to be found in Julian of Toledo *De Comprobatione Aetatus Sextae, PL.* 96, cols. 537–86.

Zacchaeus, touched the wounds lightly. When Jewish Zacchaeus claims the prophetic promises of joy for his congregation, Athanasius says, "Everlasting joy has not been and is not now upon your heads." Zacchaeus: "No one insults another by way of argument." Athanasius: "I do not insult thee. Far be it from me. But your government, your city, your temple are destroyed." It must be that the prophecies of joy are meant for the true daughter of Sion, the Church. On the other hand, popular thrillers, like some of the Apocryphal Gospels, shamelessly exploited the Jewish disaster for its horrors. In one rabble-rousing version, the Roman heroes, Titus and Vespasian, perpetuate their atrocities immediately after receiving baptism—to avenge the death of Jesus.[7]

In anything resembling a serious commentary, the Romans are not Christianized, nor is their behavior praised. But the loss of Jerusalem is invariably interpreted as God's rejection of the Jews in return for their rejection of him. Just as God punished them in the past for falling away from him, so has he punished them now for rejecting his Son. But never were they punished for any crime as for this one—the nation in exile, an end to prophecies and miracles, God's care transferred to converts from the heathen. And why? For that which they stubbornly consider an act of piety.[8]

And invariably, the Christians insist that the great saints of the past are on their side. The point is made most graphically in the apocryphal *Vision of St. Paul.* When Paul visited heaven, one of beautiful face, Moses, greeted him, and wept, saying,

> I weep for those whom I planted with toil, because they did not bear fruit, nor did any profit by them; and I saw all the sheep whom I fed, that they were scattered and became as if they had no shepherd. . . . I wonder that strangers and uncircumcised and idol-worshippers have been converted and have entered into the promises of God, but Israel has not entered; and now I say unto thee, brother Paul, that in that hour when the people hanged Jesus whom thou preachest, that the Father, the God of all, who gave me the law, and Michael and all the angels and archangels, and Abraham and Isaac and Jacob, and all the just wept over the Son of God hanging on the cross.[9]

7. "Dialogue of Athanasius and Zacchaeus," trans. F. C. Conybeare, *Expositor,* V (1897); *Avenging of the Saviour* in *Apocryphal Gospels, Acts, and Revelations,* Ante-Nicene Library, XVI (1870), 245 ff.
8. Origen *Against Celsus* II. 8.
9. Ante-Nicene Additional Volume (1896), pp. 164–65.

ALLEGORIES OF THE TWO PEOPLES

Paul, who was no respecter of persons, would have corrected even Moses in heaven on one point: the prophet ought not to have "wondered" that the strangers had entered into the promises of God. Indeed, it would have surprised no one if Moses had explained the supplanting of the Jews by the Gentiles in an allegory.

As was observed in chapter two, St. Paul calls the story of Isaac and Ishmael an allegory of the Old and the New Laws. Besides representing the two laws (we shall look at this point in a later chapter), Isaac and Ishmael represent the two peoples; and the relation between the sons of Abraham prefigured the persecution of the Church by the Jews in Paul's time and the ultimate triumph of the Church. "For it is written," Paul says, quoting Isaias,

> "Rejoice, thou barren, that bearest not: break forth and cry, thou that travailest not: for many are the children of the desolate, more than of her that hath a husband." Now we, brethren, as Isaac was, are the children of promise. But as then he that was born according to the flesh persecuted him that was after the spirit: so also it is now. But what saith the Scriptures? Cast out the bondwoman and her son: for the son of the bondwoman shall not be heir with the son of the free woman (4:21–30).

Apparently the meaning of the prophecy of Isaias was so obvious to Paul that he did not think it necessary to explain it. The church fathers briefly note that it proved that believers from the Gentiles would be more numerous than from the Jews. What seems curious is that the prophecy was considered so important and the charge of barrenness taken so seriously and repeated so often, even in *Piers*. For their part, the Jews did not let it go unanswered. There is an amusing debate in the Talmud between a Jewish-Christian and Beruria, a famous Jewish lady who died in the middle of the second century. The barren woman of Isaias, understood by the Christians to be the Church of the Gentiles before the coming of Christ, was interpreted by Beruria as the Synagogue. "Fool," she says to the Christian, "look at the end of the verse." It means that the Synagogue is to "rejoice" because her children, although few in number, are not destined, like yours, for hell.[10]

10. R. Travers Herford, *Christianity in Talmud and Midrash* (London, 1903), pp. 237 f.

The Christians searched the Scriptures and found dozens of examples of barren wives, two wives quarreling over one husband, two sons quarreling over the inheritance of the father. Always the context is a family argument, and the point of the Christians is always that the elder, the first fruitful, the Synagogue of the Jews, has been rejected in favor of the younger, long-barren Church of the Gentiles. To take just one example—which appears in literature from the early centuries throughout the Middle Ages—when Isaac prayed for Rebecca his wife, because she was barren, she conceived. And the Lord said to her, "Two nations are in thy womb, and two peoples in thy belly; and the one people shall surpass the other, and the elder shall serve the younger" (Gen. 25:23). So the elder Esau (the Synagogue, the Jews) was supplanted by the younger Jacob (Christ, the Church, the Gentiles).[11]

Literary developments and variations suggest widespread familiarity with the theme. For example, in the famous pseudo-Augustinian *De Altercatione Ecclesiae et Synagogae*, the quarrel over the inheritance of the kingdom of God is dramatized in a lengthy debate between the two churches personified as two mothers. All the arguments and prophecies, including that of Isaias on "the barren has borne," are worked into a clever legal allegory. Far less sophisticated and much nastier are the allegories which appear, unlikely as it may seem, in the moralized animal world of the *Physiologus*. For example, the "Night Raven," in this popular bestiary, is an allegory of the calling of the Gentiles, the abrogation of the law, and the rejection of the Jews.[12] For David had said, "I am become as a Night Raven in the deserted town" (Ps. 101:7). Just as the Night Raven loves night better than day, so also "has our Lord Jesus Christ loved us who dwelt in darkness and the shadow of death, that is the heathen, better than the Jews, who also have received the promise of the Father." But, says the author, it will be objected "that the Night Raven is unclean according to the Law, and how then can he appear before

11. Romans 9:10–12; *Epistle of Barnabas* XIII; *The Apostolic Fathers,* Ante-Nicene Library, I (1870); Tertullian *Answer to the Jews* VII; Cyprian *Testimonies* I. 19.
12. Trans. James Cargill, in William Rose, *Epic of the Beast* (London, 1924), pp. 213 ff.

the presence of the Saviour?" The Savior "has abased Himself" that he might deliver us. So has the Lord loved the darkness, "namely the heathen, more than the murderous and God-hating Jews, because of their apostasy; and those which in time past were no people have become the people of God."

ANGLO-SAXON ENGLAND: BEDE AND AELFRIC

The same range of attitudes and the same arguments and prophecies mark the writings of Anglo-Saxon England. With characteristic thoroughness, Bede discusses the whole Messianic question, proving at considerable length, for example, that the time for the coming of the Messias has passed. In one and another of his works can be seen also his belief that the Jews were led astray by the devil, that they were to be rejected in favor of the Gentiles, and that eventually they were to be united to Christ.

Who among the prophets were not persecuted? he asks. The evil spirit which led Saul against David was like the blind perfidy of the Jews against Jesus. The fish that assaulted young Tobias (a figure of Christ) was the devil; the incident is a parallel of the Passion. The mockery of the nakedness of Noe prefigured the mockery of the Passion of Christ.[13]

Typical of the way such parallels were developed is Bede's description of the life and character of Tobias, under which, he says, is depicted the history of the Israelites, the Church, and the Synagogue. As Tobias, that is, Israel, took Anna to wife, so the Synagogue accepted the ceremonial law instituted by Moses. The son of this union was both Israel and Christ—the first-born, the prophet promised by Moses. As the angel Raphael explained the medicine of God which would cure the blindness of Tobias and free Sara from a demon, so did God come into the world to enlighten the darkness of the Jews and lift the Gentiles from idolatry. And it is fitting that Sara should be the Church, for Sara is the name of Abraham's wife, the mother of Isaac, the son of promise. At the marriage of Tobias and Sara (Christ and the Church), the angel Raphael brought Gabe-

---

13. Bede *Allegorica Exposito* (ed. J. A. Giles) VIII. 80, 110; IX. 433; *PL.* 91, cols. 228, 245.

lus to the feast; like Gabelus, many peoples were invited to the Church of Christ. While Tobias was celebrating the wedding, his parents (the people of the Jews) sat sad at home, for they did not know the glad tidings. But when Tobias returned with great gifts and cured the blindness of his father, he was received with rejoicing. Thus the Doctors of the Church enrich with good works the substance of the people of the Jews who believe in Christ, the cornerstone of the church of both peoples.[14]

Bede finds the supplanting of the Synagogue by the Church in numerous examples of the relationship between the elder and the younger—Leia and Rachel, Ishmael and Isaac, Cain and Abel, Ruben and Juda, Manasses and Ephraim. The Song of Songs he interprets as an allegory of the growth of the primitive Church from the Synagogue and of the Church's yearning for reunion, which will be accomplished at the end of the world. For example, his interpretation of "I will not let him go, till I bring him into my mother's house, and into the chamber of her that bore me" (3:4) is that the Church will so persevere in love that the Synagogue will accept the faith. "Return, return, O Sulamitess; return, return, that we may behold thee" (6:12) is the cry of the Church to the Synagogue; return to the pure faith, to the love of Christ.[15]

Aelfric is even more interesting than Bede, for besides the conventional commentary, his occasional remarks suggest that, like Langland, he gave considerable thought to the problem of the Jewish rejection of the Messias. In attempting to explain the Crucifixion, he says that the "Jews were from God, and they were not from God." They were good by "kind," for they were Abraham's offspring; but they were evil by imitation of the devil who corrupted them. Still, "the merciful God would yet incline the minds of the Jews with great signs, to the true belief, if they themselves would, that they with penance might extinguish their sins." And he tells a miraculous tale of St. James the Apostle, in which the Jew is converted. In another context, he describes with great approval how St. Clement got "the favor of the Jewish people" by proving that "their forefathers were called friends of God," and by telling them that they would have

14. *Allegorica Expositio* IX. 428 ff.
15. *Allegorica Expositio* IX. 186 ff.

been first in God's election, "if with belief they had obeyed his commandments."[16]

But alas, many of the Jews would not believe. God gave them the opportunity to repent of the Crucifixion, and while many did, others killed St. Stephen and St. James. Therefore God permitted the Romans to destroy Jerusalem. Aelfric, however, does not dwell on this last subject, saying that "it is not fitting that we in this holy Gospel recount all the shameful miseries which befell the besieged Jews before they would yield." Apparently the good priest did not approve the horrible descriptions of the slaughter of the Jews in the *Gospel of Nicodemus* and the *Legend of Veronica*, both of which were translated into Old English. He prefers to talk about the "many good men of that nation," many thousands of whom follow Christ, with the patriarchs, prophets, and apostles. And all shall finally believe. "For the psalmist wrote concerning Christ, that he is the corner-stone which joins the two walls together," Jews and Gentiles in one church.[17]

The words of the Psalmist had long since been incorporated into one of the O antiphons of Advent, and in eighth-century England the antiphon had been incorporated into the first Old English *Advent Lyric*. While the *O Rex Gentium* antiphon calls Christ the "Cornerstone, who makest two to be one," it does not make the point that the cornerstone was rejected by the Jews. When the poet adds that the "work" has need now that "the King Himself should come, and should restore the house," he may be echoing the plea of the commentators for the union of the Church and the Synagogue.

While the theme of the calling of the Gentiles thus typically led to discussion of the rejection of the Jews, accounts of the Crucifixion did not necessarily proceed to Messianic controversy. In narratives based largely on the Gospels rather than on the commentaries, it is usually observed that all was in order that the Scriptures be fulfilled, but the point is not argued. In the long description of the Passion in the Old English *Christ III*, the word "Jews" is not even used. It is the Christians who are reproached: while Christ died for them, they are

16. *Homilies* II. 301; I. 559.

17. *Homilies* I. 403–7; *Anglo-Saxon Legends of St. Andrew and St. Veronica*, trans. C. W. Goodwin (Cambridge, Eng., 1851).

not willing even to care for the sick or feed the hungry. The cross of their sins, on which he is bound unwillingly, is harder to bear than that on which he once ascended freely.[18]

The Elene of Cynewulf

At the other extreme is Cynewulf's *Elene,* in which the search for the True Cross is alternately helped and hindered by Jews who are themselves not sure whether or not they are responsible for the Crucifixion. Cynewulf did not invent the story, and both the confusion and the lengthy controversy are probably attributable to his Latin source. But the poem is obviously no literal translation: the characters are thoroughly naturalized Anglo-Saxons, and the prophecies are rendered with the greatest freedom. Indeed, the debate between the missionary queen and the Jews is presented in such idiomatic Old English that the poet's concern over the role of the Jews in the Crucifixion seems very real.

Addressing a band of Jews learned in the law, Elene refers to the glories of Israel's past, and brings in many of the testimonies of the prophets.[19] Once beloved of God, the Jews have lost the light of the Lord because they rejected the Christ and cursed him who came to free them from the Deuteronomic curse. The Messias opened the eyes of the blind and raised the dead, but in their blindness the Jews refused to see the truth; and they continue to follow error with error. As they persecuted the prophets and followed idols in the past, now they have fought against the "truth that in Bethlehem was born the Child of God, the one-begotten King, the Prince of princes."

Evidently Cynewulf did not hold the blindness of the Jews entirely against them. To the long speech of the queen, they sadly reply that indeed they "have learned the Hebraic law, which in days of old our fathers knew, at the ark of the covenant of God," but they do not know why the queen is so "wrathful" against them. They know not what sin or wrong they have committed against her.

Only a character named Judas knows. His reasoning is curiously

18. In *The Poems of Cynewulf,* trans. Charles W. Kennedy (London, 1910; reprint ed., New York, 1949), ll. 1093 ff.
19. *Ibid.,* ll. 276 ff.

muddled (in the Latin versions as well as in Cynewulf), probably because we have here, I would guess, stories about two men popularly canonized as one.[20] The date of the story is fourth century; the Jews have no recollection of Jesus, but Judas is the brother of St. Stephen! The confusion is relevant here because it complicates the problem of why the Jews rejected Jesus. Judas testifies to his sinlessness but will not cooperate with Elene, and at the same time he wonders why the Jews crucified Jesus.

This Judas alone knows that the queen has come for the "tree of triumph," whereon, "all free of fault," suffered the Son of God, "whom our fathers hung in hatred, unstained of sin, upon the lofty cross in olden days—that was a fearsome thought!" Judas had been told the story by his father, who in turn had heard it from his. He had asked how it could befall that "our fathers seized upon the Holy One," if they "wist that He was Christ indeed." It is a good question, but we are not given an answer here. The father of Judas simply cleared himself: he had not taken part in the sin and had tried to keep the "council" from their deed. After his other son, Stephen, received the bath of baptism, the father had concluded that if the Jews would do penance, God would forgive them. Further, he had specifically instructed Judas not to fight against Jesus, nor hate nor blaspheme him.

After relating this whole story to the Jews, Judas pleads ignorance to Elene, saying that the Crucifixion happened long before he was born. We are told elsewhere in the poem that the Jews were seduced by the devil to crucify God (ll. 210–12); and when Judas is about to be converted, the same devil attempts to stop him. In another attempt to explain the inexplicable, Judas' stubbornness is attributed to his fear of the Jewish loss of power as a consequence of the Crucifixion. He tells the Jews that the Crucifixion and the hiding place of the rood must be concealed, for "no long time shall the race and worship of Israel have power upon the earth if this be known" (ll.428 ff.).

The poem has a happy ending: the Jews are converted by the miracles which attend the finding of the True Cross, and Judas becomes a bishop. But the ambiguities remain, typical of a good part of Christian thinking about the Jews. Learned in the law and heirs to

20. Alban Butler, *Lives of the Saints,* ed. Herbert Thurston and Norah Leeson (New York, 1936), V, 35 ff., 51 f.

a great tradition, yet provokingly stubborn and blind and blasphemous, they are both innocent and guilty. Justly subject to Elene's wrath for their rejection of their Messias, they are yet the bearers of the prophecies, the chosen people, whose conversion is the cause of great joy among Christians and of many honors to themselves.

Chapter VII

THE MESSIAS AND THE JEWS IN *PIERS PLOWMAN*

℟The many ambiguities in the Christian attitude towards the Jews in earlier times are reflected in the words and works of Anglo-Norman and medieval England. The same prophecies and prefigurations, the same puzzling over the whys of the Jewish rejection, the same allegory of the two peoples—all appear in a great many works with endless variations. Actually, examples from this period are too numerous and too diverse for our purpose; they do not lead to *Piers Plowman*. Even works like the rood legends and the *Cursor Mundi*, which include the most interesting allegorizations of the ancient arguments over the Crucifixion, must not detain us, for they depend on the prefigurations of the Cross which Langland never mentions. Furthermore, as we have seen, by comparison with other medieval writers, Langland was not only sparing in his use of Messianic prophecies but rather unusual in his approach. Instead of meditating on the prophecies in a devotional way, he tends to use them in arguing the kingship of Christ and the rejection of the Jews.

But though we need not seek out specific sources, we are looking for similar treatments of the prophecies and similar attitudes towards the Jews in the England of Langland's time. Although the material in *Piers* is thereby limited, it is still far from unified, because Langland's own mood varied. At one time he sounds like Gilbert Crispin; at another like Peter of Blois—or Grosseteste, or a mystery, or an allegory. Underneath a hostile passage, we sometimes sense the Jewish-Christian conflicts in England that we looked at in an earlier chapter; often both hostility and praise seem to be derived from other works. The best we can do by way of preface to *Piers* is to look briefly at the contemporary currents and crosscurrents.

CONTEMPORARY BACKGROUND OF *Piers:* THE MESSIAS AND THE JEWS

In both popular and learned works, the Christian's tone is likely to become tart when he glances at the continued Jewish expectation of the Messias. As the Christians well knew, many medieval Jews expected the Messias momentarily, and false claimants were readily followed. Apparently undiscouraged by the failure of the predictions of the previous generations, even such scholars as Rashi and Maimonides computed the "end." Maimonides, for example, wrote his "Letter to Yemen" (1172) to suggest the course to be taken with a troublesome Messianic impostor, indicating in the same letter that the true Messias might, indeed, soon be expected. It was thought by some that the Messias had been born on the day the Temple fell but that he had not yet entered on his mission; on the other hand, Abrabanel, in the fifteenth century, believed that the mission had already begun.[1]

Occasional Christian disputants pointed to the repeated failure of Jewish predictions as proof of the vanity of the continued Jewish hope. Others, like Peter of Blois, angrily observed that Jews had two sets of Scriptural interpretations, one for controversy and one for home consumption. Like his father the devil, warns Peter, the Jew is capricious: sometimes he pretends to believe only the literal meaning of Scripture; sometimes he refers all the prophecies to his future Messias.[2]

All the commentators (like Grosseteste) insist that the prophecies have been already fulfilled and cannot be fulfilled again—and that, anyhow, the time and the place have long since passed. Jesus was born in the place foretold by Micheas at the time predicted by Daniel. For performing the foretold miracles, he was proclaimed the son of David by the Jews in Jerusalem; and as Jacob and Daniel prophesied, the scepter and the crown have passed from Israel. Because the scepter has passed from Juda for a thousand years, remarks Gilbert Crispin, we say that the Christ must have come. According to Bromyard (ca. 1400), the Jews contested the fulfillment of this prophecy on the basis of the legend (part of the Alexander cycle) that the scepter of their forefathers had not passed from Israel but was hidden in the Caspian Mountains. Even if that were so, replies Bromyard, the hidden tribe would not be of Juda, and thus is of no significance.[3]

1. Joseph Sarachek, *The Doctrine of the Messiah in Mediaeval Jewish Literature* (New York, 1932), pp. 53, 305, 127, 183, 242.
2. *Contra Perfidiam Judaeorum, PL.* 207, col. 870.
3. *De Cessatione Legalium, Parts 1 and 2. A Critical Edition from the Extant*

As in earlier centuries, the loss of Jerusalem, the Temple, and the sacrifices proved also that the Jews were being punished for rejecting their Messias; and this, too, had been prophesied. Grosseteste is particularly interesting on this point because, like Langland, he links the prophecies to usury. In 1231, when Simon de Montfort expelled the Jews from Leicester in order to stop usury, the Countess of Winchester considered permitting them to settle on her property. Knowing the bishop's concern for the Jews and his zeal for their conversion, she asked his opinion about her plan. But although we might have expected him to welcome the countess' offer, Grosseteste objected, fearing that it might encourage usury, and in a letter to her he examined the proper treatment of Jews.

It is clear from this letter that Grosseteste was less angry with the Jews than with the kings who encouraged usury. Quoting the words of Isaias, he says that God will turn away from these princes when they pray to him because their hands are "full of blood" (Isa. 1:15). And he interprets a passage from St. Paul to mean that they are worthy of death. By contrast, his tone in discussing the Jews is calmly reasonable; but it is nonetheless chilling. Fair-minded, judicious, and honest as he undoubtedly was, he was apparently blind to the humanity of the people whose lives he disposed of in a few phrases of Scripture.

Like most Christians of his time, Grosseteste believed that the whole history of the Jews, past, present, and future, was prophesied. He explains that it was because of their sin of crucifying our Lord that the Jews lost Jerusalem and were dispersed among the nations of the world. But Scripture also says that they must not be killed. A type of the Jews, he says, is found in Cain, who killed his brother Abel, a type of Christ, killed by the Jews for the sake of the world. But God set a mark on Cain (Gen. 4:11) so that none should kill him, and said, "slay them not, lest at any time my people forget" (Ps. 58:12). Furthermore, as St. Augustine says, they must not be killed because they carry our Testament with them, in which is the prophecy and promise of Christ, and so they are witnesses of the Christian faith against the pagans. Above all, as St. Paul says in Romans 11:25–26,

MSS, ed. Arthur M. Lee, Ph. D. dissertation, University of Colorado (1942), New York Public Library microfilm, pp. 133, 171–86; Gilbert Crispin, *Disputatio Judaei cum Christiano de Fide Christiana, PL.* 159, col. 1033.

in the last days, when the fullness of the Gentiles has come in, all Israel (that is, the Jews) shall be saved. In the meantime, while the Jews blaspheme the Savior of the world, they are justly held captive. Out of the mercy of God, they must not be killed; out of the justice of God, they are dispersed and must labor. In order to accomplish this end, he concludes, it should be provided that they work by their hands. The sentence of God is not that they are to grow great and rich through the oppression of usury.[4]

Here is certainly a link between theory and practice that is worth examining. The background of the theory is clear enough in those works of Grosseteste that are directed to the Jews. One of the subjects discussed most thoroughly in his *De Cessatione Legalium* is the fulfillment of the Messianic prophecies, including those concerning the calling of the Gentiles and the rejection of the Jews. Furthermore, the old theme that the prophets had foretold the Jewish rejection of their Messias found new support in the *Testaments of the Twelve Patriarchs,* a recently discovered work that Grosseteste translated from the Greek in the hope of converting the Jews. According to the modern editor of the work, Dr. R. H. Charles, even before interpolation, some of the passages in this pre-Christian Jewish work predicted the downfall of the Temple and the dispersion of the Jews for their sins (e.g., Test. Levi XI); and also the salvation of the Gentiles through Israel (Levi IV).[5]

Texts such as these might easily be used to explain or to justify the contemporary plight of the Jews; that they motivated Grosseteste's policy on usury is doubtful. Grosseteste hated usury; wanting to see an end to it, he inevitably cited Scripture to support his case. In much the same way, as was noted in an earlier chapter, he defended the bishop's right of visitation in his diocese by citing the example of Moses. It seems to me—and it may well have seemed to him in happier moments—that if his counsel had been followed successfully, the position of the Jews might have improved. If usury had been ended and the Jews had gone to work as farmers and tradesmen, they would not have been the outcasts they were as usurers, however rich;

4. *Epistolae,* ed. H. R. Luard (London, 1861), vol. XXV, *Chronicles and Memorials of Great Britain and Ireland during the Middle Ages,* pp. 33 ff.

5. *The Testaments of the Twelve Patriarchs,* trans. and ed. R. H. Charles, in *Apocrypha and Pseudepigrapha of the Old Testament,* vol. 2 (Oxford, 1913).

and the day might have come when they became citizens, accepted rather than rejected by society. As for the prophecies, one might logically conclude from them (as Langland did) that, far from prohibiting usury, they predicted it as the fate of a rejected people. Actually, of course, the Jews practiced usury not because of the prophecies but because they were outsiders, exempt from the restrictions as well as the privileges of feudal law.

Contemporary Allegories of the Two Peoples

That Jews and Christians were two separate "peoples" was a social, economic, and religious fact that neither group questioned, a reality that continued to be allegorized in tract, play, and picture. A brief glance at a few of these sources suffices to reveal an attitude towards the history of the Jews that, like Langland's, is both callous and concerned. Following all the earlier commentators, Peter of Blois in his *Contra Perfidiam Judaeorum* (Chap. XXV) allegorized the Old Testament stories of Cain and Abel, Ishmael and Isaac, Esau and Jacob, Ruben and Juda—all stories of the loss of the inheritance by the first-born, all prefiguring the passing of God's favor from the Synagogue to the Church.

While Israel lost her power when Jerusalem was destroyed, it was generally assumed that the rejection of the Jews by God occurred when they rejected the Messias, that is, at the Crucifixion. That is why the figures of the Church and the Synagogue are included in so many portrayals of the Crucifixion: the Synagogue, standing at the left of the Cross, lets the crown fall, while the Church, standing at the right, holds the scepter. The opening address of the *Disputatio* once attributed to Gilbert Crispin reads like a caption to these paintings. The author says that the Synagogue, standing at the left of the Cross, lost her crown and the light of God at the very time that the Church became the spouse of Christ.

So familiar were the two figures that their influence can be seen even in works in which the meaning was lost. In Malory's *Quest*, for example, the allegory departs from the familiar argument, but the same imagery is drawn upon. In the dreams of both Bors and Perceval, for example, the elder of two sisters is probably not the Synagogue. But she echoes the argument in many ways; for one, she complains that she has been disinherited in favor of her younger sister because she put to death a great party of the king's kinsmen.[6]

In the *Stanzaic Life of Christ* (ll. 356 ff.) [7] and in the Chester play of the Nativity, there are interestingly stylized portrayals of the two peoples. Both tell how Mary herself prophesied the rejection of the Jews, a story originally found in the *Apocryphal Gospel of pseudo-Matthew* (Chap. XIII).[8] In the play, just outside Nazareth, Mary sees a vision and asks what it signifies that she sees some men "glad and mery," and "some sighing and sory." Angelus explains that "the common people" rejoice that they see "of Abrahams seede Christ come to helpe them in their need." "The mourning men" are Jews "that shall be put behynde,/ for it passes out of their kinde/ through Christ at his cominge" (ll. 441 ff.).

For their part, the Jews rather looked forward to the Messianic day when the Christians would mourn and "be put behynde." And like the Christians, they found the relations between the two peoples allegorized in the Scriptures.[9] Abrabanel, for example, explained that the Christian or Roman power grew out of the Biblical race of Edom. The soul of Esau, father of the Edomite race, passed into Jesus, and the hostility between the two peoples can be traced back to the dispute between Esau and Jacob in the womb of their mother. The combat nursed the widespread Jewish faith that "Israel would vie with other nations and ultimately triumph over them."

The Moslems fit into the family image, too, for Islam is of the race of Ishmael, the "brood of Hagar." "According to the traditional notion," Abraham Ibn Ezra (twelfth century) interpreted Christianity and Islam as brother and servant of Israel—the two conspiring together to supplant the true heir. In Ibn Ezra's allegorical explanation of the loss of Jerusalem, Israel is personified as a frail woman, and the reproaches of the prophets are accepted: her misfortunes were deserved, for she deceived her Lord. "Wherefore she was divorced. Then did her patrimony, her vineyard Zion, become the plunder of

6. Sir Thomas Malory, *The Quest of the Holy Grail*, ed. Eugène Vinaver (Oxford, 1947), II, 912 ff.

7. Ed. Frances A. Foster, EETS 166 (1925).

8. In *Apocryphal Gospels, Acts, and Revelations*, Ante-Nicene Library, vol. XVI (1870).

9. The interpretations which follow are taken from Sarachek, *Doctrine of the Messiah, passim*.

her foes." These are the same same symbols of divorce and property used by the Christians. The rabbi concludes, however, that God will restore Israel to his affections, "and will see that the servant's progeny shall not share the inheritance bequeathed to Isaac."

The status of the Gentiles in the Messianic age is varied in Talmudic literature, but the general belief was that when Israel became supreme, "the unrepentant Gentiles and inveterate foes among them would be extirpated"; and proselytes would not be accepted, their motives being suspect. Further, almost all the rabbis (with a few notable exceptions, like Rashi) set out to show that the promises of redemption were not purely spiritual and moral, as the Christians said. They insisted that the Scriptures promised an actual state, "the restitution of the Torah and the Temple in Palestine." The law of Moses, they felt, would not be abrogated in the Messianic era; on the contrary, the ceremonial, sacrificial, and agricultural laws would be in force. It followed for Jewish writers that the destruction of Jerusalem and the loss of the Temple meant that Jesus could *not* have been the Messianic king.

CONTEMPORARY NOTIONS OF THE END OF THE WORLD

The candid and learned Judaeus of Gilbert Crispin's *Disputation* questioned also the spiritual and moral redemption of Christianity. Citing the prophecy of Isaias, he demanded to know where people could be found who did not "lift swords." Christianus replies that the peace described by Isaias is of the spirit and that this peace Jesus brought to his followers. It is harder to humble the heart than to beat swords into plowshares, he says, and yet many highborn men give up great possessions for the love of God. In this way, continues Christianus, can be understood the words of Isaias that the lion and the lamb will lie down together. And following all the early commentaries, Gilbert concludes that the fulfillment of the most important prophecies is obvious to all: that Jesus was indeed the "expectation of the Gentiles" is apparent from the fact that the Gentiles do worship the God of Israel.

Most Christians took Isaias literally, and like Langland they dreamed of peace among nations as an event of the Second Coming, when Jesus would come as king and fulfill all the royal prophecies.

Then, too, the Jews would be converted, but not without a struggle.

Both Christians and Jews expected the world to end in a conflict between good and evil: in the Jewish version the conflict would be between Messias and Beliar (the devil), in the Christian, between Christ and Antichrist. The Talmud explains that when the Messias is at hand, the kingdom will be turned to the Minith, i.e., to the Christians, while the Christians expected the Jews to welcome Antichrist. There are a number of ancient legends mixed in here, but whatever his ultimate origin, the character of Antichrist was fixed by the Jewish-Christian debate. From earliest times, the Christians had said that the continued Messianic expectation of the Jews would lead them to accept Antichrist. Because they refused the truth, says St. Paul (2 Thess. 2:9–12), they will accept the lie. Scriptural warrant for this view was found also in the words of Jesus: "I am come in My Father's name, and ye receive me not: if another shall come in his own name, him ye will receive" (John 5:43).

Patristic apologetic and apocryphal legend elaborately developed the theme of a false Messias who, at the end of the world, would seduce both Christians and Jews. Aelfric, for example, says that Antichrist will be "human man and true devil, as our Savior is truly man and God." He will work signs and wonders, saying that they prove him to be god, but he will heal only those he has harmed previously.[10]

We need not go into the history and development of the theme, but it is worth observing that popular literature on the subject reveals that Christians were familiar with the Jewish hope of a Messianic king who would restore the state and the sacrifices. In the Chester play on the *Coming of Antichrist*, for example, Antichrist fulfills what were, in fact, the medieval Jewish expectations on this score. Antichrist announces that he has come to call the Jews from the Gentiles, to fulfill the prophecy of Ezechiel 36, "*Tollam vos de gentibus et congregabo vos de universis terris, et reduca vos in terram vestram.*" He explains that one has been before him, who separated

---

10. R. Travers Herford, *Christianity in Talmud and Midrash* (London, 1903), p. 207; Bede *Allegorica Expositio* (ed. J. A. Giles) VIII. 209; Aelfric *Homilies* I. 5. The source of many medieval versions of the tale was a popular tenth-century compilation of patristic descriptions of Antichrist by Adso, *Libellus de Antichristo*, *PL*. 101, cols. 1290 ff.

his people the Jews, so that they never came into their land. Now he will restore them, build the temple anew—and be honored as God therein. When the Jewish "kings" are convinced that he is the Messias, they "keep" their sacrifices; they worship him and sacrifice a lamb to him in the Temple. There is obviously some theological confusion here, but there is also ground for the Jewish complaint that the Christian Antichrist was adapted from the Jewish Messia ben Joseph. And while the true and false miracles are clumsily portrayed, the conclusion has a certain validity: the Jews accept Jesus only when Elias appears to bear him witness.

Piers Plowman: Langland's Attitude toward the Jews

In *Piers,* the Messianic king is often linked with the lost kingdom of the Jews. In fact, the disquieting aspect of Langland's choice of prophecies is that so many of them lead to derogatory remarks about the Jews. It is difficult, perhaps impossible, to reconcile this hostility with the enlightened view expressed in other contexts. We have observed, for example, Langland's belief that the unbaptized, Jews and Saracens alike, who live according to their truth, will not be abandoned by the God of Truth. He says elsewhere, with apparent approval, that Jews still live according to the law of Moses, which they think the best. But when he discusses Jesus as the Messias, then the Jews become "wretches," rightfully rejected by God and society alike.

Now anti-Semitism is a disease with many complications, and I am not prepared to give a definitive diagnosis of Langland's case. But some of the symptoms concern us here because they were, I believe, inherited as part of the argument with the Jews on the fulfillment of the Messianic prophecies. And while the cleavage is more marked in Langland than in most other writers, the tendency to praise the Jews while discussing the law and to censure them in discussing Messianic claims was typical of Christian thought.

The changes in tone are not quite as capricious as first appears. For one thing, Langland, like many other Christians, revered the law so highly that he could understand why the Jews would resist any change. For another, the law is impersonal. But the rejection of the Messias was fraught with emotional overtones, not only of the historic Crucifixion but of the continuing Jewish hostility to a beloved person. What further troubled Langland in the Jewish attitude towards Jesus was his strong sense of kinship. His Messias is not primarily the bearer of the Word to the Gentiles but the rightful king of the Jews, the heir of that David whom he admired. Perhaps that is why so often a reference to the kingship of Christ turns into an argument against the Jews and ends with a proof that the Jews were wrong—for as the prophecies foretold, the Synagogue was supplanted by the Church. Perhaps, too, that is why the tone of acrimony is lost when Langland describes the Second Coming of the Messias, for then the Jews were expected to acknowledge Christ as king.

It may also be that the emphasis on kingship was due in part to Langland's interest in politics. Christ as king is not much talked about in our time, probably because kings strike us as the stuff of musical comedies. We have to remind ourselves that for Langland and the men of his time, kings *were* politics; and that to devout men, the kingship of Christ had an obvious application to the conduct of the realm. As Professor Bloomfield points out, Langland, more than his contemporaries, "concentrates" on the kingship of Jesus, the Pantocrator, and on the transformation of society into the kingdom of God.[11] But much of Langland's extended discussion of statecraft, in the cantos on Lady Meed, for example, has only a general relevance for us here. That is, his way of drawing on Old Testament examples of good and bad rulers follows the Pauline dictum that all Scripture was written for our instruction. His frequent coupling of King David with Christ, however, and his descriptions of Christ as king of the Jews and "Conqueror" of Christians are specifically related to both the Messianic tradition and to contemporary affairs.

Similarly, his views on the rejection of the Jews are related to both the Messianic proofs and to the medieval Jewish problem. While the Jews had been expelled from England a few generations earlier, their history was not forgotten, and their presence just across the channel was, of course, obvious. Works written to and about them, both during the English settlement and later on the Continent, were read and quoted in fourteenth-century England. One of the clearest examples of Langland's combination of Messianic proofs with politics, both

11. Morton W. Bloomfield, *Piers Plowman as a Fourteenth-Century Apocalypse* (New Brunswick, N.Y., 1961), p. 100.

Jewish and Christian, is found in his description of the Second Coming. The subject grows out of a rebuke administered to the king beguiled by Meed and develops as a prophecy of the golden age when the just king will fulfill the promises of peace and justice, and so convert the Jews.

Now the question of what a man of Langland's stature thought about the Jews and why he thought the way he did has an independent interest for us. But it should be made clear at the outset that his attitude is not especially significant to *Piers* as a whole. Langland's treatment of the Messianic prophecies is not basic to his thought and allegory, as is his pondering on the Trinity and the law. In discussing the Trinity and the law, he rewove the entire fabric of prophecies and doctrine with a sure hand. When he discusses the Jewish rejection of the Messias, he falters and loses his own vision. And while he selects and assimilates the material into his own plan, he repeats stereotypes from plays and allegories in a manner far beyond his usual mode.

The Rejection of the Jews

A passage in Passus XV (ll. 572 ff.) begins with what sounds like praise not only of the law but of the Jews who believed in it. They believe in the law, Langland says, that our Lord himself wrote "in stone, for it stydfast was, and stonde sholde eure." This "parfit Iewen lawe" is *"Dilige deum et proximum."* Christ gave it to Moses to teach men until the coming of the Messias; and the Jews still believe in that law and think it the best. In the lines which immediately follow, as the subject shifts from the law to the Jewish attitude toward the Messias, the style becomes uneven and the tone angry. Apparently aware of the Jewish expectation of a true Messias, with its implication that Jesus was a liar, Langland seems to be answering the argument of the Jews and returning their hostility. They knew Christ for a prophet, he says, who saved many people. They knew

> Bothe of myracles and meruailles and how he men fested
> With two fisshes and fyue loues fyue thousande peple;
> And bi that maungerye men mi3te wel se that Messye he semed.
> And whan he luft vp Lazar that layde was in graue,
> And vnder stone ded and stanke, with styf voys hym called,
>> *Lazare, veni foras,*
> Dede hym rise and rowme ri3t bifor the Iuwes.
> Ac thei seiden and sworen with sorcerye he wrou3te,

And studyeden to stroyen hym and stroyden hemself;
And thorw his pacyence her powere to pure nou3t he brou3te;
  Patientes vincunt;
Danyel of her vndoynge deuyned and seyde,
    Cum sanctus sanctorum veniat, cessabit vnxio vestra.
  And 3et wenen tho wrecches that he were *pseudo-propheta,*
And that his lore be lesynges and lakken it alle,
And hopen that he be to come that shal hem releue,
Moyses eft, or Messye here maisteres 3et deuyneth.

(XV. 580–93)

He wrought miracles and marvels and gave the
      multitude a banquet;
Two fishes and five loaves feasted five thousand.
Men might see by that that he was Messiah, or
      like him.
He lifted Lazarus who had lain buried
Under a stone and stank. He said loudly:
Lazare, veni foras.
He bade him arise and walk before the people.
They said and swore that sorcery did it,
And strove to stone him and to destroy themselves.
But his patience brought their power to nothing.
Patientes vincunt.
Daniel had divined their undoing in his prophecy:
Cum sanctus sanctorum veniat, cessabit unctio vestra.
And those wretches regard him as though he were
      pseudo-propheta
And hold his lore a lie and blame it boldly,
And expect that he shall come who shall at last
      relieve them,
Moses again or Messiah, as their masters still
      prophesy.

(XV. 630 ff.)

This is not a reasoned argument, yet some of the traditional objections to the Jewish position are recognizable. As was customary in such controversy, the miracles are cited as proof that Jesus was the Messias. In the poem, as in the argument, the rejection by the Jews led to their self-destruction. Their "undoing" was predicted by Daniel, whose prophecy is cited and is intended to mean that when the Messias came the kingdom of the Jews ended. The last four lines glance at the continued Messianic expectation of the Jews, and the use of the word "lie" probably refers to the libelous reports circulated about Jesus by the Jews. The effect of incoherence in the passage as a whole may be partly blamed on tradition, too. So familiar was the prophecy of Daniel that Langland does not even translate it; and the way in which arguments are sprinkled with prophecies, interjected without explanation or transition, is as old as St. Paul.

That some of the bitterness was equally ancient is clear from a passage in Passus XVI which is based on the twelfth chapter of Matthew, the chapter in which Jesus calls his antagonists a generation of vipers. The rendering in the poem is a choice example of Langland's technique of translating the Bible into the vernacular. According to Matthew, some of those who witnessed the miracles recognized them as a sign that Jesus was the Messias and asked, "Is not this the son of David?" In *Piers*, those who witnessed the miracles call Jesus the "leche of lyf and the lorde of heigh heuene" (XVI. 118). In Matthew, the Pharisees say that Jesus casts out devils with the help of the prince of devils; Jesus replies that a kingdom divided against itself cannot stand and that Satan does not cast out Satan. In *Piers* the Jews "Iangeled" and judged that Jesus worked by witchcraft and with the devil's might. Jesus himself calls the Jews "cherles" and says that Satan is their Savior.

That the Jews followed Satan and that his own people crucified Jesus troubled, as well as angered, Langland. He may have meant to include himself among those Christians censured by Dame Study (in Passus X. 101 ff.) for questioning overmuch. She complains that she has heard important men, while they were eating at the table, carp as though they were clerks. Discussing the Crucifixion and other such subjects, they go so far as to lay "fautes" on the Father. Augustine, she says, counsels such arguers not to ask more than is fitting. Never wish to know why "god wolde suffre Sathan" to seduce his people, or why God was willing to permit Satan to betray Jesus. All was according to the will of the Father, and the only right course is to believe loyally in the lore of Holy Church. Dame Study's authoritarianism contains some satire, and the dreamer does not really drop the subject as a result of her rebuke. But when he returns to it elsewhere, as in the description of the Passion in Passus XVIII, it is only to confirm the lady's conclusion that the part of the Jews in the Crucifixion is a mystery.

It should be observed, by way of a caveat, that the clashes between those who accept and those who reject the Messias are less significant in the whole context of the canto on the Passion than they may appear here. In Langland's vision of the Crucifixion, of the debate between the four daughters of God, and of the harrowing of hell, it is the universal meaning of Christ's sacrifice that is explored, and the role of the Jews as crucifiers is of only secondary importance. Far more important is the role of Faith-Abraham, who is both the Jewish herald of the fulfillment of the prophecies and also the father of all Christian believers.

Indeed, the joyous acceptance of Jesus as the Messias dominates the brief preface to the Passion, in which Langland adapts the Messianic psalms of the son of David, used in the liturgy of Palm Sunday, to the imagery of *Piers Plowman* (XVIII. 8 ff.). The scene is set in Jerusalem, with the children chanting *"gloria laus"* to Jesus while "olde folke" sing hosanna with the organ playing. Then "one semblable to the Samaritan and some-del to Piers the Plowman" arrives barefoot, riding on an ass, like a squire coming to be dubbed knight. Faith, the herald, cries from a window *"a fili David!"* and the "Olde Juwes of Ieruslalem for Ioye thei songen, *Benedictus qui venit in nomine domini."*

Then the dreamer asks Faith aside "what al that fare be-mente," and "who sholde Iouste in Iherusalem." Faith's answer is a deep one that touches on the cosmic meaning of the Passion and which, incidentally, would seem to exonerate the Jews. For one thing, he explains that Jesus will joust in Piers's armor, that is, in a human body, so "that Cryst be nou3t biknowe." It would seem to follow that the Jews could not have been guilty of willful deicide; as a matter of fact, earlier in the poem, Langland had mentioned Christ's forgiveness of the crucifiers, who knew not what they did. Further, when the dreamer asks whether Jews or Scribes will joust with Jesus, Faith replies, neither, but the foul fiend, and Falsehood and Death (l. 28).

Christ's triumph over sin and death is one of Langland's major themes, and of course it dominates this canto, with its long contest with the devil. Even in the description of the Crucifixion most closely based on the Gospels, the motif is carried out. Pilate comes to see how "doughtilich" Death can do, and when the crucifiers mock Jesus on the cross, they say that if he would come down, they would believe that "Lyf" loves him. When the "lorde of lyf and of li3te" closed his eyes, day withdrew, the sun darkened, and in the darkness Life and Death battled.

It is in this same vein that Faith begins his denunciation of the Jews, saying that they have chosen darkness and death. Provoked by their forcing the centurion to pierce the side of Christ, Faith berates them as "caytyues, acursed foreuer." When this darkness is over, he cries, his death will be avenged; and you, "lordeynes, han ylost for Lyf shal haue the maistrye" (XVIII. 92, 102). Then he foretells the rejection of the Jews in a passage influenced by the literary and social history of the Church and the Synagogue, and by the allegorical portrayal of the conflict that is seen in the art of the Middle Ages.

The Church and the Synagogue

The representation in art of the centurion piercing the side of Christ explains two curious aspects of the scene in the poem. Unlike the Gospel account, in *Piers Plowman* the Jews are responsible for the centurion's act, and Faith is particularly angry with them for this "foule vylenyne" (XVIII. 94). The C version (XXI. 85) is more startling—Longinus is called "this blynde Iuwe." Whether this was a slip or a deliberate modification of history, it can be traced to the frequent association in art of the centurion and the Synagogue. In the numerous personifications of the Church and the Synagogue as two ladies, the Synagogue holds the lance, which has become one of her attributes. In some of the paintings of the Crucifixion in which the two ladies stand on either side of the Cross, Longinus also appears. In one twelfth-century illumination, he holds the lance while the crowned Church catches in a chalice the blood that flows from the wound of Christ.[12] Is this centurion Jew or Gentile? How did the Synagogue get the lance? If the scene in *Piers* may be taken as a

12. See Urban T. Holmes and Sister M. Amelia Klenke, O.P., *Chrétien, Troyes, and the Grail* (Chapel Hill, N.C., 1959), pp. 110–14. It should be noted that in some commentaries and paintings, Longinus symbolizes the Church of the Gentiles: as Longinus had been blind until the blood from the wound of Christ gave him sight, so the Gentiles lived in the darkness of idolatry until Jesus brought them to the light of the God of Israel. That is why in some paintings of the Crucificion, in which the Church and the Synagogue stand on either side of the cross, the Church is represented by the centurion, the Synagogue by a man with a sponge. When Langland called Longinus a Jew, however, he must have had in mind the more popular personifications discussed in the text.

125

gloss, the Roman centurion has become a Jew who receives his sight at the same moment that the Synagogue receives her blindfold, and her guilt is symbolized by the transference to her of the lance. In the poem, it is after the centurion's eyes are "vnspered" by the blood springing down from the lance that Faith predicts the rejection of the Synagogue, her loss of crown and kingdom.

The crown and the scepter, so frequently portrayed in medieval iconography, were no doubt supplied originally by the royal imagery of the prophecies, especially those of Jacob and Daniel. In *Piers*, Daniel's prophecy appears at the end of this passage:

> "And ʒowre fraunchise, that fre was, fallen is in thraldome,
> And ʒe, cherles, and ʒowre children chieue shal ʒe neure,
> Ne haue lordship in londe ne no londe tylye,
> But al bareyne be and vsurye vsen,
> Which is lyf that owre lorde in alle lawes acurseth.
> Now ʒowre good dayes ar done as Danyel prophecyed,
> Whan Cryst cam, of her kyngdom the croune shulde cesse;
> *Cum veniat sanctus sanctorum, cessabit vnxio vestra.*"
>
> (XVIII. 103–10)

> "And your franchise among the free has fallen
>   into thralldom,
> And you churls and your children shall never
>   thrive after,
> Nor have lordship in the land or land in tillage,
> But all shall be barren and live by usury,
> Which is the life that our Lord in all his laws
>   holds cursed.
> Now your good days are done, as Daniel prophesied
> That when Christ came the crown of their kingdom
>   should be broken.
> *Cum veniat sanctus sanctorum, cessabit unctio vestra.*"
>
> (XVIII. 106 ff.)

Did Daniel have such deep significance for Langland that he quotes him again here, just as he did in Passus XV? Usually when he repeats a phrase (like "Let us make man in our image"), it is in order to explore its meaning more deeply. But there is no development of Daniel's prophecy here. Indeed, there is no reference to the "seventy weeks" or to the destruction of Jerusalem, as there would be had Langland been studying the text or the commentaries. Further, from the wording of the prophecy, it is quite certain that his familiarity with Daniel can be traced not to the Vulgate but to the popular theater.

As was pointed out many years ago by M. Sépét, the wording of the prophecy in the popular prophet plays is quite different from that in the Vulgate.[13] The reading in the plays follows the wording of the pseudo-Augustinian *Sermon against the Jews,* which, as was observed earlier, was the source of the first prophet plays. It is this reading that occurs, for example, in the Anglo-Norman *Adam,* in the Towneley *Prophets,* in the *Pageant of the Shearmen and Taylors,* and in the *Pageant of the Weavers;* it is also used in the *Cursor Mundi,* in the *Three Kings of Cologne,* and in *Piers.*

In the original tract, and in most of these works, Daniel is but one of the prophets called upon to give testimony to Christ. While by the fourteenth century many of the prophecies had lost their controversial tone, Daniel's had become almost an epithet, which served to summarize one point of the Messianic argument. From the earliest days of the Church, the prophecy of Daniel had been used to prove not only that with the coming of the Messias Jewish power would end, but that the fulfillment of the prophecies showed that the time for the coming of the Messias had passed. Placed at the end of the Daniel passage in Passus XVIII of *Piers,* the prophecy has the effect of a catch-phrase that everyone would understand.

Still another link with the traditional phraseology of the Church and the Synagogue is Langland's use of the word "barren" in this same passage. "All shall be barren," says Faith-Abraham, in what is surely an odd way to speak of a people's future. It may be remembered, however, that St. Paul had cited Isaias' text on barrenness in his famous allegory of Ishmael and Isaac as the two peoples and the two laws. The charge of barrenness had been repeated throughout

---

13. The Vulgate reads: "Septuaginta hebdomades abbreviatae sunt . . . ut . . . impleatur visio et prophetia, et ungatur Sanctus Sanctorum." The Sermon reads: "Cum venerit Sanctus Sanctorum, cessabit unctio." The various prophet plays apparently repeat the form used in the sermon (Marius Sépét, "Les Prophètes du Christ," *Bibliothèque de l'école des Chartes,* XXVIII (1867), 22). Professor Karl Young adds that this same form appears in the Beauvais *Daniel* and in the *Daniel* of Hilarius, and he says that it "must derive either from the pseudo-Augustinian Sermon or from the prophet plays themselves" (*The Drama of the Mediaeval Church,* (Oxford, 1933), II, 304–5). I have found the same reading in so many works that I wonder if there was not a variant Biblical tradition.

the centuries in debates and commentaries to prove that the Church of the future would have more believers than the Synagogue.

While repeating the insult, Langland, however, develops it quite differently and links it with usury, which itself was considered "barren" in medieval thinking. When Faith prophesies that all shall be barren, he is predicting the practical consequences to the Jews of their rejection of Jesus: they will neither plow nor own their land, but instead will "live by usury." It is an interesting commentary on commentaries that Langland and Grosseteste should have come to such different conclusions on the basis of the same Scriptures. Both men hated usury and both condemned Christians who encouraged it (Grosseteste the English kings, Langland the popes at Avignon). That it is Faith-Abraham who predicts the rejection of the Jews here is also Langland's own touch, and a characteristic one: freely transcending time and history, Abraham both quotes Daniel and forecasts the medieval condition of the Jews.

Later in this same eighteenth canto, just before the harrowing of hell, there is still another reference to the rejection of the Jews. At the very brink of hell, the four daughters of God have been debating whether the light they see can really conquer sin and death and rescue the descendants of Adam from hell. They are quite abruptly interrupted by one "with two brode eyen," called Boke. "A bolde man of speche," he bears "witness" out of both Testaments to the many times this Lord of light has conquered the elements and shown himself creator of all things. For this Jesus is a Giant, he says, who comes to break down the bars of hell and have out whomsoever he pleases. He concludes by saying:

> "And I, Boke, wil be brent but Iesus rise to lyue,
> In alle myȝtes of man and his moder gladye,
> And conforte al his kynne and out of care brynge,
> And al the Iuwen Ioye vniognen and vnlouken;
> And but thei reuerencen his rode and his resurexioun,
> And bileue on a newe lawe be lost lyf and soule."
>
> (XVIII. 252–57)

> "I, Book, shall be burnt, [unless] he shall rise
>   living,
>   In all the might of a man, and be his mother's
>   gladness,

> And comfort all his kindred, and cleanse their
> sorrow.
> All the joy of the Jews will be disjointed and
> shattered—
> Unless they reverence his resurrection and do
> the rood honour
> And believe in a new law, they lose soul and body."
>
> (XVIII. 261 ff.) [14]

There really seems to be no logical or aesthetic reason for bringing in the disbelief of the Jews here. I wonder if the reference resulted from a simple association of ideas and phrases—if the references to mother and kindred recalled a comparison of believers and unbelievers such as that which appears in the Chester *Nativity*. In that play, as we saw earlier, Mary sees a vision of two groups of Jews, some glad and merry, others sighing and sorry, the latter to be "put behind" for their disbelief. In much the same vein, Book goes on from the "gladness," "comfort," and "joy" of mother and kindred to the shattered joy of those who refuse to reverence Jesus.

Christ the Conqueror

The theme of the victorious Christ is expanded in Passus XIX in a curiously argumentative way, which begins by adapting the old royal imagery to medieval warfare and deteriorates into a cold-blooded defense of the *status quo* of medieval Jews. In the previous canto, Jesus was the knight gaining his spurs in the tournament of the Crucifixion. In the legend of Longinus, he was described as a knight and a king's son. Here he is the king, and his title of Christ is interpreted to mean conqueror. Conscience is explaining to the questioning dreamer that knight, king, and conqueror may be one person

14. There is some difficulty of interpretation in the first line of the passage quoted here. Where Wells translates "but" or "bote" as "but," I have substituted "unless," following a suggestion made by Richard L. Hoffman, " 'The Burning of Boke' in *Piers Plowman*." *MLQ*, XXV (March, 1964), 57–65. Our meaning of "but" simply does not make sense here; at least, I cannot conceive any context in which Langland would present the destruction of the Book of the Old Testament as some sort of corollary to the Resurrection. Hoffman suggests that "but" was used in the sense of "unless." In his translation of the B text, Professor J. F. Goodridge translates "bote" as "if" (London, 1960). In the C text edited by Salter and Pearsall, the line is: "And yet I, Boke, wol be brente, bote he aryse to lyve" (l. 264); in a note (p. 164) the editors translate as "And I, even I, the Book, will gladly be burnt if he does not arise again to life."

(XIX. 27 ff.). To be called a knight is noble, "for men shal knele to hym"; to be called a king is fairer, for he can make knights. To be called a conqueror, however, comes of special grace, both of "hardynesse" of heart and of courtesy; a conqueror can make free men foul thralls if they violate his laws. Then Conscience applies this mystique to Jesus and the Jews; or perhaps the mystique arose out of Langland's need to justify the treatment of the Jews. It is not his usual way to praise conquerors, or for that matter, success, but here he says:

> The Iuwes, that were gentil-men Iesu thei dispised,
> Bothe his lore and his lawe now ar thei lowe cherlis.
> As wyde as the worlde is, wonyeth there none
> But vnder tribut and taillage as tykes and cherles.
> And tho that bicome Crysten by conseille of the baptiste,
> Aren frankeleynes, fre men thorw fullyng that thei toke,
> And gentel-men with Iesu for Iesus was yfulled,
> And vppon Caluarye on crosse ycrouned kynge of Iewes.
>
> (XIX. 33–41)

> The Jews who were gentle held Jesu in dishonour,
> Both his lore and his law, and are now low villains.
> Though this world is wide not one is living
> Out of toll or tribute, as tramps and scoundrels.
> And those who become Christian because of baptism
> Are franklins and freemen by the faith which
>   they have taken,
> And are gentlemen with Jesu, for Jesus had baptism
> And was crowned king of Jews upon the cross
>   at Calvary.
>
> (XIV. 34 ff.)

This is only the old argument of the rejection of the Jews put in contemporary terms: those who reject Jesus are tramps, those who accept him are franklins. Unfortunately, the new dress makes the old figure uglier than ever, for whereas the citation of prophecies at least seems impersonal and inevitable, this Christ is a conqueror directly responsible for cruelty.

To Langland, of course, it did not seem to be cruelty but justice. Conscience explains:

> "It bicometh to a kynge to kepe and to defende,
>   And conquerour of conquest his lawes and his large.

And so dide Iesus the Iewes, he Iustified and tauȝte hem
The lawe of lyf that last shal euere;
And fended fram foule yueles, feueres and fluxes,
And fro fendes that in hem were and fals bileue.
Tho was he Iesus of Iewes called gentel prophete,
And kynge of her kyngdome and croune bar of thornes.
And tho conquered he on crosse as conquerour noble;
Myȝt no deth hym fordo ne adown brynge,
That he ne aros and regned and rauysshed helle.
And tho was he 'conquerour' called of quikke and of ded;
For he ȝaf Adam and Eue and other mo blisse,
That longe hadde leyne bifore as Lucyferes cherles.
And sith he ȝaf largely alle his lele lyges
Places in paradys at her partynge hennes,
He may wel be called 'conquerour' and that is Cryst to mene."

(XIX. 42–58)

"It becomes a king to keep his kingdom steadfast,
And a conqueror to conquer and to give laws and
    bounty.
And so did Jesus with the Jews; for he justified
    and taught them
The law of life that shall last forever.
He fended them from evils, fevers and fluxes,
And from fiends that were within them and
    false believing.
Then the Jews called Jesus a gentle prophet,
Also he was king of their kingdom and bore a
    crown of thorns.
He conquered upon the cross as a conqueror who
    is noble.
No death might destroy him or bring down his
    sovereignty,
But he arose and reigned and ravished hell.
Then he was called conqueror of quick and dead folk;
For he gave Adam and Eve and many others their
    deliverance,
Who had lain long years in Lucifer's bondage.
He gave places in Paradise at their departure
    from the living
With a liberal largess to all his loyal liegemen.
Well may he be called Christ, for conqueror
    is its meaning."

(XIX. 42–58)

131

Obviously, there is nothing "Aryan" in Langland's resentment against the Jews. As in the Old English epics, Jesus is the chief or baron, the Jews his followers, tied by blood and history and oaths of fealty. It was they who knew him in the flesh; he taught them and cured them and delivered all their ancient heroes; he fulfilled their prophecies and was their Messias. If nothing more, they owed him loyalty as his liegemen.

Still, only the blindness of prejudice could have kept Langland from seeing that his view was basically un-Christian, as he himself understood Christianity. Indeed, the inconsistency is implicit in this very passage, in which he proceeds to recommend as blessings to the Christians the poverty and sorrow just described as the curse of the Jews:

> Ac the cause that he cometh thus with crosse of his passioun,
> Is to wissen vs there-wyth that whan that we ben tempted,
> There-with to fyȝte and fenden vs fro fallyng in-to synne,
> And se bi his sorwe that who so loueth Ioye,
> To penaunce and to pouerte he moste putten hym-seluen,
> And moche wo in this worlde willen and suffren.
>
> (XIX. 59–64)

> This has caused his coming with the cross of
>   his passion.
> He would advise us with it that whenever we
>   are tempted
> We may fight with it and defend us from falling
>   into evil.
> We see by his sorrow that whosoever loves joy
> Must put himself to penance and to poverty of spirit,
> And have much woe in this world and a will to suffer.
>
> (XIX. 59–64)

This, indeed, is the Christian message that Langland preaches throughout the poem—not that baptism is the way to prosperity, or that suffering is for outsiders. Unlike many Christians, Langland did not even believe that the Church should be rich; in an earlier canto, he laments the Donation of Constantine as the beginning of the worldly power of the Church, and he goes so far as to suggest that property be taken away from the Church by the state in order to remove temptation from the clergy. Only with the Synagogue does he suggest that thralldom is a sign of the rejection of God.

The strangest part of the paradox is that Langland seems to be echoing in part the Jewish view in the ancient controversies over the Messianic king. That view was that Jesus could not have been the Messias because he was not the temporal ruler who was to set up a state and punish the enemies of Israel. The Christian answer was not that Jesus was a conqueror who punished his enemies but that, as Langland says here, he "was crowned king of the Jews upon the cross." Throughout the poem, especially in the scenes of the Crucifixion and the harrowing of hell, he insists that Christ's victory was in death, and that the true follower of Christ must take the way of the Cross.

The Messianic Promises

When Langland goes on to "carpe more" of Christ and how he came by that "name," it is clear that Christ means Messias; for Langland tells us how Jesus fulfilled the Old Testament prophecies and revealed himself as greater than David, of whose royal line he was descended (ll. 65 ff.). When Jesus was born in Bethlehem, "as the boke telleth," angels came singing out of heaven. Then the three kings arrived with their gifts to show that he was acknowledged "soeuereigne / Bothe of sonde, sonne, and see." Then was the prophecy fulfilled, "*Omnia celestia terrestria flectantur in hoc nomine Iesu.*" It was when he made the lame leap and the blind see and fed the famished five thousand, thus comforting those in his care, that he won the title of Do Better. Then throughout the country for his deeds of mercy he was called by the common people "*fili David Iesus.*" Langland explains that the deeds of David were the most valiant of his time, and the maidens sang, "*Saul interfecit mille, et David decem milia.*" Therefore, for the greatness of his deeds of mercy, the country from which Jesus came called him "*fili David.*" And no man was so worthy to be "kaisere or a kyng of the kyngedome of Iuda," or a justice over the Jews.

These are the old Messianic proofs, selected and modified to suit the new allegory of Do Better. More broadly, the allegory is certainly intended as a mirror for magistrates. For Langland believed that rulers in both Church and state could do well, better, and best only if they took Christ as their model. In this canto, the prophecies and the discussions of king and conqueror all lead to the setting up of the Church, in which Christ the king deputizes power to the pope to reign in his name. In the last canto, we see why the Church of Langland's time was in such bad case—far from following Christ, the pope had broken both the Old and the New Laws.

The Messianic Kingdom

In this last canto, we are in the last age of the world, in which Langland saw a long struggle between Christ and Antichrist. This was the current world view, but unlike other histories of the world which began with the Creation, *Piers* does not conclude with a vision of the final conflict and the fulfillment of the prophecies of the Second Coming and the Last Judgment. For whatever spiritual and aesthetic reasons, Langland leaves his pilgrims in the fourteenth century.

In Passus III, however, there does occur a fervent description of the Messianic era at the end of the world. As in the later cantos, the prophecies occur in a political context in which the Messianic king is held up as a model for earthly rulers. And sorely do they need a model. So corrupt is society that vicious Lady Meed seems beautiful and desirable to the scions of both Church and state. Indeed, so respectable are the bribery and falsehood she personifies that the king suggests a marriage between Meed and Conscience, and when the latter indignantly refuses, the lady is much offended. She defends herself in a masterly Machiavellian speech which, by the way, suggests so little love for conquerors on Langland's part that we wonder why he went to such lengths later on to apply the term to the Messias.

Referring to the late French wars, Meed sneers at Conscience for making cowards of strong men and keeping them from burning and pillage (C. IV. 236 ff.). When the king came to France, Conscience stopped him from felling foes, although fortune willed it. Like a caitiff, Conscience counseled the king to leave the heritage of France in the hands of his enemy. This was not fair to his followers, the lowliest of whom expected at least a barony to live in as a freeman when a new land was conquered. Obviously, if a king wishes to conquer, he ought never to ask Conscience for counsel. Had her advice been taken, the king would have been lord of that realm and helped all his kin. And hers is a socially accepted doctrine: everybody knows that emperors and earls, popes and prelates, all take presents with mutual approval. With a final touch of irony, Langland has the king say, "By Cryst," in my judgment Meed is worthy "the maistrye to have."

In his reply, Conscience explains the difference between just wages and grasping for gold, and between just kings who deserve love and loyalty and those whose wish and will are their only law. Seeking authority for his view, he then tells the story from the Book of Kings of how God's vengeance fell on Saul when Saul spared Amalek because he coveted the king's goods and how Saul perished because he followed Meed instead of God.

Since Conscience fears, he says, to anger his rich and powerful audience, he will forbear drawing what is really the quite obvious moral. Instead, he describes a world without Meed, which is, in fact, the Messianic dream. Some day Christ will come again as king, and Christians will behave so well that even the Jews will recognize the Messias in the fulfillment of the prophecies of a golden age.

The Old Testament prophecies are woven into a brilliant series of antitheses, in which the future hope is set against the present horror. As Saul was set against David, so all the evil that Saul prefigured will be daunted by the Christ whom David prefigured:

> "I Conscience knowe this for kynde witt me it tauʒte,
> That resoun shal regne and rewmes gouerne;
> And riʒte as Agag hadde, happe shul somme.
> Samuel shal sleen hym and Saul shal be blamed,
> And Dauid shal be diademed and daunten hem alle,
> And one Cristene kynge kepen hem alle."
>
> (III. 282–87)

> "I, Conscience, conceive, for Common Wit taught me,
> That reason should reign and rule the kingdoms.
> And what Agog had shall hap to others.
> Samuel shall slay him, and Saul be convicted,
> And David will be diademed and daunt all.
> One Christian king shall keep the earth."
>
> (III. 407–12)

The master of mankind will no longer be Meed but love and lowliness and loyalty. Whoever trespasses against truth shall be judged by law alone, not by lawyers in silken hoods and fur robes bought by Meed. Such love shall arise,

"And such a pees amonge the peple and a perfit trewthe
That Iewes shal wene in here witte and waxen wonder glade,
That Moises or Messie be come in-to this erthe,
And haue wonder in here hertis that men beth so trewe."
                                        (III. 299–302)

And such a peace and perfect truth be with the
    nations
That Jews will wonder whether finally
Moses or the Messiah has come among them,
And wonder in their hearts how men are so true.
                                        (III. 424–27)

The famous Messianic prophecy of Isaias that men "shall beat their
swords into ploughshares" and that "Nation shall not lift up sword
against nation" is then transposed into contemporary terms:

Alle that bereth baslarde, brode swerde or launce,
Axe other hachet or eny wepne ellis,
Shal be demed to the deth but if he do it smythye
In-to sikul or to sithe to schare or to kulter;
    Conflabunt gladios suos in vomeres, &c.;
Eche man to pleye with a plow, pykoys or spade,
Spynne, or sprede donge or spille hym-self with sleuthe.
                                        (III. 303–8)

All who bear baselards, broad swords or lances,
Axes or hatchets or any other weapons,
Will be doomed to die unless they smithy them
Into sickle or scythe, share or coulter:
Conflabunt gladios suos in vomeres, etc.
Men shall practice ploughing, picking or spading,
Spin or spread dung, or sloth shall destroy them.
                                        (III. 428–34)

Instead of hunting, priests will pray for the dead and read their
Psalter—"dyngen" upon David, daily till evening. Neither king nor
knight, constable nor mayor shall crush the commons, and there shall
be one justice for all, without bribes or falsehood. And again, "ba-
tailles shal non be"—"*Non levabit gens contra gentem gladium, etc.*"
He concludes with a reference to the supernatural portents that will
herald the end and convert Jews and Saracens and with a quotation
from Proverbs:

"And er this fortune falle, fynde men shal the worste,
By syx sonnes and a schippe and half a shef of arwes;
And the myddel of a mone shal make the Iewes to torne,
And saracenes for that si3te shulle synge *gloria in excelsis, &c.,*
For Makomet and Mede myshappe shal that tyme;
  For, *melius est bonum nomen quam diuicie multe.*"

                                        (III. 323–27)

"But before this fortune befall men they shall
    find the worst,
By six suns and a ship and half a sheaf of arrows,
And the middle of the moon shall make the Jews
    Christians,
And Saracens at that sight shall sing *Gloria in
    excelsis,*
And Mahomet and Mede meet with disaster.
For, *melius est bonum nomen quam divitiae multae.*"

                                        (III. 450 ff.)

Viewed logically, the apocalyptic tone seems extraneous to the
alleged intent of the canto. The just king, David or Christ, is held up
as an ideal that rulers should follow in the present, not await at the
end of the world. Indeed, Conscience begins the passage, probably
with only a trace of irony, by saying that the doctrine was taught him
by Common Sense—as though justice and mercy were a modest
proposal, the merits of which would be obvious even to these habitual
grafters. And in the following passus (IV), the king does at last scorn
Meed and agree to rule with the help of Conscience and Reason.

But visions go deeper than, if sometimes contrary to, logic. The
Second Coming had been much brooded upon over the centuries, and
it meant many things to many men. For Christians of Langland's
temper, the most important promise of the Messianic prophecies,
whether of the First or Second Coming, was not, say, the birthplace
of the Messias or his riding on the clouds of glory, but his fulfillment
of the ideal of justice and mercy, foreshadowed by David. While
Langland mentions the portents traditionally associated with the end
of the world, he does not follow, either here or at the end of his
poem, with the final dramatic conflict so popular in the mysteries.
Nowhere does he mention the Jewish hope of a revival of the
sacrifices in the temple, nor are the horrors at the end of the world
related to a Jewish Antichrist. The Antichrist against whom the

Christian is warned to prepare in the last cantos is comprised of the sins of Christians. And the great miracle at the end of the world that will convert the Jews will be the "pure and perfect truth" of Christians.

It is really the same miracle that Langland elsewhere demands of Christians in the present. Just as he believed that Church and state must be reformed now, even if the golden age cannot be achieved, so he believed it to be the duty of Christians to try to convert individual Jews now even if the whole people would not be converted until the end of the world. As was observed in an earlier chapter, his suggestions on procedure followed those of the apologists and missionaries to the Jews: the Jews must be preached to, and taught the doctrine little by little, so that they would see that the New Testament did indeed fulfill the Old. And most important for Langland, Jews could be converted by the good example of Christians. "If priesthood were perfect," he says, "all would be converted who are contrary to Christ's laws and who hold Christendom in dishonor."

Langland speaks with two voices. In one, he seems to understand the difficulties in the way of Jewish acceptance of Christianity and to blame Christians for a good part of that difficulty. He sees that the Jews reject Christianity on principle, because they think the law of Moses "best," and it is his considered belief that God judges non-believers according to their lights. In the discussion of the salvation of non-believers in the last few hundred lines of Passus XV, the Jews are criticized less harshly, for the most part, than the Christians. The refusal of both Jews and Moslems to accept Christianity is blamed on the priests, who neither preach to them nor give a good example in their lives. "There would be no more debate if beadsmen were faithful," if those who should show the way were first in holy living. So writes the satirist and reformer, in the voice we prefer to hear.

In the other voice, he thunders at the Jews for rejecting the Truth. In part, he censures them for their disbelief and disloyalty, much as he censures Christians for their greed and hardness of heart. But in this mood, the why of the Jewish denial angers as well as troubles him, and he does not pretend to know a reasonable explanation. He sees that even to say that they were seduced by the devil does not explain why God permitted such a tragedy. It is a mystery, he says, not to be questioned. The refusal of the Jews to see that the Messianic prophecies have been fulfilled and cannot be fulfilled again must be accepted along with the fact of their consequent rejection. Jesus was the Messianic king of the Jews: he was born in Bethlehem according to the Book; the three kings paid him homage, according to the prophecies; he performed the miracles expected of the Messias; he was proclaimed the son of David by the Jewish people; he was crowned king of the Jews on the cross; and he delivered the patriarchs and the prophets from their long bondage. But they rejected and continue to reject their king, who has in turn rejected them. So it was prophesied and so it is, as Daniel said and as anybody can see. For those who persist in disbelief are usurers and outcasts, while those who are baptized are freemen and franklins.

Langland is not so much contradicting himself as voicing the perennially ambivalent attitude of Christians towards Jews. Throughout the poem, his shifts in tone follow a traditional pattern. The passages on the Jewish rejection of Jesus are touched with the ancient bitterness of the Messianic controversy, and in them he fails in the charity which, he himself believed, could alone save both Christians and Jews. When his subject is the law, his boundless admiration for the traditions of the Hebrews colors his attitude towards later Jews. And like St. Paul and the Fathers, like Aelfric and Gilbert Crispin and Grosseteste, he yearned for the reunion which the Second Coming of the Messias would bring. Then, as Bede had said, Christians will so persevere in love that the Synagogue will accept the Church.

Chapter VIII

THE FULFILLMENT OF THE LAW: FROM THE APOSTOLIC AGE THROUGH THE MIDDLE AGES

❲Whatever their feelings about contemporary Jews, medieval Christians reverenced the laws and lawgivers of the Old Testament; indeed, they claimed them for their own. They believed that the moral law had remained unchanged, that the ceremonial law foreshadowed the sacraments, and that both were fulfilled, not abrogated, by Christ and the Church.

In the traditional teaching, the difference between the Old and the New Laws was never the difference between bad and good, between justice and mercy, between the "eye for an eye" of the Old Testament and the "other cheek" of the New. On the contrary, the Christians of both the medieval and the patristic periods insisted that the same morality was preached in both Testaments. They believed, however, that it was through the New Law, as promised by the prophets, that the Gentiles were called by Jesus Christ out of the darkness of idolatry to the light of the God of Israel. By his Passion Christ opened the gates of heaven for all men, and by his sacrifice he fulfilled the sacrifices of the Old Law for all men and for all time. Thus both the Jew and the Greek were liberated from the letter of the law and its accompanying nationalism. For the universal and eternal meaning of the law, as understood by the patriarchs and the prophets, is that you shall love the Lord your God and your neighbor as yourself. Love is therefore the fulfillment of the law, and Jesus, Love Incarnate, the end of the law. Such has been the fundamental teaching of the Church from St. Paul to Pope Paul VI—and, as we shall see in the next chapter, it is the fundamental teaching of *Piers Plowman*, reiterated in precept, examined in dialogue, and assimilated in allegory throughout the poem.

RIGHTEOUSNESS AND RITUAL

Throughout history Christians have meditated on the revelation of the doctrine in Scripture and history and have felt the need to explain how and why their interpretation differed from that of the Jews. According to St. Paul, Tertullian, Origen, and St. Augustine, to name a few, the Jews understood the law only superficially. In their preoccupation with food and drink, they ignored "the grandeur of the ideas contained in the law and the prophets," and they mistook the temporal and carnal for the eternal and spiritual. The very history of the Jews proves, said the fathers, that the ceremonial law is not unchangeable, as the Jews believe. If it were, what of the saints *before* Moses? Was salvation denied Adam, Abel, Enoch, and Noe because they were uncircumcised and did not keep the Sabbath? Certainly not. Before the written law of Moses, there was the unwritten law of God, understood and kept by the patriarchs. Otherwise, whence was Noe "found righteous" or Abraham the "friend of God?" [1]

It is the righteousness of God that is unchangeable, not the ritual. The law was given in mercy to raise up a fallen nation—to a people who in the very face of God worshiped a golden calf and offered their children to devils. God enjoined the Sabbath as the only way to make an idolatrous nation think of him and commanded abstinence from certain meats so that, when men ate and drank, they might have to think of God. But that law was intended to bind only until the coming of the Messias, who was to give a new covenant. When the Messias came, he fulfilled the Old and instituted the New.

It is clear from even this brief summary that the conflict over the law was basically the conflict of two attitudes towards God, which might be called the priestly and the prophetic. The two are not necessarily mutually exclusive, but their combination is rare, and the history of both religions records the inevitable struggle of the prophetic battle for righteousness against the priestly code of salva-

---

1. Origen *Against Celsus* II. 4; Gal. 3, 6; Heb. 11:9; James 2:23; Justin *Dialogue* 19, 20; Irenaeus *The Demonstration of the Apostolic Preaching* (trans. J. Armitage Robinson) 35; Tertullian *Answer to the Jews* II, III.

tion through ritual. While the battle has been waged within both Church and Synagogue, in the Jewish-Christian debate the Jew takes the priestly side, for he is defending the absolute necessity of circumcision and sacrifice, while the Christian appeals to the prophets to prove that God is not pleased with sacrifice and cares only for justice and mercy.[2] But while in controversy with the Jews, the Christian apologist stresses the spirit, at home he may be all for the letter. Indeed, every "renewal" in the Church has been, in effect, an attempt of the prophets to resist the priestly tendency to rely on Masses and fasting instead of on charity.

It is not that Christians questioned the theoretic primacy of the spirit but that the emphasis shifts with the character of the writer. Curiously enough, the priestly tendency was nurtured by the very arguments which were used to prove to the Jews that the old ceremonies were types and symbols of the new. Writers who had a special tenderness for ritual devoted so much of their discussion of the law to the development of the sacraments of the Church from those of the Synagogue that circumcision and baptism assume more importance than justice and mercy. So popular was this ancient argument that, even when it was kept in its secondary place, it seems an inextricable part of the discussion of the law.

Only Langland, it seems, managed to extricate it. As we shall see in the next chapter, he obviously knew all the arguments, for his concepts, his heroes, even the images of his allegories were molded by the tradition; but he does not argue with the Jews, and he barely mentions the ceremonial law. So entirely prophetic was his view that he concentrates on the spirit rather than the letter not only in the New Law but in the Old, and the historical differences stressed by others are entirely subordinated by him to the eternal unity of the laws of Abraham, Moses, and Jesus. Set against the general background of apologetic and literary discussions of the law, his omissions

2. For example, in the *Dialogue* (8, 9), Justin tells Trypho that when he was a pagan philosopher, a Christian had kindled a flame in him so that he "was seized with an ardent love of the Prophets." In reply, Trypho does not invite him to the Jewish study of the prophets, as it seems he might, but says, "first be circumcised, and then, as commanded, observe the Sabbath, and the feasts, and the new moons of God, with all that is written in the Law, in which case you may perhaps find mercy with Him." He says further that the Christians do not excel the heathen in their lives, *because* they do not observe circumcision, etc.

are significant, for they can mean only that he deliberately excluded the priestly view.

St. Paul

The most important single figure in that background is St. Paul. In the Epistles are epitomized not only the doctrine but its history, from the controversy with the Jews to the tendency within the Church itself to lapse into ritual. The story of the Galatians, for example, illustrates most vividly how difficult it was—and would be—for simple Gentiles to grasp the prophetic doctrine of the fulfillment of the law. For soon after their conversion by Paul, the Gentile Galatians were seduced by Judaizers, and they began to practice circumcision and to observe the feast days of the Jews. O senseless Galatians, cried Paul, "Are you so foolish that, whereas you began in the spirit, you would now be made perfect by the flesh?" (Gal. 3:3)

Paul is harder to follow than many later writers, partly because many of his references are apparently brief allusions to points that had been expounded more fully in oral teaching, partly because even his full explanations are mystical and allegorical. But it was the mysticism, as well as the lesson, that caught the imagination of Christendom. And while Langland omits Paul's contrasting of the Old and the New Laws, his thought and phraseology are permeated by the Pauline explanation of the faith of Abraham, of the spiritual meaning of the law and the promise, and of the necessity for the grace of Christ to fulfill the law of Moses.

It was Paul who established Abraham in the Christian tradition as the symbol of faith and as the father of the Gentiles. He never tires of repeating his dictum that Abraham became the friend of God through faith, *before* circumcision. What do the Scriptures say? Paul asks the Romans (4). "Abraham believed God: and it was reputed to him unto justice." Abraham received the "sign" of circumcision as a seal of faith because, against all hope (he and Sara both being very old), he believed God's promise to make him a father of many nations. This was a promise made not through the law, but through faith: Abraham was to be the father not only of those of the circumcision, the Jews, but of "those that follow the steps of the faith," the Gentiles.

143

The Israelite descendants of Abraham, Paul concedes, have a glorious history. They served God, and to them were given the testament and the law; theirs were both the fathers and Christ himself, according to the flesh. But the flesh is less important than the spirit, and therefore the true children of Abraham are those who follow him in faith. "For it is not he is a Jew, who is so outwardly; nor is that circumcision which is outwardly in the flesh. But he is a Jew that is one inwardly, and the circumcision is that of the heart, in the spirit not in the letter" (Rom. 2: 28–29).

Paul believed that the story of Isaac and Ishmael was an allegory that showed that the blessing promised to Abraham was spiritual freedom. Abraham had two sons, one by a bondwoman, the other by a free woman. Ishmael, the son of the bondwoman, was born according to the flesh; while Isaac, the son of the free woman, was born according to the promise. Followers of Christ "are not the children of the bondwoman but of the free: by the freedom wherewith Christ has made us free" (Gal. 3, 4).

The promise given to Abraham was not annulled by the law given later to Moses. God forbid, exclaims Paul, that anyone should think that God did not mean the law. Still, the law was set "because of transgressions" and was meant to last only until the seed would come to whom the promise was made. The law, he says in an oft-repeated phrase, was only "our pedagogue in Christ." "As long as the heir is a child," he is under tutors until the time appointed by the father. So were we, when we were children. But when God sent his Son "made of a woman, made under the law, that he might redeem them who were under the law," we became sons of God (Gal. 3:17–4:7).

If a law could give life, then justice would have come by the law. But all men stand in need of salvation, for all have sinned, the Gentiles without the law, the Jews within it. Paul cites Scripture (Psalms, Isaias, Proverbs) to prove that no man is just in himself, nor is he just through the law; only God is just. But the power of the Gospel brings salvation to everyone who believes. In Christ all are equally children of God. "There is neither Jew nor Greek: there is neither bond nor free: there is neither male nor female. For you are all one in Christ Jesus" (Gal. 3:28). The justice of God is now made known by Christ, "outside the law," but "witnessed by the law and the prophets." The followers of Christ do not destroy the law through faith, but establish it. For it is only faith in Christ that delivers men from the law of sin and death and gives them the strength to fulfill the commandments and to live in peace with God. He who loves his neighbor has fulfilled the law; love is the fulfilling of the law (Rom. 3).

THE FATHERS

The "witness of the prophets" was fully explored by the Fathers who, in turn, were drawn upon by later writers. All repeated Paul's assertion that the only acceptable circumcision is a circumcised heart, and they multiplied examples from Scripture to prove that it was the prophetic view that God was not pleased with circumcision and sacrifice. The Christians loved the passages from the Psalms, and from Amos, Isaias, Jeremias, and Micheas, which proved that salvation lay not in the priestly code of ritual but in righteousness. A favorite, for example, was the text from Micheas (6:6–8) which says that thousands of rams cannot appease God, but that the Lord requires a man "to do judgment, and to love mercy, and to walk humbly" with his God. And Jeremias (31:31–33), it was believed, had not only prophesied the new covenant but had said it would be written in the hearts of men.[3]

Now that we have the new covenant, went the patristic writings, the time for the carnal observances of the old has passed. Useful as those observances were in the history of the Jews, they were also intended to be prefigurations of the sacraments of the Church. Christ changed them not by arguing but by fulfilling them in his life. He was born under the law, he received the sacraments of the law, and then he instituted the sacraments of the New Law. He was circumcised in the flesh; he instituted baptism, the spiritual circumcision. Like all Jews, he celebrated the Passover; at the same time, he was the sinless Lamb who was sacrificed for all men; and he left us the memorial of the Last Supper to offer continually to God instead of a bloody sacrifice. In brief, argued the Fathers, the sacraments of the Synagogue are continued in a better, more spiritual way in the

3. Cyprian *Testimonies* I. 10; *De Montibus Sina et Sion, PL.* 4, cols. 989–1000.

Church, and Christians keep the law in a deeper way than do the Jews.[4]

As the missionary Church converted increasingly large numbers of pagans, the prophecies of the calling of the Gentiles were recited more and more fervently. David became a beloved figure because it was thought that he had not only prophesied the new covenant but had rejoiced in the Gentile part in it. "Sing ye to the Lord a new Canticle," David had sung. "The Lord has made known his salvation: he has revealed his justice in the sight of the Gentiles. All the ends of the earth have seen the salvation of our God. Sing joyfully to God, all the earth" (Ps. 97). And so, said the Fathers, it has happened. The eternal word of God, previously revealed only to the Jews, has gone out to the Gentiles. The prophecies have been fulfilled not through the law of Judaism but through the covenant of Christ. Even to the very ends of the earth, to "the parts of Britain unreached by Rome," the word of God has been carried.[5]

ANGLO-SAXON ENGLAND

The learned commentaries of Anglo-Saxon England follow so closely the patristic ones we have been looking at, that many of them might well have been written in second-century Antioch or fourth-century Carthage. On the other hand, the differences between eighth-century England and, say, eighth-century Rome were felt keenly by even the most academic Englishmen. To these first- or second-generation Christians, the calling of the Gentiles from idolatry aroused something more than scholarly interest. For they were the prophesied Gentiles, and the promises of Scripture were fulfilled in them. From Rome the pope wrote to that far-off corner of the world, to King Oswy, expressing his joy in the conversion of the English. Who would not be delighted, he writes in a letter quoted in Bede's *Ecclesiastical History*, that "your nation has believed in Christ the Almighty God, according to the words of the divine prophets, as it is written . . .";

4. *Epistle of Barnabas* VIII. Tertullian *Answer to the Jews* V. Irenaeus *Apostolic Preaching* 25. Origen *On John* X. Augustine *Tracts on St. John* XI. 8; *On Christian Doctrine* II. 41; *Tractatus adversus Judaeos*, PL. 42, cols. 52–56. Eusebius *Proof of the Gospel* I. 7, 10. Gregory Nazianzen *Orations* I, III.

5. Tertullian *Answer to the Jews* VII.

the rest of the letter is a string of prophecies of the calling of "them that sit in darkness" to the light of righteousness.[6]

That the position of the English in the universal Church should have been jeopardized by their interpretation of Mosaic law is, by the way, not the least surprising part of the story. The fact is that the English church was almost split from within by Judaizing—that, at least, was what the Roman church called the practice of the Irish in the controversy over the date of Easter. Having been called to the God of Israel, the Irish thought they ought to observe Easter at the same time as the Jews observed Passover. In the course of the argument, Colman, an Irishman, took the side of those first Jewish-Christians who did not "cast off all the observances of the law which had been instituted by God." But Wilfrid triumphantly insisted that the celebration of Easter on Sunday does not "abolish the law, but rather fulfills it."[7]

Commentary, Homily, and Allegory

Viewed against the background of the *Ecclesiastical History*, Bede's concern with the Old and the New Laws in his expositions of the Bible seems less academic and derivative than at first glance. It was certainly a subject which preoccupied him, and it would take a fair-sized volume to summarize the relevant commentaries. And always, in explaining the differences in the interpretations of the law, he insists that the law was not abrogated but fulfilled by Christ.

He delighted especially in finding Old Testament allegories of the two laws, the two peoples, and the two churches, some of which were popular throughout the Middle Ages. He finds the allegory in almost every episode of the life of David, who was a figure of Christ. For example, Saul clothed David with his garments, the helmet of brass and the coat of mail, as the Incarnate God accepted the legal observances of the Jews—for the sword of Saul is the law given by Moses. But law and ceremony are narrow and confining, and in order to fight Goliath (the devil), David put away the arms of Saul, as Jesus had put away legalisms. Yet, Saul asked Jonathan: "Why cometh not David to meat neither yesterday nor today?" And the

6. (Trans. John Stevens, rev. Lionel C. Jane) III. 29.

7. Bede *Ecclesiastical History* II. 19; III. 25; V. 21. Cf. *Letter of St. Columba to St. Gregory* in Gregory the Great *Selected Epistles* IX. 127.

Jews ask: "Why do Christians not follow the carnal law of circumcision and sacrifice?"[8]

When Abigail went with five damsels to marry David, she prefigured the marriage of the Synagogue, the five books of the law, with Christ. But David also took to wife Achinoem of Jezrahel, as Christ accepted the Gentiles after the Jews. Like the Church, David, when persecuted by the Jews, went among the Gentiles. Inevitably, the transference of the kingdom from Saul to David as a result of Saul's disobedience to God is a figure of the transference of the kingdom of God from the Jews to the Christians.[9]

Elcana, too, is a figure of God, who is wedded to both the Church and the Synagogue. Elcana had two wives: Phenenna, the Synagogue, had the law and the prophets while Anna, the Gentiles, had no such fine children. But Elcana said to Anna, "Why weepest thou? Am I not better to thee than ten children?" For, explains Bede, the love of God himself is better than the Ten Commandments. Anna, insulted by the priest in the temple, is the humble church, insulted by the Jewish teachers; her silent prayers which were scorned by the priest are the inner, spiritual prayers of the Church. Finally Elcana knew Anna, and a son was given by God. So the Church conceives children, that is, converts, and instructs them in the spiritual life.[10]

Like Bede, Alcuin too is interested in the two laws. As might be surmised, many of the questions asked in his *Questions and Answers on Genesis* concerned the changes in the law. Alcuin's framework is interesting, for it suggests that the questions were genuine ones raised by Biblical students; but the answers are traditional enough and need not detain us. A word must be spared, however, for Alcuin's commentary on the Epistle to the Hebrews. The Epistle itself is hard reading. Because it was written to already converted Jews—who had received the meat but seemed once again to need milk (5:12)—the prophecies and proofs are recited with little explanation. Alcuin's commentary (based on Chrysostom's) fills in the arguments and is a highly articulate exposition of the relationship between the two laws. It is quite clear from Alcuin, for example, why Melchizedek was so popular among Christians. The high priest was a type of

8. *Opera Omnia,* ed. J. A. Giles (London, 1844), VIII, 99, 100, 134.
9. *Ibid.,* pp. 193–96, 104.
10. *Ibid.,* VII, 368 ff.

Christ: he was not in the regular priestly succession; he was a priest before the institution of circumcision; and his offering was not the blood of an animal but bread and wine.[11]

The question that arises in our minds is how widely known were these ideas on the law. Statistics would be difficult to establish, but we can see in the vernacular writings of the time the same deep appreciation of the law, and the same stress on the concordance of the Scriptures as in the Fathers, and as in Langland. Both sermons and poetry are steeped in the doctrinal arguments we have been looking at.

The example of Aelfric suggests that the most likely channel of popular information was the pulpit. Indeed, Aelfric's captive audience of pupils and parishioners may have thought his preoccupation with the law excessive. It does seem to a reader of the homilies that Aelfric never hesitated to interrupt a train of thought with a lesson on why the customs of the Christians differed from those of the Jews. In his preface to the Old English translation of Genesis, he gives what may be taken as one reason for this emphasis. He expresses the fear that some "dysig" man reading Genesis might follow the marital customs of the patriarchs. For example, Jacob had four wives, two of them sisters. (It is interesting to observe, by the way, that Justin Martyr accused the Jews of citing the example of Jacob to justify their taking of many wives.) The unlearned must be taught to understand that the Old Law is not to be taken literally, but as a betokening of the New.[12]

As the dangers of misinterpretation did not keep Aelfric from translating the Bible, so the difficulties of St. Paul's style did not keep him from giving his congregation the full Pauline text. On the Feast of the Circumcision of Jesus, Aelfric explained what circumcision is, why it was given to Abraham, how it prefigured baptism, and how Christ fulfilled the law he had established himself. While Christian men do not observe circumcision bodily, "nevertheless, no man is truly a Christian, unless he observes circumcision in spiritual conduct." If this sounds foolish to anyone, Aelfric apologizes, let him

11. Alcuin, *Expositio in Epistolum Pauli Apostoli ad Hebraeos*, PL. 100, cols. 1031 ff.

12. *Preface to Genesis*, ed. S. J. Crawford, EETS 160 (1922), pp. 77, 80; Justin *Dialogue* 134.

"chide God, who established it, not us, who say it." And he says it again: "If we observe this spiritual circumcision, then are we of Abraham's kin, in true faith." [13]

Many feast days called for similar explanations of the fulfillment of the law. On Easter, Aelfric's sermon dealt with the sacrifice of Easter "both according to the Old Testament and according to the New." On Pentecost, he explained how fifty days after the Passover God gave Moses the law on Sinai, just as fifty days after the Resurrection, the Holy Spirit came into the hearts of the apostles. On the Feast of the Dedication of a Church, he gave a long description of Solomon's Temple. All God's churches, he said, are betokened by the one temple Solomon reared under the Old Law. As Solomon was a type of Christ, so the queen of Sheba was a type of Holy Church; and the camels she brought with her signified the heathen, who were humpbacked through covetousness and deformed by sins. On the birthday of St. John the Baptist, Aelfric explained that John is the ending of the Old Law and the beginning of the New, for he was sent before the Lord as the Old Testament was sent before the New. And at the marriage of Cana, "the wine ran short because the old law ceased in Christ's presence from fleshly works, and was turned to ghostly morals." The Lord could have filled the empty vessels with wine but preferred to use water, to manifest "that he came not to overthrow the old law or the prophets" but to fulfill them.[14]

In a way that was to remain popular throughout the Middle Ages, Aelfric, like Langland, interpreted a number of New Testament parables as allegories of the two laws and the two peoples. The five loaves with which Jesus fed the multitude betoken "the five books which the leader Moses appointed in the old law. The lad who bare them, and tasted not of them, was the Jewish people who read the five books, and knew therein no spiritual signification, before Christ came and opened the books." [15]

On Palm Sunday, Aelfric explained that the "tied ass and its foal betoken two peoples, the Jewish and the heathen," both tied with ropes of sins, both unbound by the preaching of the apostles. The "tamed ass" betokened the Jewish people, tamed under the Old Law;

13. *Homilies* I. 91 ff.
14. *Homilies* II. 263 ff., 245, 259; I. 311 ff.; II. 579-95; I. 355; II. 57, 59.
15. *Homilies* I. 187; II. 397.

the wild foal signified the untamed heathen. Those who walked before Christ as he entered Jerusalem that day and those who walked behind all sang Hosanna to the Son of David. Those who went before were the prophets and patriarchs before his Incarnation; those who went after were those who "inclined to Christ after his birth, and daily incline to him; and all these sing one hymn; because we and they all hold one faith." Indeed, "we sing the hymns which the Jewish people sang before Christ." [16]

And what does the parable of the wedding feast mean to Aelfric? "The certain man" who prepared the feast and invited man is Christ, who sent servants to invite mankind to the eternal feast. When the first-invited guests, the Jews, refused, the servants called the poor and maimed and blind and halt—the Gentiles. But one room was yet empty. That room, explains Aelfric, is for us, "who from all the world come to the feast." [17]

Poetry and Story

The joy felt by the English at having come to the feast is most movingly expressed in poetry, particularly in the Old English *Advent Lyrics*. The Advent liturgy, on which (as we saw earlier, the poems are based, is itself highly poetic, and is, in turn, based on the Messianic prophecies. Indeed, four of the seven antiphons elaborated in the *Lyrics* are based on prophecies of the calling of the Gentiles. What the elaborations do, in part, is to explain the antiphons by a poetic paraphrase of the arguments on the law.

In the "O Emmanuel" antiphon, for example, Christ is addressed as King and Lawgiver and Expectation of the Gentiles. Not only does the poet explain the relation between the giving of the new law and the mission to the Gentiles, but he brings in Melchizedek to prove that Christ was not only king but priest (Poem VI; *Christ*, 130–63). In his development of the "O Jerusalem" antiphon, he presents the whole Christian interpretation of the meaning of Jerusalem, the spiritual city loosened from the bonds of the law (Poem III; *Christ*, 50–70). And in the "O Clavis David," the poet understands that the Key of David was Christ, who opened the true meaning of the Scriptures. He "illumined" the "teachings of ancient

16. *Homilies* I. 207–9, 215–19.
17. *Homilies* II. 377.

day, which lay concealed beneath the veil of night" (Poem II; *Christ*, 18–49).

Quite similar in meaning to this last passage is one in the *Exodus* which has been considered obscure.[18] Following the description of the giving of the law to Moses, the author says that

> as yet people find in the Scriptures every law which the Lord laid upon them with true words on that journey. If life's interpreter, the radiant soul within the breast, will unlock with the keys of the spirit this lasting good, that which is dark shall be made clear, and wisdom shall go forth. It has the words of wisdom in its keeping, earnestly teaching the heart, so that we shall not lack God's instruction, the mercy of the Lord. He will reveal more to us, now that wise men declare the more lasting joys of heaven.[19]

What this passage tells us is that the law of Moses still to be found in Scripture is eternally true, or the law given on that journey was a "lasting good." But the full meaning was dark and had to be opened by the keys of the spirit. The words of Wisdom, of Christ in the New Testament, teach the heart and enlighten us "more" than the Old Testament did the Israelites; and Christian teachers now declare the more lasting joys of heaven.

A further example can be found in a poem called the *Seasons of Fasting*, which begins with the Jewish people under Moses and dwells at length on Elias. Clarity was not a distinguishing characteristic of the author of this poem; but it may be said in his defense that the whole subject of the dating of the Ember days was complicated by the Church's desire to be the fulfillment of the Synagogue in every detail. St. Augustine had written: "A candid mind . . . cannot but be anxious . . . to ascertain what is meant by the fact that Moses and Elias and our Lord himself, all fasted for forty days." Our author is clear enough in telling us that "that great nobleman" Moses fasted before he received the law from God and that great earl Elias fasted before ascending Mount Horeb. If we hope to see God as they did, we must fast as they did. (Aelfric makes the same point.) But for the connection between Moses and the Ember days, we had best look elsewhere. The medieval author of the *Speculum Sacerdotale* also begins his discussion of the fasts with a brief history of the Jews; he

18. G. P. Krapp, ed., *The Junius Manuscript* (New York, 1931), p. 216.

19. In *The Caedmon Poems,* trans. Charles W. Kennedy (London, 1916; reprint ed., Gloucester, Mass., 1965).

explains that while we fast in penance for Christ's suffering for our sins, we fast not at the same time as he, but at the four times of the year commanded in the Old Law.[20] This is probably what the earlier author meant but did not quite say.

THE LATER MEDIEVAL PERIOD

The extensive medieval literature explaining the various fasts derived from the Old Law need not concern us here, for it was a subject which did not interest William Langland. But it is worth noting that even seemingly small-minded men always stressed the unity of the two Testaments and identified themselves with the Jews of old. In Septuagesima, for example, we not only fast but abstain from singing the Alleluia, the Gloria, or the Te Deum, for at that time we remember the Babylonian captivity of the people of God. And how can we sing in the land of exile? [21]

Like the tracts on fasting, the numerous medieval works on the sacraments are often more priestly than prophetic. While they do not neglect to point out that the sacraments of the Church fulfill in a spiritual way those of the Synagogue, they have something of a legalistic tone of their own. The point of some of these detailed parallels is not really that the spirit is more important than the letter, but that one set of sacraments is as necessary for salvation as another once was. The author of the *Miroure of Mans Salvacionne*, for example, considers the fate of children who died without circumcision or baptism—apparently making no distinction between the two.[22]

One wonders if this habit of beginning explanations of baptism with circumcision, of the Eucharist with the Passover, etc. was responsible, in part at least, for the not infrequent accusations of "Judaizing." St. Bernard, as well as other famous doctors, warned Christians (much as St. Paul warned the Galatians) not to "envy Israel according to the flesh." Not that he was a rabble-rouser; on the contrary, Jews have always been grateful to him for his restraint of "Christian" mobs who

20. *The Anglo-Saxon Minor Poems,* ed. Elliott Van Kirk Dobbie (New York, 1942) ; Augustine *On Christian Doctrine* II. 25; *Speculum Sacerdotale,* ed. Edward H. Weatherly, EETS 166 (1936), pp. 52–63.

21. *Speculum Sacerdotale,* p. 40.

22. *The Miroure of Mans Salvacionne,* ed. Alfred H. Huth (London, 1888), pp. 47, 99.

zealously desired to massacre Jews. But there were Catholics who frequented synagogues and participated in Jewish customs—and wished they had been born Jews. Perhaps their desire derived from a misreading of the Pauline semantics that even Aelfric found confusing. Many a medieval Christian must have been slow to catch Bernard's distinction between the Jews who boasted of their descent from Abraham and those who "are truly Jews, not in the letter, but in the spirit, the seed of Abraham"; or the difference between him "who is a Jew in secret, from him who is one openly: the circumcision in the spirit from that which is only in flesh." [23]

Grosseteste's De Cessatione Legalium

At the time of the Jewish settlement in England, the law was debated vigorously, and all the arguments and texts appeared in tracts and debates. We need not repeat them here, but, as we have seen, there is one work, Grosseteste's *De Cessatione Legalium,* whose importance went far beyond its original purpose of converting the Jews. Widely read and copied for Christian consumption throughout the Middle Ages, it is, in fact, a comprehensive statement of the Christian doctrine of the law. Not only does it include all the arguments and all the prophecies, but it is a reasoned and reasonable work in the tradition of St. Augustine, explaining the revelation of the law in history in a way that might serve as an introduction to *Piers Plowman.*

Like the poet, the theologian saw the laws in the perspective of eternity. Time is of great importance to us, Grosseteste says, but not to God. The Old and New dispensations are one with him in eternity; they only seem to be of different ages to men who live in time. Man's law, like man, is finite and changing, and so the various ordinances were suited to man's varying needs. It follows that the change in the ceremonial law does not imply the inconstancy of God.

In discussing the changes that appear in the Old Testament, Grosseteste presents the old argument of the just men who lived before Mosaic law, but he does so in the philosophic dress of Augustine. He describes first the "natural and universal law" which was observed by our first parents, who were truly rational before they sinned. From the Fall to the time of Noe, there was both natural and positive law:

23. *Life and Works,* ed. John Mabillon, trans. Samuel J. Eales (London, 1896), vol. III, Sermons X. 11; XI. 1; XIII. 1.

that is, there were specific precepts, but they were few and simple. Noe added the positive prohibition against eating blood; Abraham added circumcision. Sacrifice, too, was part of natural law, because it is an expression of man's gratitude to God. As Augustine says, man in the beginning had natural law written on the tables of his heart, and the written law on tables of stone was necessary only when his heart hardened. Thus the natural law was followed by the written law, and later a multitude of precepts was added to the Mosaic law itself.

The law was good. Under it, the head of the Israelites was Christ, while at that time the head of the Gentiles was the devil. Before the advent of Christ, it was necessary that there be natural law and then legal law. Both were part of the slow revelation of God to men, and both were preparation for the sacraments given finally by God Incarnate. But the law was not adequate to extricate men from long habits of sin that prevented them from exercising true free will, that is, from living freely in the grace of God. The written law helped bring men out of the darkness, but the Passion of Christ was needed to bring them into the light. Until the Passion, the whole human race, including the Synagogue of patriarchs and prophets, could not enter the door of paradise—not through free will, or natural law, or written law.

But, Grosseteste believed, since Christ brought us out of sin into freedom, we must cease to cling to the old chains. What seemed great to a poor ward under tutor and authority seems trifling to the heir when, upon reaching years of discretion, he receives the treasure. So the legal sacraments of the Old Law must cease in the Passion of Christ, so that the benefit of the liberation of love may be fully realized.

The moral law is eternal; the ceremonial law historical. Christ fulfilled the law in both senses. He observed circumcision and the Passover while at the same time he instituted baptism and the Eucharist and fulfilled and preserved the eternal moral law of love: "Thou shalt love the Lord thy God with all thy heart, and with all thy soul, and with all thy mind." So is Christ truly the cornerstone which supports the two buildings of the Two Testaments.

Through Christ, all the nations have been blessed. Through him, the Gentiles have been called from the service of the devil to the everlasting covenant of God, that is, to morality and righteousness.

155

Through him, the Gentiles are called from diverse mores to concord. The promise to Abraham has been fulfilled: the earth is full of the knowledge of God.

Vernacular Works

Grosseteste's style was not much copied in vernacular works, but there is more evidence than we have time to glance at to prove that his doctrine was familiar. In the literature of the later medieval period we find many casual interjections of the fragments of the argument as well as detailed discussions of one point or another; and there are allegories of the law in art, in sermons, in poems, plays, and romances.

Wherever we look, the Christian boast is not that they are "Aryans" but that they are the children of Abraham. As Orm says, Christ came so that all the heathen folk should turn to the right life, to follow Abraham's God, Abraham's truth, Abraham's holy life, to dwell in bliss with Abraham. In prayer, Christians refer quite naturally to "oure fader" Abraham. And from the time of Gildas, there was never a lack of prophets to reproach these spiritual Israelites. "Haa!" cries a fourteenth-century preacher, "Good Lord God, where is the faith of Abraham, the good hope of Isaac, the prudens of Jacob, the chastity of Joseph?" [24]

The Drama

The full argument concerning Abraham appears, point by point, in the *Stanzaic Life of Christ*. And the Chester play of the *Histories of Lot and Abraham* dramatizes the Christian interpretation of the story of Abraham and Melchizedek. After Melchizedek receives gifts from Abraham and Lot (tithes, we are told), he gives bread and wine to Abraham, evidently in the form of Christian communion: "*offerans calicem cum vino et panem super patinam.*" The "Expositor" says he will expound what this may signify so that the unlearned standing by may understand. In the Old Law, when these two good men were living, "of beastes were their offeringe, and eke their sacramente."

24. *Ormulum*, ed. R. M. White and Robert Holt (Oxford, 1878), ll. 9815 ff.; *The Prymer or Prayer-Book of the Lay People in the Middle Ages*, ed. H. Littlehales (London, 1891), pp. 27, 84; *Middle English Sermons*, ed. Woodburn Ross, EETS 209 (1940), p. 252.

But the gift of Melchizedek signifies the New Testament. Since Christ died on the rood tree, we remember his death in bread and wine, as he commanded at the Last Supper. In signification of this, Melchizedek gave bread and wine to Abraham. Here Abraham symbolizes the father of heaven, Melchizedek a priest to minister the sacraments (ll. 57 ff.).[25]

One would rather expect that as Abraham explained circumcision as a type of baptism, so Moses would explain how the Passover prefigured the Eucharist. The parallel is described often enough, but not usually by Moses. In the Hegge play of *The Last Supper*, for example, it is Christ himself who explains the sacrifices in the two laws and makes a very lengthy speech in which he shows the spiritual signification of every detail of the Passover. Nor is the popular image of Moses closely linked with the ritual aspects of Mosaic law. When Moses appears or is discussed, it is usually as the great teacher of the moral law.

The trend of popular thought can be seen most readily in the numerous plays on the Disputation in the Temple. These begin to be debates on the Old and the New Laws, but they never develop as such. In both the *Pageant of the Weavers* and the York play, the Jewish Doctors of the Law stress the inviolability of the Mosaic ordinances. In the Weavers play (ll. 857 ff.), the doctors insist that anyone who stands against any "article" must be slain. When the Child enters, they want to send him home because he is too young to study the law. He responds that he has been where "all our law was first wrought."[26] But in all the versions (York, Towneley, Chester, and Weavers), when the Ten Commandments are discussed, the argument ceases and the differences are forgotten. The Christ Child and the Jewish doctors are united in the belief that the most important commandment is to honor God and love your neighbor as yourself. Jesus adds that that is the *whole* law, but nobody disputes him. It is quite true, of course, that there was no debate over the enduring validity of the commandments. But the playwright is evidently no longer thinking of the debate over the law; his intent is simply to instruct the audience. As a matter of fact, after saying that

25. In *Chester Plays,* ed. Thomas Wright, Shakespeare Society, vol. XVII (1843).
26. In *The Weavers' Pageant and the Shearmen and Taylor's Pageant, Two Coventry Corpus Christi Plays,* ed. Hardin Craig, EETS 87 (1947).

the whole law is comprised in the command of love, the child recites the Ten Commandments in much the same way as does Moses himself in the Hegge *Moses*. There, when Moses gives the commandments to the Israelites, he turns and preaches them in a sermon to the audience.

In the York *Entry into Jerusalem* there is an interesting echo of the argument that the new dispensation was to be written on the hearts of men. In their discussion of the new prophet, one of the "citizens" of Jerusalem tells the others how Jesus taught a new law in the temple and plainly said that "the olde shall waste, the new schall gang, that we shall see." Yes, comments another, he knows all the laws of Moses and the prophets, and he tells them so that any man may "feel" them, and know their inner meaning (ll. 141 ff.).[27]

Lydgate: Pilgrimage of the Life of Man

The Moses who appears in Lydgate's *Pilgrimage of the Life of Man* (a translation of Deguilleville's *Pélérinage*)[28] is greatly concerned with the old and the new rites, but, far from contrasting them, he unites them to the point of confusion. In an allegory of the sacraments of confirmation, priesthood, and the Eucharist, Moses, rather than Christ, is the symbol of righteousness and mercy; he fulfills the law himself, and Holy Communion is received by Christians at his "table." This identification can be explained in part by the fact that, in commentary, Moses was not only the teacher of the law but a type of Christian bishop. Grosseteste, as was observed in an earlier chapter, cited the example of Moses in defense of the bishop's right of visitation in his diocese. So here, Moses is both the Jewish prophet and a Christian bishop, who confirms the pilgrim. A maid named Reason explains that anointed Christians should be pitiful and take no vengeance, for as the prophet Moses (Deut. 32:35) said in his saws, vengeance belongs to God alone. The vicar named Moses, evidently a Christian bishop, asks when he may use his horns to punish. Reason explains that he must always temper judgment with mercy. Remember, she says, whose vicar you are: he was humble, meek, and debonair, charitable and not contrary—and you shall fol-

27. In *The York Plays*, ed. Lucy Toulmin Smith (Oxford, 1885).
28. Ed. F. J. Furnivall and Katherine B. Locock, EETS (Extra Series) 77, 83, 92 (1899–1904).

low his example. Surely she means Christ here, we think, but no—
"thys was that holy Moyses" who led all Israel in peace through the
sea and made them good passage. A marginal note reads: "*erat
Moyses vir mitissimus.* Numbers 12:3." Reason tells this Moses: if
you will lead your fold from Pharao to liberty, then you will truly be
called Moses. And then Moses ordains priests and gives them *Grace
Dieu* (ll. 1380 ff.).

In the discussion of the Eucharist (ll. 2321 ff.), we are told that
while eating of blood was forbidden in the Old Law, Moses went to
dinner expressly to eat flesh and blood "contrarye to that commande-
ment," in order to help all men. There was bread and wine on the
table; Moses summoned Grace Dieu and turned them into flesh and
blood. He then called his officers to dinner and gave them power to
change, as he had, bread into flesh and wine into blood. Between
Moses' communion table and the people, we are told, stand penance
and charity, both necessary to men before they can approach the
righteousness of Moses. The allegory is extraordinary; the point is
not. Through the grace of God, given to all men by Christ, and now
by priests in the Eucharist, all men can come to the God of Israel.

Rood and Grail

In some of the allegories derived from the doctrine of the law, the
Old Testament proofs are woven into highly imaginative settings.
The legends and romances are too complicated and controversial to
go into here, but some of the symbols are obvious enough even out of
context, and a few of them will suggest the prevailing mode of
thought.

In the legends of the rood, for example, the queen of Sheba is present at the building of Solomon's Temple. Her presence would have
seemed entirely appropriate to medieval readers. For Solomon was a
figure of Christ, the Temple a prefiguration of the Church, and the
queen herself a figure of the Church of the Gentiles. As the queen
came from Ethiopia to hear the wisdom of Solomon, so now the
peoples come from the ends of the world to hear the true Wisdom.[29]

In the Grail legends (in Lovelich's translation of the *Estoire del*

29. *Legends of the Holy Rood,* ed. R. Morris, EETS 46 (1871), pp. 33 ff.; *Kalendarium et Temporale,* ed. Francis Proctor and Christopher Wordsworth (Cambridge, Eng., 1879–86), 1455 ff.

St. Graal the explanation is clearer than in Malory's version of the *Quest*), Solomon constructs a ship rather than a temple. The substitution, which was necessary for the plot, raises no problem in symbolism, for not only was a ship a conventional figure for the Church, but Noe's ark was as popular a prefiguration of the Church as Solomon's Temple. The two edifices had been linked as figures of the universal Church by Bede in his *De Templo Salomonis;* and the wood of the tree was popularly supposed to have gone into the building of both ark and temple. The sword which is placed in the ship is an allegory of the fulfillment of the Old Testament in the New, for it is the sword of the divine word, of the spirit (Eph. 6:17; Apoc. 1:16). It is, in fact, the Old Testament which is deposited in the temple-ship. The blade is David's, the handle and sheath Solomon's, but it is not for Solomon to complete the "hangings"—they will be added in the time of the good knight, Christ. The reason Solomon cannot complete the sword is that he could only imperfectly interpret the word of God since the Psalms and the Solomonic writings would not receive their full meaning until the coming of Christ. When the ship is finally launched, with Solomon watching from the shore, a company of angels explains that the ship signifies God's New House.[30]

Perhaps the most striking point in these works is that they all realize, to a greater or less degree, the meaning of "fulfillment." It is always clear that the New House of Christianity is the old temple-ship baptized. All the variations in imagery only prove that Christ and the Church built on Moses and the Synagogue. The doctrine is portrayed in a medallion on a window at St. Denis—the prophets pour grain into a mill while St. Paul turns the grindstone and receives the flour.[31]

30. Albert Pauphilet, *Etudes sur la queste del Saint Graal* (Paris, 1921), pp. 146 ff.

31. Emile Mâle, *Religious Art in France in the Thirteenth Century,* trans. Dora Nussey (London, 1913), pp. 171 f.

Chapter IX

THE FULFILLMENT OF THE LAW IN *PIERS PLOWMAN*

¶Langland's concept of the law followed the traditions of the Fathers and was shaped by the liturgy and literature we have been looking at. But Langland did not "borrow" from them as, say, the commentators seem to have borrowed from each other, or the plays seem to have derived from other plays, poems, and sermons. It is rather as though all this background was his raw material, refined over the years and submerged in his concept of God before finally emerging in his poem.

In *Piers,* as God is and always has been love, so the law of God teaches and always has taught love. When Langland mentions the law given to Moses, he points out that it was written on stone to signify that it was to endure forever. So say all the commentators. But the commentaries, the sermons, even the plays and poems proceed to explain that while the moral law is eternal, the ceremonial law was changeable. Certainly Langland was familiar with all the arguments known to anybody who ever attended a mystery or listened to a sermon. And one would think that the changes in the law would appeal to his historical taste. But so entirely prophetic is his concept, so preoccupied is he with the grandeur of the ideas contained in the law and the prophets, that he never discusses the ceremonial law. When he contrasts the spirit and the letter, he is comparing two interpretations of Scripture, rather than the rites of the Jews and the Christians. His Abraham does not teach circumcision, nor does his Moses teach the observance of the Sabbath. Indeed, his Moses does not teach the Ten Commandments, but, like Jesus, says that the law is to love God and neighbor.

What need, then, for Christ or for a New Law? The need arose from the fallen nature of man. If Adam had not sinned, that is, turned away from the love of God, there would have been no need for Christ, and no history of the law. But after the Fall, heaven was closed to men, whose intellects and wills were clouded. God continued to reveal himself, and the patriarchs and prophets understood and followed the law. Even they, however, were denied heaven and had to await the coming of Christ to pay for the sin of Adam. And before Christ, most men neither understood nor were able to fulfill the law in their lives. With the coming of Christ, heaven was opened for all men, and all that was veiled became clear.

While the Old and the New Laws are one with God in eternity, in history, the Old Law guided men until the Incarnation, when Christ fulfilled it and opened the spiritual meaning of the letter. In the allegory of *Piers Plowman*, Abraham and Moses are the Faith and Hope who go before Charity, Charity himself having taught them the law of love. In the course of the poem, the patriarch and the prophet prophesy and await the coming of Christ, who will open heaven and whose Grace will give men the strength to fulfill the law in their lives.

In the first allusion in the poem to the law of Moses, it is identified with the love of God; indeed, the word "law" is not used. The point of the passage in Passus I is that Truth is love and is the same in God and in the hearts of men who love God better than themselves and avoid sin. This Truth is taught by all of God's works:

> And alle his werkes he wrouȝte with love as him listed
> And lered it Moises for the leuest thing and moste like to
> heuene.
>
> (I. 150–52)

> All his works are wrought with love and freedom;
> He taught love in the law of Moses; it is
> most like heaven.
>
> (I. 150–52)

What Langland means is that God taught "it" to Moses when he gave him not only the commandments to avoid sin but the exhortation to "love the Lord thy God with thy whole heart, and with thy whole soul, and with thy whole strength" (Deut. 6:5). Langland does not develop the point here, but his mention of it is crucial. In this basic outline of the meaning of the mountain and the field of folk, the law of Moses is included as an essential part of the revelation to men of the truth and love of God. The law is not just the Ten

Commandments, useful as he later shows these to be, but part of the triune Truth that is God.

The first mention of the priestly law, the "law of Leviticus," occurs in a suitably less elevated context. It occurs in a passage in which Will is defending himself to Reason for not working with his hands (C. VI. 22 ff.). He explains that he has gone to school and that he prays and sings psalms for the souls of those who furnish him with food and lodging. According to his thinking, men should not constrain clerks to common labor, for by the law of Leviticus, which our Lord ordained, clerks should neither "swynke" nor sweat nor fight. No doubt the Old Testament law, established by God, applies to Christian priests, and Langland may actually have been such a priest. But Conscience is not particularly impressed with his excuse; nor was the poet, who chose the sweating plowman as his hero.

THE PLAN OF THE POEM

I wonder if this handling of Leviticus is intended to mark the low point of the pilgrim's moral development and also to place him in the time of the Old Law. It is here, in Passus V, that the dreamer begins to seek to understand how to Do Well, and in his personal development he follows the history of the human race. He and the other pilgrims are just starting on the long road of salvation. They hear the teaching of Truth, which has always been the same, but they cannot grasp it all at once, and they must follow it, step by step, just as it was gradually revealed by God. Christ is referred to here, as he is in the Old Testament, but he does not appear until late in the poem, as he does in the New Testament. There is always the danger of pushing such a framework too hard, especially with Langland. There is something rebellious in the poet's nature that makes him argue with priests and sneer at rhetoricians. On the other hand, he does enjoy the subtleties of his plan, whatever liberties he may take with it. In Passus V, the shape of the plan becomes quite clear, and the allusion to Leviticus (which was added in the C version) may be an ironical part of it. The clerk does not cite the highest Jewish or Christian law partly because he has not reached a high plane himself, perhaps also because he is being fitted into the history of the Jews.

Be that as it may, the allegory of the rest of the passus is clear enough. The dreamer's confession of wasted time is followed by the confessions of the Seven Deadly Sins. Then Repentance prays for mercy for all sinners in a most Christian prayer which dwells on the suffering of Christ for men's sins. But this is only the beginning of the pilgrimage, and the pilgrims must travel a long road before they are ready for the mercy of Christ. The journey is mapped out in the rest of this passus and in the following one.

Immediately after the conclusion of Repentance's prayer, we are told that then "Hope" took a horn and blew on it: Blessed are they whose sins are forgiven. There is no further mention of a character named Hope until the pilgrim meets Spes-Moses in Passus XVII. That this Hope is the same Moses is, I think, one of the subtleties of his plan that Langland enjoyed. It would not have seemed an obscurity to a medieval reader, for it was a commonplace of commentary that the law of Moses gave "hope" to a people fallen in sin. In his brief appearance here, Hope rejoices in the repentance of the sinners.

Furthermore, the action of Passus V foreshadows that of Passus XVII and XVIII. In both sets of cantos, the Old Law is shown as a necessary preliminary to the New, and the teaching of Moses precedes that of Christ. In the later cantos, the pilgrim meets Spes on the road to the Crucifixion before he meets Christ, and Spes prepares him for the meeting by teaching him to love the worthless as well as the worthy (XVII. 44). In the earlier section, the pilgrims are not ready to meet Christ. But in Passus V, Hope blows his horn to assemble the repentant scoundrels to seek Truth, and the pilgrims are told to take the road of the Ten Commandments before they can arrive at the castle of Christendom.

That there can be no short cuts on this journey is made plain by the meeting of the wandering folk with a professional pilgrim. He has been to Sinai and to our Lord's sepulcher, but all the signs in his hatband do not point to the place where Truth is dwelling (VI. 523 ff.). Nor can the pilgrims shorten the way with money. When they proffer wages to Piers to lead them, he swears that Truth would only love him less if he touched a farthing. They must take the long way through the Commandments, which Piers summarizes in a paraphrase of Spes's *"Dilige Deum et proximum tuum"* in Passus XVII. Here (V. 568 ff.) he says that they must "go thourgh Mekenesse" until Christ knows surely that they "louen owre lorde god leuest of alle thinges" and their neighbor next. Maintaining the road-map image, he then turns the commandments into colorful contemporary language. "And so boweth forth bi a broke Beth-buxum-of-speche/ Tyl ȝe fynden a forth ȝowre-fadres-honoureth." Wade and wash in that water, but avoid the croft "Coueyte-nouȝte mennes-catel-ne-her-wyues"; and so on through the Ten. Only at the end will they come to a "courte as clere as the sonne" with a moat of mercy encircling the manor, the walls crenelated with Christendom, and Truth sitting in the tower. This tower of Truth is, as it were, a flashback to Passus I, in which were the same field of folk, the same castle, and the same Truth taught in the law of Moses and Christ.

Having heard the route, the folk understand that it is a rough way without a guide (VI. 1). Piers offers himself, but only after his half acre is harrowed and sown. This will mean a long delay, says a lady in a veil. But the folk accept it as necessary, for they must learn to work together, each giving according to his ability and receiving according to his need.

The practical moral problems that arise are answered out of both the Old Testament and the New. What is to be done, for example, with the wolvish wasters who will not work? They, too, are blood brethren, for God bought all men; but they fight and ruin everything. Hunger explains that the lowly and unfortunate must be helped even if they cannot work, but bold beggars should be brought down with a bean diet until they do work. "Miȝte I synnelees do as thow seist?" asks Piers. Yes, answers Hunger, "or ellis the bible lieth;/ Go to Genesis the gyaunt, the engendroure of vs alle" (VI. 232–34). Our Lord commanded that we should labor in sorrow. Solomon says the same, and so do Matthew and Holy Church.

This brief dialogue between Piers and Hunger is typical of Langland's style. More than a device to give variety, it is a dramatization of two plausible answers to a serious question. For Piers's question really troubled Langland, and Hunger's answer is cold, if just. So in the passus that follows the same problem is discussed more fully, and while Langland censures bold beggars who maim their children to turn them into beggars, there is no mistaking the warmth of his compassion for the needy, "charged with children" and pressed with rents, and for the blind, the old, the witless—for all God's poor (C. X. 71 ff.).

THE PARDON OF PIERS

It is to reward the compassionate and make amends to the poor that Piers's pardon is given. But the meaning of pardon leads to another debate, which is continued intermittently, in one guise or another, until the end of the poem.

There is no question that this pardon (in Passus VII) is good, for it is given to Piers by Truth for the comfort of those who help him harrow or sow his acre and also for all those who rule rightly—kings, knights, and bishops. Even merchants have remissions "in the margyne" of this pardon; for although the pope holds it against them that they do not keep holy days and that they swear too much, still Truth, under "his secret seel," pardons them if they use their profits to help hospitals and prisoners and such. Lawyers who plead for money get the least possible pardon, and dishonest beggars get none at all. But true laborers and all the unfortunate who "lyuen in loue and in lawe for her lowe hertis" (l. 64) shall have the same absolution that was sent to Piers, for they have their penance and purgatory now.

So far all is clear enough; but a priest appears from nowhere to raise difficulties for Piers—and for the reader. Let us see this pardon, he says, and translate it into English. His translation cannot be dismissed as a fraud, because the dreamer stands behind him and sees for himself that, as the priest says, the charter consists only of two lines in Latin. "I can no pardoun fynde," says the priest,

> But "Dowel, and haue wel and god shal haue thi sowle,
> And do yuel, and haue yuel hope thow non other
> But after thi ded-day the deuel shal haue thi sowle! "
> (VII. 112–15)

> But Do Well and have well, and God shall
>   have your soul,
> And do evil and have evil, and you may
>   hope only
> That after your death day the devil
>   shall take you.
> (VII. 217–20)

But how can this be? Neither Piers nor the priest is lying: we are expressly told both that Piers's pardon was provided by truth and also that the bull construed by the priest was written in witness of truth. It must be that these are two interpretations of the word of God. There is, in fact, no contradiction between the morality taught in Piers's pardon and in the two lines (from the Athanasian Creed) that the priest can see. But the priest sees only the letter, while Piers foresees the spirit. The priest symbolizes the Old Law, Piers the New (both being true); while the Old Law was a lasting good, its full meaning was hidden until it was revealed by Christ. The priest's termination is legalistic, for he says he can construe each word; Piers, on the other hand, emphasizes the lowly hearts of the poor and the intentions of the merchants who, significantly, do not observe the holy days.

Even more significant is the fact that this remission is in the margin and that the seal on the pardon is secret. Nobody is lying, but while neither the priest nor the dreamer can see what is in the margin, Piers can. The seal is secret, that is, hidden from men's eyes, as Christ was hidden in the prophecies of the Old Testament. Surely the point here is the same as that in the debate between the four daughters of God (which we shall look at in a moment), in which Righteousness and Truth, who hold to the letter of the law like the priest, do not know what is in the letter that Peace has received from her lover, Charity. Like Peace, Piers receives a secret letter (VII. 23); like her letter, Piers's pardon is a prophecy of the new law of Charity which can be sealed only by the blood of Christ.

Like Peace and like the prophets, Piers must await the coming of Christ. When in the A and B verions Piers tears up the pardon, he says that he will pray and do penance—like the prophets. His tearing up of the pardon in "pure tene" may reflect his frustration when he realizes that he cannot make the pardon effective. In a similar "tene" later in the poem (XVI. 86), he flings apples at the devil, although he knows only Christ can hurt him. Certainly, in the large plan of the poem, it is still a long time until the Redemption.

When the prophecies are about to be fulfilled, the dreamer meets Moses on the road to Jerusalem. The prophet is also carrying a "letter" which, he explains, is the law given him on Sinai. Is it sealed? asks the dreamer. No, replies Moses; he seeks now him who has the seal in keeping (XVII. 1–9). When the law of Moses is sealed or fulfilled, by Christ, the pardon is extended to both prophets and pilgrims, and the doctrines of the priest and of Piers (like those of the four daughters of God) are reconciled.

It may well be, as Nevill Coghill suggested some years ago, that all of the implications of the pardon were not clear to the poet himself when he wrote the early version.[1] Apparently after much pondering, he omitted the tearing up of the pardon in the C version. But he retained the wrangle between Piers and the priest, and thus his acknowledgement that its meaning is not easily taken.

He tells us that often this vision has forced him to wonder if what he saw while asleep were possible (VII. 142 ff.). In the midst of this poem of dreams, he has the audacity to say that he is a doubter of dreams, for they often deceive men. At some length he cites Cato and the canonists against, and Daniel and Joseph in favor of, belief in dreams. Actually, this aside on the truth of dreams is a half-satirical excuse for an attack on the prevailing practice of pardons. Not, mind you, that he himself would say anything against pardons, but he cannot help thinking of the vision in which the priest deemed that, at the day of doom, Do Well "passeth al the pardoun of Seynt Petres cherche." He adds hastily that the pope has power to grant pardons, so he himself believes ("lordes forbode ellis!"), but "to trust to thise triennales trewly me thinketh / Is nouȝt so syker for the soule certis, as is Dowel" (ll. 173 ff.). Therefore he warns the rich, do not break the Ten Commandments on trust of your bought pardons. At the Last Judgment, though you have pocketfuls of pardons, unless Do Well help you, "I sette ȝowre patentes and ȝowre pardounz at one pies hele!"

For all the vehemence of the conclusion of this Passus VII, it would be a mistake to think that Langland had decided in favor of the priest against Piers. True, there is no ambiguity in his bleak view of the practice of pardons in the contemporary Church. As against that practice, Langland indeed prefers the Old Law of the Ten

1. Nevill Coghill, *The Pardon of Piers Plowman*, Sir Israel Gollancz Memorial Lecture, British Academy (London, 1945). On the pardon, see also R. W. Frank, "The Pardon Scene in *Piers Plowman*," *Speculum*, XXVII (1951), 323–24; John Reidy, "Peris the Ploughman, Whiche a Pardoun He Hadde," *PMASAL*, L (1964), 535–44; Marshall Walker, "Piers Plowman's Pardon: A Note," *English Studies in Africa*, VIII (1965), 64–70.

Commandments. But that practice represented only the corruption of Piers's doctrine of mercy. In the end, Piers is the hero and his pardon the foreshadowing of the ultimate pardon of Christ.

With Passus VII, the first part of the vision ends, and as the commentators have pointed out, this is the turning point of the poem.[2] It seems almost that as the poet brooded over the meaning of the pardon his poem became both deeper and broader and the interior development of the dreamer gradually became related to the history of the salvation of the world. In that history, the ensuing cantos signify the time of prophetic preparation for Christ. Piers is absent, praying and doing penance, and the dreamer prepares himself for the coming of Christ.

THE INSTRUCTION OF THE DREAMER

The dreamer has a long way to go before he will be ready to meet Christ. His slow moral and intellectual development is portrayed in the following section of the poem in a series of moral discourses and lively debates. What he learns from Will, Thought, Wit, Study, Clergy, and Imagination is ultimately useful, but not at the moment satisfying or truly effective because he still lacks the grace of Christ. Without Piers to guide him, he often misunderstands and misuses the gifts of God.

In the course of the dreamer's moral instruction, the subject of the law frequently arises, and one aspect or another is discussed, always according to the Scriptures. In Passus IX, for example, Wit is teaching the dreamer about the soul, and part of his explanation is a little allegory of the fulfillment of the law. Lady Anima lives in a castle guarded by a Constable named "Sire Inwitte" (Conscience), who has five sons by his first marriage: Sires Sewel and Saywel, Herewel, Sire Worche-wel-wyth-thine-hande, and Sirè Godfrey Gowel. As in all the commentaries, the first wife is no doubt the Old Law, and the sons are apparently personifications of the moral teaching of the Old Testament. There are five of them because there are five books of the law;

2. John Lawlor, *Piers Plowman: An Essay in Criticism* (London, 1962), p. 70; Coghill, *Pardon of Piers*, pp. 56 ff.; J. F. Goodridge, ed. and trans., *Piers the Ploughman* (London, 1960), p. 11; T. P. Dunning, "The Structure of the B Text of Piers Plowman," *RES,* VII (July, 1956), 230–31.

the analogy was probably suggested to Langland by the popular allegorical interpretation of the five loaves in the New Testament miracle as the five books of the law. When Wit says that these five are set here to save the Lady Anima until God comes or sends for her "to save her for ever," he is expressing the role of the Old Law in the redemption of mankind. As he says later in this passus, Do Well is to do as the law teaches.

The Old Testament is, in fact, drawn upon very heavily in the description of Do Well in this and in the following passus, not because of the difference between the laws but because the basic moral law is derived from the Old Testament. The fear of God is the beginning of wisdom, says Solomon; and who "dredeth God, he doth wel" (IX. 94). When Wit adds that he who dreads God out of love does better, he is not discrediting Solomon, who continues to be praised. Dame Study, for example, bewails the fact that men love their riches better than all the wisdom and wit of Solomon (X. 13 ff.). And quoting from the Psalter and from Tobias, she warns the rich to share their wealth.

Similarly, when Clergy condemns Christian priests for committing the sins they preach against, he condemns them out of the Old Testament and out of the New, making no distinction between them (X. 274 ff.). These clerics who should Do Best, he says, are responsible for the faults of the people. For the Gospel speaks of the blind leading the blind, and Samuel tells how all Israel bitterly bought the sins of two bad prelates. Priests should rather do as David counseled —and Pope Gregory, too. Scripture proves that riches are an impediment to heaven by the witness of St. Paul, Solomon, Cato, the Apostles, and "patriarkes and prophetes and poetes" (X. 340).

It may be Scripture's lumping together of rich Jews and Christians that provokes the dreamer into raising a point here that is discussed a number of times later in the poem. He objects that the baptized must be safe, be they rich or poor (X. 347). But Scripture has understood the prophetic meaning of the law and will concede no priestly reliance on ritual, not even the sacrament of baptism. She says that Jews and Saracens *in extremis* may be saved by baptism, for their loyal belief would take them to heaven. But Christian men "with-oute more may nouȝt come to heuene." For Christ "confermed the lawe" and whoever wishes to arise with him must love and believe "and the lawe fulfille," that is, love God above all things and be kind to Christians and to the heathen. Unless they clothe the naked and feed the hungry, their storing of silver will sit against them.

The dreamer is not ready for this "longe lessoun," for which he is little "the wyser." He rashly inveighs against learning and cites famous men who taught wisdom without practicing it. To make his point, he uses, in his own way, the popular identification of Noe's ark with the Church (X. 399 ff.). He thinks it will be with many as it was with the laborers who built the ark but were not saved on it. God grant that it may not fare so with those who teach the Faith! For Holy Church is God's house, built to shield us from shame as the ark did the animals. The clerks, who are carpenters of the Church, had better work well and so come into the ark lest they drown in the deluge of doomsday.

In the following passus (XI. 107 ff.), the discussion of the merits of learning and the meaning of the law is resumed. Scripture begins her teaching with the famous text: "*Multi*" were summoned to a supper—but the porter plucked in "*pauci*" and let the rest go roam! Like the commentators, the dreamer interprets this to mean that Christ called all to come—Saracens, schismatics, and Jews. He dares hope, therefore, that he will be among the chosen. Yes, agrees Scripture, our books tell us that mercy and meekness can amend all men. "ʒee, baw for bokes!" cried one who had broken out of hell. This is Trajan, the famous pagan emperor who was saved by the tears of St. Gregory. Trajan's point here is that all the learning in the Church and in the world did not save him. He was saved not by bead-bidding or by the singing of masses but by his love and living in truth.

Scripture accepts the doctrine of love but modifies the argument against learning. The doctrine of love and loyalty *can* be learned— from the Bible, from the law of love given to Moses:

> Loue and leute is a lele science;
> For that is the boke blessed of blisse and of ioye:—
> God wrouʒt it and wrot hit with his on fynger,
> And toke it Moyses vpon the mount alle men to lere.
>
> (XI. 161–64)

> Love and loyalty is the lofty science!
> For this is the Book blessed with bliss and
>   joyfulness;

God wrought it and wrote it with his own finger,
And gave it to Moses on the Mount that all men
should learn it.

(XI. 168–71)

Law without love is indeed not worth a bean. But the love of God and of all men is taught by St. John, and the Gospels stress especially the love of the poor. Under the New Law, even more than under the Old, men ought to care for one another. In the Old Law, men were men's sons, mentioned always as issue of Adam and Eve. Since the Crucifixion and the Resurrection, we are all brethren of the God-man and must therefore love as brothers.

Some seventy lines later (Scripture is still speaking) is a passage that begins with what seems like a basic difference between the laws. Scripture remarks that although Solomon said that it is best to be neither rich nor poor, a "wyser than Solomon" taught us that God likes best a life of perfect poverty (XI. 262 ff.). Lengthier than the passage from Luke, however, is a similar one from David. For David said that those who serve God willingly will never lack a livelihood. If priests were perfect, they would listen to David and take no silver for masses, nor meat from usurers, "neither kirtel ne cote theigh they for colde shulde deye." (XI. 276). Again Scripture links Jesus and the apostles with Job and Abraham (C. XIV. 1–25). Jesus and the apostles chose poverty and patience. When Job and Abraham had lost their riches, patience relieved their poverty, and so the joy of father Abraham and Job the gentle has no end.

The battle of the books is concluded in Passus XII (ll. 70 ff.), in which Imagination sets the dreamer straight. True, grace is a gift of God, begotten of love, and neither clerks nor nature knows its secrets. Yet knowledge is to be commended, especially the knowledge of the clergy. The example Langland gives is adapted from the popular belief that, in the story of the woman taken in adultery, Christ wrote a message in the dust. It was sometimes said in commentary that this was the second time that Christ wrote the law, the second being a clarification of the first. Imagination seems about to compare the laws, for he cites the Mosaic stricture on stoning a woman taken in adultery. But the only moral he deduces is that Christ "of his curteisye" saved her through learning. It was through the letters ("carectus") that he wrote that the accusers discovered that they were more guilty than she; so learning comforted the woman. Finally, he points out that the learning of Christian priests serves the laity, just as *"Archa Dei* in the olde lawe Leuites it kepten," and no layman might lay hands upon it.

In order to refute the dreamer's "crabbed" contention that the unlearned are more readily saved than the learned, he tells also the Christmas story of the angel, the shepherds, and the star (XII. 149 ff.). The angel, he says, appeared "to pastours and to poetes" and sang a song of "solas, *Gloria in excelsis Deo!*" While the rich were snoring in their houses, "it schon to the schepherdes a schewer of blisse." "Clerkes" understood it well and came with their presents and did homage. Now we can see how the learning of the wise men is relevant here, but how do the shepherds present an example of learning? Langland does not explain, but probably behind this mixed allusion was the allegorical exposition of the story, according to which the shepherds represent the Jewish people while the three kings represent the heathen. In this interpretation, the shepherds, rather than the kings, represent learning. For the shepherds were near-by not only geographically, but by virtue of their knowledge of the law. That is why the message was made known to them in words, while to the remote heathen it was made known by a star.

Imagination is more to our taste in his broad views on the salvation of the unbaptized. He debates the point with the dreamer who, having rashly condemned the clergy for their lack of charity, now runs to the dullest of them for authority for his own uncharitable opinion. He insists that "alle thise clerkes" say in their sermons that neither Saracens nor Hebrews can be saved. Imagination frowns most severely and points out that the true God would never abandon those who live as their law teaches but will give them "mede" for their "truth." And "with that he vanesched" (XII. 275 ff.).

THE DINNER PARTY

Imagination's place is taken in Passus XIII by Conscience and Patience, and Piers himself makes a fleeting appearance. Beginning with a highly comical dinner party, this passus includes a variation of the earlier argument over the pardon of Piers and relates it to the

Redemption to come. Both the conversation and the dramatic appearance of Piers foreshadow that Redemption and suggest that it is soon to come.

At the dinner party given by Conscience, a great Master of Divinity is the honored guest. He sits at the main table with Conscience and Clergy, while the inconsequential dreamer and a poor creature named Patience are seated by themselves at a side table. While the master, who is famous for his sermons on penance, gorges himself with food and wine, Patience and pilgrim get a sour loaf. In the after-dinner conversation, the famous friar explains Do Well, Do Better, and Do Best in terms that do not satisfy the company. Clergy comments that one Piers Plowman says that Do Well and Do Better "aren two infinites" which, together with faith, discover Do Best, who will save men's souls. Conscience does not know about this, but he trusts the plowman not to speak against Holywrit. Then (in the C text only, Passus XVI), Piers himself makes an abrupt and brief appearance in which he says that Patience conquers all; and he advises those assembled to love God and their enemies without reservations. Patience then propounds a riddle. He shows the others a package with the words *"ex vi transitionis"* on it, which contains Do Well within it. No misfortune, he says, will ever trouble them if they carry this bundle. *Caritas nihil timet.*

The Doctor brushes aside both riddle and moral. But Conscience departs at once to be a pilgrim with Patience. Clergy is not so easily convinced and advises Conscience to stay. He himself will bring a Bible and from a "boke of the old lawe" will prove the fine points of doctrine which Patience has never mastered. But Conscience would rather have perfect patience than half of Clergy's books, and he hopes, with Patience, to remedy the woe in the world, to make kings and countries turn to peace, and to turn Saracens and Syrians, and all the Jews to the true faith and one belief.

Obviously this is a highly allegorical party, and its meaning is complex. Among other things, we have returned to the themes of the spirit and the letter, the Old and the New Laws, the disputed pardon of Piers, and the conversion of the Gentiles.

The friar embodies all the anti-clericalism of the last four books. He does not practice what he preaches; he is rich and uncharitable and thoroughly professional. He represents *not* the Old Law, the law of love given to Moses, but the priestly interpretation of the law. Do Well, he says, is "do as clerks techeth." The low level of his comprehension is symbolized by his diet. While Conscience and Clergy are served separate dishes of the meat of Augustine and Ambrose and the Evangelists, and Patience and the dreamer get a sour loaf of the penitential psalms, the master eats only mashed meats. In other words, he has no stomach for the strong meat of Christian doctrine or for the patristic interpretations of the Scriptures. The great glutton sates himself with baby foods that make no demands on his mind or heart.

Dramatically set against him is Piers. Both Clergy and Conscience talk as though Piers's teaching is new to them: Clergy says he will have to wait and see, and Conscience is unable to argue one way or the other. They believe, however, that Piers's new law of the infinity of love is not against the teaching of the Bible, which they know well. In other words, this is the New Law of Christ, which does not abrogate but fulfills the Old. That the learning of Clergy is at this point in the poem the Old Law is made explicit in Clergy's offer to explain the Old Testament to Conscience. Since Conscience is of the heart, the very promise of the New Covenant appeals to him, and he departs to seek its meaning with Patience.

It needs no learned gloss to explain the importance of Patience in the pilgrimage ahead. Here he is very closely united with Piers, even appearing at the dinner looking like Piers Plowman, in his palmer's clothing. And in his mystical appearance at the dinner, Piers cries, "*Pacientes vincunt*."

But the riddle of Patience is indeed a riddle. Professor Goodridge has suggested that "*ex vi transitionis*" means "through the power of the passing-over," and is a reference to the Passover. This would fit the calendar part of the riddle ("In a signe of the Saterday that sette firste the Kalendare, / And al the witte of the Wednesday of the nexte wyke after" [ll. 153–54]), which apparently refers to Holy Saturday, Easter, and the Wednesday of Easter week. The Easter liturgy, of course, referred to the Passover as a prefiguration of the Eucharist and taught that all the sacrifices of the Old Law were fulfilled in the Passion of Christ.[3] The perfect love hidden in Patience's bundle is the New Law, which fulfilled the Old and gave men

3. Goodridge, *Piers,* pp. 306–7.

power to Do Well in their own lives and to make peace in the world —if they would but untie it. (The friar refuses even to try.)

The reason Patience propounds the doctrine as a riddle is, I think, because in the Biblical progression of the poem, this whole scene is set before the Incarnation. Like the prophets, Patience can speak only in riddles; indeed, his riddle is a prophecy. As the New Testament is hidden in the Old, the Passion of Christ is both concealed in Patience's package and prophesied in the cryptic words *"ex vi transitionis."* Also included in his prophecy is the calling of the Gentiles. It is because Conscience understands that the New Covenant is to carry the word of God to the whole world and bring all peoples to the God of Israel that he hopes, with Patience, to make peace between kings and popes and bring Jews and Gentiles to one faith. Finally, as the utterances of the prophets prepared men for the coming of Christ, so the riddle of Patience prepares the dreamer for the coming meeting with Christ and moves him to resume his pilgrimage.

The dreamer still has some way to go. It is one of Langland's ironies that, at the dinner party, the dreamer is seated most impatiently beside Patience and can barely contain his rage against both food and company. For the first time, however, he does hold his tongue, and when he leaves, he is strengthened by the company of Conscience and Patience.

HAUKYN

The need all men have for these two virtues is suggested by the character of the first person they meet, a remarkable fellow called Haukyn, the Active Man. With his racy speech and his coat stained with sins, Haukyn brings to mind the motley crew of pilgrims, the repentant Seven Deadly Sins of Passus V. It is made clear almost immediately that Haukyn, like the earlier pilgrims, is not ready for the pardon which Piers tore up in Passus VII, the true meaning of which remains hidden in Patience's bundle. Haukyn comments satirically that if only he had a clerk who could write, he would petition the pope for a pardon to bring down boils (XIII. 247 ff.). He would be happy to make bread and cakes for everybody if the pope's pardon would heal a man as it really should; since the pope has the power that Peter himself had, he has "the potte with the salue." More

176

soberly, he admits that the power of miracle is missing not because the pontiff is guilty but because men are unworthy to have the grace of God. No blessing may help us unless we amend. No mass can make peace among Christians until pride is purged through pestilence and famine.

In brief, this pilgrim, like the earlier ones, like every man, would like a cure-all to guarantee health and wealth and heaven, too. He half realizes, however, that hardships are a necessary evil. (So Piers had found to his sorrow that only hunger would make some of his alleged followers work.) To be worthy of Christ's pardon, Haukyn and the other pilgrims must be willing to renounce comfort and do penance. Then they will see that in his little bundle Patience does have the salve that cures pain: the perfect love of the New Covenant which casts out fear.

What *is* charity? asks the dreamer. Anima's lengthy reply (in Passus XV) is, in part, a prologue to the ensuing cantos; it prepares both the dreamer and the reader to understand the meeting with Christ which is soon to follow. Anima believes, first of all, that the meaning of charity can and must be taught. Indeed, he bitterly censures priests who, through their lack of charity, not only lead Christians astray but also fail to convert Jews and Saracens. It is not the fault of the priests, however, that even the best of them cannot supply the vision of God. When the pilgrim cries out that he would "know" charity, Anima replies that without the help of Piers Plowman, he will never see him. No clerk, no earthly creature, not through words or works, can ever tell you, but only "Piers the Plowman, *Petrus, id est, Christus*" (XV. 206). This cryptic expression is a prophecy of the Incarnation, in which Christ was embodied and God seen by men. At the same time, Anima wants it clearly understood that the words and works of the law and the prophets teach the same charity. He says that our Lord himself wrote the law of the Jews in stone, so that it should stand forever. "*Dilige deum et proximum* is parfit Iewen lawe" (l. 574), and it was given to Moses, to teach until the coming of the Messias.

There is no suggestion here of the New Law superseding the Old. The law of charity stands forever, and Moses was its teacher before the coming of Christ. But it is through Christ that we "know" charity, and by charity all the peoples of the world could be united.

Add to this the point that Christ opened the gates of heaven to all men, and we have an outline of the meaning of the tree of charity in Passus XVI and of the allegory of the Good Samaritan in the following cantos.

Behind Langland's tree was the popular tree of Jesse,[4] a familiar symbol in medieval art which adorns many a church window and illuminated manuscript. Springing from the root or "rod of Jesse," it traced the genealogy of Christ, showing the patriarchs and prophets on the lower branches and the Virgin and Child at the top. Langland's tree represents the genealogy of charity. Mercy is its main root, pity its stock; charity is its fruit, which grows through God and good men. But as the fruit dropped down, the devil gathered it all—Adam, Abraham, Isaias, Samson, Samuel, and St. John the Baptist. He bore all these good men to limbo with nobody to stop him until *"Filius"* went to rescue them.

FAITH-ABRAHAM AND SPES-MOSES

In explaining the meaning of the tree, Piers tells the dreamer the story of the life of Jesus and then vanishes. Distraught, the dreamer wanders east and west, like "an ydiote," until he meets Faith-Abraham, then Spes-Moses, and finally, the Good Samaritan, all traveling the same road. Obviously, the dreamer must learn from Abraham and Moses, from Faith and Hope, before he is at last ready to meet Charity face to face.

Faith and Hope are no fanciful appellations for the patriarch and the prophet, but terms that arise almost inevitably out of the Christian doctine of the fulfillment of the law. For Abraham, who lived before the law, won the favor of God not through circumcision but through faith, and so became the father of the Gentiles. Further, his association with Melchizedek foretold the end of the sacrifice of blood. Then the law of Moses raised and gave hope to a fallen people, and so prepared the way for charity.

It is clear from Abraham's recital of his autobiography (XVI. 225 ff.) that Langland was entirely familiar with the doctrinal argu-

---

4. For a most useful summary of "tree" symbolism, see Ben H. Smith, Jr., *Traditional Imagery of Charity in Piers Plowman,* Studies in English Literature, vol. XXI (The Hague, 1966).

ment, but his use of it is unique. As we have seen, in plays and poems as well as in sermons, it was apparently *de rigueur* to explain that circumcision prefigured baptism and to argue a little with the Jews about whose father Abraham really was. Langland uses the word "tokenes" to describe Abraham's obedience, his circumcision of his followers, the promises of God to him, and his worshiping with bread and wine. "Token" has the same meaning as the old "betokened"; Aelfric, for example, had said that circumcision "betokened" baptism. And in *Piers*, it is these tokens that make Abraham the "herald" or prophet of Christ. But what they explicitly betoken for Langland is not the change in the ceremonial law but the love and loyalty of Abraham which unite him to Christ.

The theme of the union of love and faith runs through Abraham's story. "First," he says, God tested his love to see whether he loved him or Isaac better. Describing the circumcision of his followers, he says that they "Bledden blode for that lordes loue." (He does not add a comparison with baptism, nor does he hint at any change in the law.) When God called him the foundation of the faith, he knew that Abraham would save from the fiend the people who believed in him. Therefore he has been God's herald on earth and in hell, where he has comforted those who await deliverance. Now he seeks him, for he has heard from John the Baptist that he has seen him who will save them. Then he shows the dreamer the "preciouse present" in his bosom, all those who are waiting in limbo until he comes of whom he has spoken; "Cryst is his name" (1. 265). This naming of Christ for the first time at the end of a long passage which obviously refers to his Old Testament appearances is a dramatic way of announcing the Incarnation. It also completes the portrait of Abraham as a figure of unchanging faith in the unchanging God of Israel.

While the dreamer is still weeping over the plight of those in Abraham's bosom, he sees another running rapidly on the same road taken by himself and Abraham. This is Spes-Moses, who is a "spye" looking for the knight who gave him "a maundement" (XVII. 1 ff.). He carries with him the letter that that champion (the preincarnate Christ) gave him on Mount Sinai; and now he seeks him who has the seal, that is, the Cross with Christ hanging on it. When it is sealed (with Christ's blood), he knows that Lucifer's lordship will last no longer.

The writ is described in almost the same words as were used for the law of the Jews in Passus XV. On a piece of granite are two words: *Dilige Deum et proximum tuum.* "This was the tixte trewly," for the dreamer took good heed of it. And there was a glorious gloss in gilt letters: *"In hijs duobus mandatis tota lex pendet et prophetia."* This "gloss" was made, of course, by Christ (Matt. 22:40), when he said that on the two commandments "love God and your neighbor" hang all the law and the prophets. To make Christ simply a commentator on the law, and his commentary a part of the original writ, is a graphic way of portraying the fulfillment of the law by love, and the unity of Moses and Jesus.

As his questioning of Moses reveals, however, the dreamer sees only the superficial differences in the laws. "Which of 30w is trewest" and best to believe? he asks. Abraham has saved those who believed and are sorry for their sins. "What neded it thanne a newe lawe to bigynne,/ Sith the fyrst sufficeth to sauacioun and to blisse?" (XVII. 30–31). It is easier to have faith, as Abraham teaches, than to love the worthless as well as the worthy, as Moses teaches. The problem posed here is, in part, that of justification by faith as opposed to works —Abraham representing faith and Moses works, as in St. Paul. But the very wording suggests a greater question. If Abraham and Moses, separately or together, could guarantee salvation, what need was there for Christ? The dreamer has not yet met Christ, but his final words to Moses anticipate both question and answer. When he says that those who "lerneth thi lawe wil litel while vsen it!" he is expressing the Pauline doctrine that men lack the power themselves to live according to the law. In fact, the whole passage raises questions which are answered in the allegory of the Good Samaritan which follows.

THE ALLEGORY OF THE GOOD SAMARITAN

The parable of the Good Samaritan has been a favorite since the earliest days of Christianity, and a history of its exposition would reveal both continuity of doctrine and changing tastes in Biblical interpretations. Contemporary popularity of the parable is derived from its social significance. Year after year, on the twelfth Sunday after Pentecost, the preacher in the American pulpit is likely to equate the Samaritan with the outsider—the Negro, or Jew, or even Communist; [5] the priest and the Levite are pictured as self-righteous Catholics who piously pass by the man (also Catholic) lying in the highway after being struck by an automobile. This is certainly a valid interpretation, but it is no closer to the mind of the primitive Church than Langland's allegory, in which priest and Levite are Abraham and Moses, and the Good Samaritan is Christ.

The point of the parable was not just that a member of a despised group might be virtuous, but that the stranger actually fulfilled the law of Moses better than those trained in it. The parable was told, after all, as an explanation of the meaning of the law. When a certain lawyer, testing him, asked Jesus what he must do to possess eternal life, Jesus countered with another question: "What is written in the law? How readest thou?" The lawyer answered, "Thou shalt love the Lord thy God with thy whole heart and with thy whole soul and with all thy strength and with all thy mind: and thy neighbor as thyself." When Jesus agreed, the lawyer asked, "And who is my neighbor?" The story told in reply was offensive enough in making the neighbor a Samaritan. But when Jesus concluded by telling the lawyer to "Go and do in like manner," he was, in effect, telling a Jew that he could learn how to follow the law from one who was despised for being outside of it (Luke 10:25–37).

Given the patristic fascination with the law, the ancient equation of the Good Samaritan with Jesus led easily to the interpretation of the parable as an allegory of wounded mankind, saved not by the law-givers and the prophets but by Christ. There are variations in the telling, but in all, the point is the same: good as the law was, it was not sufficient for salvation.[6] The Jews were not sunk in the mire as were the Gentiles, for they knew God and they awaited Christ. But even they could not enter heaven, and all others lay prostrate in sin. The allegory was so popular that it was sometimes used without the parable: a number of homilies teach the basic idea, while borrowing symbols from chivalry as well as from the Bible. In these, Christ comes as messenger or physician or knight to "restore goodness" and

5. E.g., "The Good Communist" is the title suggested for the parable in a parish bulletin, *My Parish Guide,* Catechetical Guild (St. Paul, August 29, 1965).

6. Smith, in *Traditional Imagery,* analyzes some of the Latin commentaries, e.g., *Glossa Ordinaria,* by Rabanus Maurus, Honorius of Autun.

to give men "strength and might" to fulfill the law of God. In a twelfth-century homily, Christ is the final messenger of the King, the other messengers being Abel, Seth, Noe, Samuel, and other Old Testament "teachers and inviters." Though we name many laws, says the homilist, all are one in God's will, and "each of them raiseth up and perfects the others." [7]

Most complete is a twelfth- or thirteenth-century homily on the Nativity, which opens with the parable of the Good Samaritan followed by an interpretation similar to that of Augustine, Bede, and Langland, but related in a simple style appropriate to the pulpit. Here the man who went down from Jericho to Jerusalem represents Adam. He fell among thieves but remained half alive because he was sorry for his sins. The priest who failed to help him

> betokens the world that was from the beginning and lasted even unto the time of Moses the prophet. In this world there was neither law nor law-expounder, and though the patriarchs as Abel and Noah, Abraham and Isaac, were good men, being enlightened of the Holy Ghost, yet all this goodness could not preserve them from going into hell,

and all this time this wretch lay wounded. After the priest came the deacon—Moses the prophet—who brought the law and taught men how to serve God and perform his will; but all this could not save them from hell. After the deacon came the foreign man, from the foreign land of heaven, and he had pity on the wounded man. What need had mankind that God should become man? Man had lost the right of speaking before God, and Christ as man won it back for him. He brought the wounded man to an inn. "What is this inn? It is holy church. What is holy church? All Christian folk." What are the two pence? "These are the two laws, the old and the new." [8] The same interpretation occurs in a poem by Adam of St. Victor, and in the *Miroure of Mans Salvacionne.* In the latter, and also in a number of sermons, we are told that Christ took the order of knight when he came to fight the devil, the weapons, of course, being spiritual. [9]

7. *Old English Homilies,* ed. R. Morris, EETS 29, 34 (1868), p. 234.

8. *Ibid.,* pp. 78 ff.; Augustine, *Quaestionum Evangeliorum, PL.* 35, col. 1340, cited in D. W. Robertson, Jr., and Bernard F. Huppé, *Piers Plowman and Scriptural Tradition* (Princeton, N.J., 1951), p. 198.

9. Adam of St. Victor, *Liturgical Poetry,* with translations by Digby S. Wrangham (London, 1881), vol. I, seq. viii; *Miroure,* pp. 18, 19.

Langland's handling of this material sounds so colloquial and unstrained that it might be considered artless. Actually, it is a remarkably successful tour de force. For the poet not only dramatizes the parable but assimilates the traditional elements into his own allegory of Faith, Hope, and Charity and into the pilgrimage of the dreamer.

As Abraham, Spes, and the dreamer go on their way "wordying" together, they see a Samaritan riding rapidly on the very road that they had taken, coming from a country that men call Jericho and hastening to a joust in Jerusalem (XVII. 47 ff.). The Samaritan overtook the others, and together they came upon a wounded man who had been waylaid by robbers. He was half-dead, naked as a needle, and helpless. Faith saw him first but veered around him and would not come nearer than nine furrows. Hope hurried behind. He had boasted how he had helped men with Moses' covenant, but when he saw that sight, he stepped aside as much in dread as a duck fears a falcon! But the Samaritan alighted from his horse and went at once to the poor creature. He perceived by his pulse that the man would die unless a savior came speedily. He unbuckled his two bottles, washed the man's wounds with wine and oil, and held him on his horse until they arrived at the *Lex Christi*, an inn six or seven miles from the New Market. Then he gave the host two pennies to care for the man until he returned, mounted his charger, and rode rapidly on the highway to Jerusalem.

The dreamer then pursues the Samaritan and offers himself as his groom. Then he tells him how Faith and Hope had fled. Let them be excused, said the Samaritan, for they could not help much. Neither Faith nor Hope nor any medicine can heal that man without the blood of a babe born of a maiden. And he will never be strong until he has eaten that child and drunk his blood. No one in this world has gone through that wilderness unhurt except Faith, Spes, and myself —and others I loved—and now you. Outlaws hide in the woods, and the one who saw me on my horse named *Caro* (which I took from mankind) hid himself in hell; but three days from today, that scoundrel will be in chains.

In the future, the Samaritan explains, Faith will be forester in this wood and will direct men to the road he took to Jerusalem. Those who are too feeble to learn from Faith will go to Hope, who will be the innkeeper's man. Hope will heal them by leading them to love in accordance with his law ("lettre"), which is the belief of the Church. For the child has been born in Bethlehem whose blood will save all who live with Faith and follow his comrade's teaching (ll. 113 ff.). This passage beautifully solves the problem of faith and works and the Old and the New Laws raised by the dreamer in his earlier questioning of Moses. Even after the Resurrection of Christ, in the time of the New Law of the Church, most men are neither pure enough nor strong enough to live by faith alone. They need the help of the moral law; and the teacher of the doctrine of the Church, the keeper of the inn called "The Law of Christ," is Moses.

The lesson is repeated even more plainly by the Samaritan when the dreamer, apparently having missed the point of the allegory, asks him whether he ought to believe Abraham or Moses. Christ tells him quite simply to follow both. "Sette faste thi faith," he says, according to Abraham; and as Moses has bidden you, I bid you also. Love your fellow Christians evermore, even as yourself.

It is Abraham, again, who is the herald and the explicator of the Passion in the following passus (XVIII). He explains to the dreamer that Jesus in Piers's armor, that is, God in the body of man, is about to joust in Jerusalem to fetch from the fiend the fruit of Piers Plowman. The dreamer asks him who will joust, Jews or scribes? Neither, replies Faith, but the foul fiends, Falsehood and Death. The Passion and the harrowing of hell are, in fact, represented as a battle between Christ and Satan, between life and death, light and darkness, truth and falsehood.

THE FOUR DAUGHTERS OF GOD

Before the victory is finally won in the depths of hell, there is a long pause in the action, during which the law of God is justified both to men and to the devil. At the very threshold of hell, the dreamer overhears a debate between the four daughters of God. This debate attempts to reconcile justice with the mercy of God in much the same way as the Christians in debate with the Jews attempted to reconcile the Old and the New Laws. The point is not that justice is taught in the Old Testament and mercy in the New, but that Christ clarified and fulfilled the highest teaching of the Old Testament. For what is clear to Mercy and Peace is veiled from Righteousness and Truth;

while they know only the story of Genesis Peace has a "letter" of foreknowledge from Charity himself. And like the traditional debates between the Church and the Synagogue, this debate is, as the dreamer says, "secundum scripturas" (XVIII. 112).

At the opening of the debate, Truth says that she is startled by the sight of a great light over hell and wonders what it means. Do not marvel, says Mercy; it signifies mirth. She tells Truth the story of the birth and life of Jesus and observes that patriarchs and prophets often preached that what was lost through a tree would be recovered through a tree. Your talk, replies Truth, "is but a tale of Waltrot!" Adam and Eve, Abraham and all the other patriarchs and prophets can never be brought out of hell by that light. And Truth quotes from Job that what is in hell can never be redeemed. Peace and Righteousness then repeat much the same argument. Peace has come to welcome Adam and Eve, Moses, and many others, who will now have mercy. She invites her sister to dance with her and quotes from Psalm 30 that joy comes in the morning. She knows what is about to happen because Charity is her lover and has sent her a letter saying that she and Mercy will save mankind. Here is the patent, she says, and she quotes not the New Testament (as we might expect) but the fourth psalm. Righteousness is so indignant that she suggests that her sister is drunk. (Incidentally, in the *Disputation*, in which the disputants are mother and daughter, the mother accuses the daughter of being drunk on the wine of the marriage in Cana.) Righteousness is angry because she has recorded the judgment that God gave in the beginning against Adam and Eve; their pain must be perpetual, she says. Let them chew as they have chosen!

At this point a character called Book interrupts. He supports the view of Peace and Mercy by showing that all the elements bear witness to the divinity of Jesus, who can therefore release from hell whomever he pleases. And he concludes (as we saw in an earlier chapter) that unless the Jews believe in Jesus and a New Law, they will be lost.

THE HARROWING OF HELL

In the scene of the harrowing of hell which follows, the debate is continued first by Lucifer and Satan and then by Jesus and the devils

185

(XVIII. 270 ff.). Lucifer complains to Satan that if this Lord and Light delivers mankind, he robs him by force. By right, he argues, those who are in hell belong to him, body and soul, because Truth himself said that if Adam ate the apple, all would die and dwell with the devils. Therefore, he concludes, the "lawe" will not allow this Light to do anything. Well, says Satan despondently, part of what you say is true, but you got Adam and Eve by treachery and lying; that which is got by deception is not duly got. A devil named "Gobelyn" adds that God will not be beguiled, and he fears that they have no true title to mankind. And he reproaches Lucifer for his lies, through which they first fell from heaven and through which they are now about to lose Adam and all their rule.

Then the light breaks the bars of hell, and Jesus enters. Before he delivers all those awaiting him, he justifies his action to Satan, out of the law. It is true, he concedes, that he had said that if Adam and Eve ate the apple they would die, but he did not condemn them to hell forever. It was your deceit, he tells Satan, that made them do the deed. You got them by guile, against all justice; you robbed my palace, paradise, in the form of an "addre." Now the Old Law grants that guilers should be beguiled, a tooth for a tooth and an eye for an eye. Ergo, all that man has done wrong, I, man, will amend, member for member, life for life, by the Old Law of amendment; and by that law I claim them. Do not believe, he admonishes Lucifer, that I fetch them against the law. It is by right and reason that I here ransom my subjects. *"Non veni solvere legem, sed adimplere."*

That Christ's death was necessary to atone for the sin of Adam is a commonplace enough idea. But Christ's insistence here that he does not abrogate the Old Law of an eye for an eye seems extreme, not only because in the Gospels Christ explicitly substituted for it the injunction to turn the other cheek, but also because in *Piers* the law so consistently means Moses' law of love. It is, in fact, so extreme a development of the doctrine of the fulfillment of the Scriptures that I think its possible derivation is worth a side glance.

In the early centuries of the Church, pagan opponents argued that the ethics of the two Testaments were quite different; and they delighted in compiling the least savory portions of the Old Testament for the embarrassment of Christians who asserted the moral unity of Jesus and Moses. For the most part, when Jewish disputants accused

Jesus of abrogating the law, they meant the ceremonial law, and there is little or no argument over practical morality in Jewish-Christian debates. The usual view is expressed in a literary exercise of Abelard's, entitled *A Dialogue between a Philosopher, a Jew, and a Christian,* in which the philosopher scores both Jews and Christians by attacking the Old Law as primitive and tribal.[10] Occasionally, however, a Jew did argue that Christian ethics were un-Jewish. A good example is a medieval rabbinical tract in which the author states his objections to Christianity, using the words of the Gospel. The rabbi attacks the Sermon on the Mount by saying that in it Jesus destroyed the moral law, despite Christian affirmation to the contrary. The command of Jesus to love your enemies and not to insist on an eye for eye is contrary to the specific word of Scripture, and to God's command to destroy the Canaanites.[11]

Whatever Langland's source, this is just the argument that his Christ expects the devil to use against him in the case of Adam and Eve. Far from saying that he brings a higher law of mercy, his Christ accepts the justice of the law. Careful not to depart from the Old Testament, he turns the argument to the injustice of Lucifer. You robbed me, he says, and the Old Law grants that guilers be beguiled; and he quotes from Psalm 7 that he who digged a ditch has fallen into it. Righteousness had said of the children of Adam, let them chew as they have chosen. Christ tells the devil, "Thou art doctour of deth, drynke that thow madest!" (l. 362).

This does not mean, however, that Langland is teaching an ethics of revenge. In what seems to be a further development of the point (in the following passus, XIX), there occurs one of the usual Christian answers to the pagans and to the "certain Jew." In defending the unity of the laws, Origen in the third century and Nicholas de Lyra in the fourteenth (in an answer to the rabbi) pointed to the teaching of the prophets against revenge and excerpted appropriate passages from the Scriptures.[12] A favorite was "Vengeance is mine, says the Lord"; and it is this verse that Langland uses to condemn the pope

10. Abelard, *Dialogue entre un philosophe, un juif, et un chrétien, Oeuvres choisies,* trans. Maurice de Gandillac (Paris, 1945).

11. The rabbi's arguments are cited and answered in Nicolas de Lyra, *Biblia Sacra* (Lyons, 1545), VI, 282 f.

12. Origen *Against Celsus* VII.

for his failure to forgive his enemies. What makes it seem possible that Langland was thinking along the same lines as the apologists is that in the passage in question he brings in the two laws somewhat gratuitously. The pope is one of those who do not wish to observe the conditions of Piers's pardon; instead, he leads the people to battle—and spills the blood of Christians "aȝeyne the olde lawe and newe lawe." As Luke witnesses: "*Non occides, mihi vindictam, etc.*" (XIX. 442–44). The New Law is thus represented as "Thou shalt not kill" and the Old by "Vengeance is mine." The choice of texts seems curious, especially since Luke is obviously quoting from the Old Testament; but it is just the sort of choice the apologists made to emphasize the unity of the Testaments. Whether or not Langland was borrowing from them, he shared their way of looking at the Scriptures.

It is with a similar stress on the unity of the Scriptures that the scene of the harrowing of hell ends. When Christ leads from hell all who loved him, the angels sing, and the four daughters of God embrace. Let no one perceive that we have quarreled, says Peace. For in Christ, Truth and Righteousness, Mercy and Peace—the Old and the New Testaments—are united. And they sing from the Psalms: Mercy and Truth are met together, Righteousness and Peace have kissed, and behold, how good and joyful it is for brethren to dwell together in unity. The dreamer awakes, and calls Kit, his wife, and Calote, his daughter, to go to Mass, for it is Easter Sunday.

The Fulfillment of the Law by the Church and by Christians

This note of theological harmony persists throughout the rest of the poem, in spite of the moral discord that prevails in the world that Langland portrays. There is little to suggest that the characters in the last cantos are morally better than those sinners who set out to seek Truth in Passus V. But this bitter realism does not mar the joyful realization that Christ *has* come and that the long search for the meaning of Truth is over. It remains for the dreamer and all men to fulfill the law that has been sealed with Christ's blood, and so to become worthy of Piers's pardon before the end of the world. To this end, they must follow the example of justice and mercy given by Christ and taught by him to his Church.

In describing the founding of the Church (with Piers as builder, in Passus XIX), Langland, like most medieval writers, brings in the fulfillment of the Old Law in the New. Characteristically, he reinterprets a popular commentary to suit his own deepest meaning. According to the Fathers and to contemporary commentators and poets, when Christ changed water into wine at the marriage in Cana, he changed the Old Law into the New. In *Piers*, Conscience tells the dreamer that at a feast of Jews, Jesus turned water into wine and "then God began graciously to Do Well." Wine, he says, is "lykned to lawe and lyf of holynesse," but then the law was lacking, for men loved not their enemies (XIX. 105–8). Langland does not say that Christ changed the law; this is the same law which Moses described to the dreamer before the Passion. But by Doing Well, by practicing the forgiveness that Moses preached, Christ fulfilled what was lacking.

Forgiveness and restitution, mercy and justice, the New and the Old Law—all are united in the final pardon which Christ gives to Piers in Passus XIX, and which is referred to again and again in the last two cantos. It was when Christ taught Do Best to the apostles after his Resurrection that he gave Piers power to pardon all manner of men, "in couenant" that they should acknowledge the pardon of Piers Plowman, with its *"redde quod debes"* (XIX. 177 ff.). "Pay what you owe" is a key phrase, as its repetition in this and in later passages indicates. And its meaning is as stern as it sounds. It means that Christians, following Christ, must fulfill the Old Law of justice —without which mercy cannot exist—as well as the law of love. In this same passage, Conscience says that at doomsday, Christ will reward him who *reddit quod debet* and punish those who pay badly. And in much the words of the sour priest who impugned Piers's pardon earlier, he concludes that "The gode to the godhede and to grete Ioye,/ And wikke to wonye in wo withouten ende."

In Langland's prophetic view, pardon is not easier under the New Law than under the Old. By the Passion of Christ, heaven was opened to all who do well, but more is required of Christians than of others, because more has been given them. Under the Old Law, the prophets had said that circumcision and sacrifice were not enough. They insisted on the covenant: *because* God brought the Jews across the Red Sea and fed them manna in the desert, *therefore* they must care for the widowed, the fatherless, and the poor. The Christian prophet says likewise that baptism and pardons must not be counted on. The pardon of Christ is also a covenant: because Christ has redeemed men and shown them the way and the truth and the life, therefore they must make restitution and forgive their enemies.

Throughout the poem, under both laws, God is portrayed as love and mercy. Abraham teaches faith and love, Moses teaches forgiveness, and Christ is portrayed as yearning for the salvation of all men, all his brethren, the unbaptized as well as the baptized. But his is not a sentimental love but the love of Righteousness of the God of Israel. You cannot have love without righteousness, the New Law without the Old.

When the Grace of the Holy Spirit distributes gifts, we are told that Piers the Plowman, his reeve, will receive payments, *"redde quod debes"* (XIX. 253 ff.). In order to fulfill his role as purveyor of Grace, Piers must till Truth with a team of oxen, the four Evangelists. The four horses with whom he will harrow after the sowing are the four Doctors of the Church. These four harrowed all Holy Scripture with two harrows that they had, an old and a new, that is, the Old Testament and the New. Grace also gave Piers the cardinal virtues to sow in men's souls. Piers sowed these four seeds and so harrowed them with the Old Law and the New Law that love might wax. The Barn to hold the harvest is, of course, the Church. Conscience, who must guide the Church, invites all Christians to receive the Eucharist, if they have paid "to Pieres pardoun the Plowman, *redde quod debes*" (1. 388).

The passage that follows this invitation explains the method of paying debts. For one thing, it means that each must forgive the other in accordance with the Our Father: Forgive us our debts, or trespasses, as we forgive those who trespass against us. For another, it means that men must pay all that they owe to others in order to be forgiven. But the Christians whom Conscience is addressing do not wish to observe these conditions. The brewer who waters his beer intends to continue robbing his customers. And the pope leads the people to battle and spills the blood of Christians, against the Old Law and the New. Obviously, Conscience is describing the sacrament of penance, which requires the penitent to make restitution and to forgive his enemies. So he "pays what he owes" to both men and God and practices both justice and mercy. What Conscience is also saying is that in order to partake worthily of the sacraments, men must fulfill the law in their lives.

Throughout the poem, the pardon of Piers is described as a medicine to cure the sick. Haukyn wants a medicine for boils, and Patience carries in his bundle a cure for pain and fear. The Samaritan tells the dreamer that no medicine can heal wounded mankind without the blood of a babe born of a maiden. That blood has been shed, and the grace of the sacraments freely offered; but men can still refuse the medicine, and with it the cure.

In the last canto, that is, in the last age of the world, Conscience calls a doctor well acquainted with shriving and asks him to salve the sick, wounded by sin (XX. 302 ff.). Shrift took sharp salve and made men do penance for their misdeeds and saw that Piers was paid, "*redde quod debes.*" But some disliked this leechcraft and shopped around for a surgeon in the city who had softer plasters. When Friar Flatterer physics the wounded, for a little silver he glosses over his shriving until the patient wholly forgets contrition, which is the sovereign salve for all sins. Pride and Sloth take over, and there are no justice, no mercy, no love among men. Once again, Conscience becomes a pilgrim and sets out to seek Piers the Plowman to conquer pride; and the dreamer awakes.

Was Langland concluding, then, that Christ died in vain and that the Church founded by him was a total loss? Modern readers sometimes think so, but medieval readers probably did not. For one thing, they did not expect an operatic ending with organs playing and cherubs flying. In the medieval arts, the last act was supposed to include a bitter struggle with Antichrist, and Langland's picture of the struggle is only less conclusive than the rest, for he stops short of the Second Coming. Furthermore, in the medieval view in general, and in Langland's vision in particular, there is little "progress" in the nineteenth-century sense, according to which mankind evolved from savagery, and morality and civilization broaden from precedent to precedent. There is development in Langland's view: God is revealed and the Scriptures are fulfilled in time. But while Revelation has a history, truth does not evolve—nor does morality.

In explaining the meaning of the mountain and the field of folk in Passus I, Holy Church explains that the Truth that is on the mount is the same Truth that good men practice in the field. As the triune God was always the same, so was his law of love. Indeed, the law is one aspect of that Truth, and it was written on stone to last forever. For Langland, as for Grosseteste, the Old and the New Laws are one with God in eternity.

But men live in time, and the Scriptures were fulfilled in history, in a cosmic drama in which the eternal pierced the temporal. The sin of Adam disturbed the moral order of the universe and closed heaven to mankind. But the law was still operative, and there were always men who understood and lived by it. When Trajan lived in love and loyalty, he did well according to the true law, by whatever name he called it. The name and the knowledge were revealed most abundantly to the patriarchs and the prophets, and all the virtues can be learned from the example of the Old Testament saints. Even the evangelical virtues of patience and poverty can be learned from Job. Finally, the Passion of the Son of God restored the balance. Christ made restitution for the sin of Adam and so fulfilled the law of an eye for an eye and won pardon for mankind. At the same time, in his life and his death, he fulfilled the law of love of Moses and the prophets and illumined the teaching of the God of Israel for all men.

But while baptism opens a door for Christians, it does not automatically push them through. The whole history of mankind, *sub speciae aeternitatis,* must be repeated in the moral development of every man. Men are not born better in the fourteenth century A.D. than in the fourteenth century B.C. There were men who did well under the Old Law, and there are men who refuse to do well under the New. The law has been fulfilled by Christ; heaven has been opened to men, and the grace to fulfill the law is given to all who ask. But the road to heaven is still through the commandments, through the faith and morality of Abraham and Moses. So at the end of the poem the wicked are condemned by the Old Law and the New; and the dreamer, enlightened by Abraham and Moses and Christ, and strengthened by the sacraments of the Church, must fulfill the law in his own life in order to gain the pardon granted to Piers.

Chapter X

EPILOGUE: THE RELEVANCE OF *PIERS PLOWMAN*

⸿ One of the pleasures of reading *Piers Plowman* is that it seems so medieval and so modern at the same time. Sights, sounds, and smells, characters and customs—all evoke a bygone age in which we recognize our neighbors, our betters, and ourselves. What is most startling is that we can recognize the new Christian of the twentieth century in the old poet of the fourteenth. I mean not simply that the Christian ideal is always basically the same but that Langland's particular way of grasping that ideal—his questioning, satirical, prophetic anti-establishment way—is much the way that is disturbing the churches of today.

Whether he is demanding reform within the Church, or searching the old doctrines for new meanings, or paraphrasing a parable in contemporary jargon, Langland is kin to the restless Christians of our time. Like them, he complained bitterly that the Church had failed in both teaching and living the faith and that both clergy and laity had lapsed into comfortable reliance on the forms rather than on the meaning of religion. He believed that Christianity was not primarily a completed system of theology but a way of salvation to which each generation has to be converted anew. So he thrashed out the ancient and recurrent problems, such as the meaning of the Bible in contemporary life, the ways to Do Well, Better, and Best, and the relations between Christianity and other faiths.

As in fourteenth-century England, so in twentieth-century Rome and Germany and America, the "other faith" that Christians are really concerned with is Judaism. And while present opinion is, in general, immeasurably more enlightened than Langland's, the same questions still arise. Even a brief glance at the debates and decrees of the recent Vatican Council reveals that all the emotions which once confused and troubled Langland, especially those connected with the role of the Jews in the Crucifixion, continue to confuse and trouble even men of good will.

No doubt the impetus behind the conciliar discussions was a sense of collective guilt among Christians for the terrible history of persecution of the Jews. But the prelates could not merely apologize. First they had to explain (as they did easily with Hinduism and Islam) the relationship between the two religions, preferably without offending the Jews, expurgating the Gospels, or discarding the doctrine of the fulfillment of the Scriptures.

The first part of the council's declaration on the Jews is, in fact, an expression of the ancient doctrine of the fulfillment of the Scriptures, couched in ancient terms, with little "updating." It might indeed, have been written by Langland, or by Grosseteste, Bede, or Augustine. Describing the "bond that ties the people of the New Covenant to Abraham's stock," it touches lightly, but unmistakeably, on the prefiguration of the Church, the calling of the Gentiles, and the ultimate conversion of the Jews. "All who believe in Christ," the council fathers say, are "Abraham's sons according to faith." The Church cannot forget that she "feeds upon the root of that cultivated olive tree into which the wild shoots of the gentiles have been grafted." Most of the apostles and disciples sprang from the Jewish people, and through his cross, Christ reconciled Jews and Gentiles. "In company with the prophets," the Church awaits that day on which all people will address the Lord in a single voice. In brief, the council follows the ancient tradition of the Church in extolling the "spiritual patrimony common to Christians and Jews."

Aside from a few expressions of annoyance over the references to conversion, this first part of the decree attracted scant public attention. The excitement was over the content and wording of the passages dealing with the causes and cures of anti-Semitism. Apparently the "progressives" felt that an important cause of hatred is the belief among Christians that the whole people of the Jews was guilty of the death of Christ and that persecutions have been justified further by the contention that the Jews were "rejected by God or accursed, as if this followed from the Holy Scriptures." The decree therefore enjoins catechists and preachers not to teach these things and pleads with all to "end hatred, persecution, and displays of anti-Semitism, directed against Jews at any time and by anyone."

Would that Langland had been so instructed, the reader of *Piers* must feel. For Langland considered the Jews both rejected and accursed, and he cited chapter and verse to prove that their plight was foretold in Scripture. But the alleged deicide of the Jews (whether we use the word or not) was not the root of Langland's anti-Semitism, and the prophecies were probably a justification rather than a cause.

For one thing, Langland made the same point as the council, that Christ "underwent His passion and death freely, because of the sins of all men and out of infinite love." For another, he realized that the crucifiers did not recognize the divinity of Jesus because of his "disguise" in the armor of Piers. Finally, he did not deduce the mass guilt of the Jews from the actual crucifixion; indeed, he cited Jesus' forgiveness on the cross of his crucifiers. What did anger him was the continued disbelief and hostility of the Jews and their continued expectation of a true Messias who would prove Jesus false. Now it is really no answer to this to say that the whole people of the Jews was not guilty. Is it permissible to hate the Sanhedrin or to persecute those who approve their decision?

Langland would still be wrong if it were proved that the Jews alone were responsible for the Crucifixion—and for all the blasphemies of the ensuing centuries—and for the persecution of the Church in Russia and in China; or if tomorrow all the Jews reverted to usury in order to fulfill the prophecies. The guilt or innocence of the Jews (or the Communists, or anyone else, for that matter) is not the yardstick by which to measure Christian conduct: only the teaching and example of Christ should be the rule.

Langland was wrong not because his interpretation of history or prophecy is outmoded but because his own principles should have taught him to love those he considered enemies. Certainly men of good will must make every effort to reduce enmity and must work for "mutual knowledge and respect," through Biblical studies and "fraternal dialogues." But the particular Christian failure, in the twentieth century as in the fourteenth, has been not the neglect of such efforts but the failure to extend to the Jews what Piers called the "infinity" of Christ, the love which extended to his crucifiers, and which alone can destroy the roots of hatred.

In his better moments, in describing salvation and the law, Langland did include the Jews in the brotherhood of man, and his general concept was not narrow. He stated as clearly as does the council that all men, not just believers, are brothers, created in the image of God the Father, and that the cross of the Son is the "sign of God's all embracing love." Langland had, too, what we call the ecumenical spirit; that is, he saw that Truth is God, wherever it is found, in Plato, Aristotle, or Trajan, in good men everywhere. As a matter of fact, there was nothing new in the doctrine; Langland may have learned it from the description of Truth in the opening verses of the Fourth Gospel.

The broad outlook, however, was all but lost in the narrow partisanship that followed the Protestant, the French, and the Russian revolutions. Even twenty years ago, the fact that the Communists were in favor of something—even something like justice or mercy— was sufficient to put Catholic zealots on the other side. Langland himself was suspect because he had been quoted and claimed by the Protestants. After all, he was a married deacon who believed in the disestablishment of the Church. He was suspect also as a social and economic radical, whose harping on the social message of the Gospel sounded like that of left-wing novelists, and whose attacks on the clergy were regarded as intemperate.

Rivaling the Catholics in narrowness, the secularists similarly divorced politics and economics from religion. Taken out of context, Langland's "realism" appealed to them, and it was by virtue of their vices that such fellows as Robert the Robber and Lousy Harvey slipped into college anthologies. In fact, few writers have excelled Langland in describing the seamy side of life, and it is a measure of his literary success that, after six centuries, some of his readers relish his method more than his message.

One cannot go far in *Piers,* however, without encountering the message, and it is Langland's combination of radicalism with orthodoxy that is especially relevant for Christians who march on picket lines and choose to live in slums. Among all the new voices crying out the old social gospel, Langland would have been most in tune with those who borrow their phrases from the Old Testament. There is a surprising number of these; quite suddenly, it seems, Church bulletins and family magazines quote the prophets, especially those who stormed most rudely at their co-religionists for relying on the forms of religion while practicing business as usual. Never entirely dead, this prophetic spirit flowers perennially in both Judaism and Christianity—and is often transplanted into the garden of unbelievers, who may call it by another name. In our own revolutionary age, it is precisely Langland's prophetic denunciation of social injustice and religious hypocrisy that ensures him a hearing among readers of diverse beliefs. His compassion for the poor and the outcast, his rage against the rich and the great, and his despair over the complacency of the clergy all suit the temper of our times.

What is often forgotten by the Marxists, and even occasionally by avant-garde Christians, is that the basis of this criticism is not a social contract among men but a covenant with God. According to the covenant, it was *because* they were chosen by God that the Israelites were obliged to care for the poor, the fatherless, the widowed, and the alien. In the Judaeo-Christian tradition, those to whom the law of God has been revealed must fulfill it in their lives. Because Christians have been promised much, Langland insists, much is demanded of them. If they hope to enter heaven, the rich must share with the poor. Like the prophets, he insists over and over again that God is pleased not with sacrifice but with a merciful heart which is shown in deeds, not words.

For Langland, the means and the end, morality and theology, are one. Doctrine is the articulation of the knowledge of God revealed to men. As the justice of men derives from the justice of God, so the Trinity, the Incarnation, and the law are aspects of the God of Love, whom men understand only insofar as they love their fellows. The same Truth of Trinity, the same law, the same Jesus Christ bind in love and mercy the king, the pope, and Lousy Harvey.

In brief, sociology and theology and Scripture are unified in *Piers* not only by a consummate literary skill but by a prophetic spirit that was both traditional and personal. Even Langland's harshness, his preference for the rough word and the homely image, and his very rhythms of speech echo Amos and Hosea and the Christ who overthrew the money-changers and cried woe upon the hypocrites. So Langland cries out upon the rich who would buy their way into heaven with Masses; even chastity without charity, he says, will be chained in hell. He condemns especially the clergy, from friars to popes, for failing to show in their words and works the love of God which alone can save the world. The phrases vary, but matter and manner were old in Gospel days and are still fresh in ours.

197

That is not to say that Langland's enthusiasm for the patriarchs and the prophets would qualify him for a post on a modern commission of Biblical experts. Archaeology was unknown to him, his acceptance of the historicity of the Scriptures was quite uncritical, and his exegetical methods are obsolete. On the other hand, the fourteenth-century poet and twentieth-century student have more in common than these differences would suggest. However far apart they may be in time and manners, Christians steeped in the Scriptures share what Vatican Council II called a "store of sublime teaching about God, sound wisdom about human life, and a wonderful treasury of prayers."[1] Langland might have known the Bible by heart, so freely does he quote, transpose, and allude, so frequently does he draw on Biblical characters and episodes. At the very least, he would be delighted by the renewed zeal of the Catholic Church for the Bible. More crucial, perhaps, he would have shared the belief of the scholars that ultimately truth can lead only to the Truth.

As he objected to irreverent dinner-party sniping at the difficulties of Scripture, so he would not countenance the flippant tone of some contemporary "debunking." But he was saved from a narrow literal reading both by his own native penetration and by the traditional exegetical methods that characterized discussion of the fulfillment of the Scriptures. Concerned primarily with the meaning of the Word, he had no interest in the measurements of Noe's ark or Jonas' whale. Further, his mystical and allegorical interpretations often transcended the letter in a way at least as daring as the "literary forms" of the new critics. Piers, Abraham, Moses, David, and Job are all friends of God, figures or prophets of Christ, and all are united in a vision of the Trinity quite broad enough to encompass outer space.

And broad enough, certainly, to include the Qumran Covenanters. When the Dead Sea Scrolls were discovered some years ago, militant secularists rushed into print to announce the end of the Christian claim to uniqueness.[2] But as everyone once knew, the Christians

---

1. Decree of the Constitution on Divine Revelation promulgated at Vatican Council II, *New York Times*, November 19, 1965.

2. Edmund Wilson, *The Scrolls from the Dead Sea* (New York, 1960), pp. 98, 108. For the relation between Christianity and Jewish apocalyptic literature, including the Dead Sea Scrolls and the *Testaments of the Twelve Patriarchs,* see D. S. Russell, *The Method & Message of Jewish Apocalyptic* (Philadelphia, 1964).

never claimed originality; they claimed the Scriptures and the Synagogue. Invariably they pointed to the similarities between the Church and the Synagogue, not only in morals but in ceremonies and pious practices. The Qumran community described in the scrolls would have been taken as still another figure of the Church, another proof that the Church developed from and fulfilled the Synagogue. Had Grosseteste discovered the scrolls, he would have used them as he did the *Testaments of the Twelve Patriarchs* which were discovered in the thirteenth century—that is, he would have offered them to the Jews as further evidence of the unity of the two Testaments and the two religions, needing only the cornerstone of Christ to make them one. The Jews would not have been converted, but neither would the Christians have been confused.

Fourteenth-century Christians did not have to reconcile evolution with Revelation, but I think that Langland would not have been especially shocked by Darwin, or even by Teilhard de Chardin. He saw more clearly than most the similarities between men and monkeys, and he thought nature rather more reasonable than mankind. Actually, he was not interested in the appearance of Adam and Eve, in what they ate or wore in the garden. And whether the Creation took seven days or seven trillion years makes little difference in his sweeping view of the Revelation of God in history and eternity. For Langland, the mystery of creation was the transformation of matter by spirit, what he called the descent of love into the clay to create the image of God in man.

In Langland's vision, while the events of history occur in sequence in time, they are also present all together in an eternal now which includes men living in the twentieth century as well as in the fourteenth. Through his juxtaposition of texts and through his allegory, Langland makes Abraham, Moses, Jesus, and the dreamer contemporaries. The dreamer's question about the nature of man is answered by the stories of the Creation and the Incarnation. For the union of God and man in Jesus illuminates the union of spirit and matter in Adam—and in the dreamer. In the face of all the diversities in faith and morals, the dreamer would know what is truth, what is law, and whom we should believe. These are the riddles of the universe, and Langland finds the answers in the books of Genesis and Deuteronomy, opened by the key of Christ. The same triune God who created

the stars and the suns of the universe and who is beyond the comprehension of men is yet known to them through love. This love, which
distinguishes men from monkeys, was gradually revealed to men.
The Faith of Abraham and the Law of Moses were fulfilled in the
Charity of Christ, and all are one in eternity. Yet all are worked out
in time, not only in the past but in the present; for every man must
fulfill the Scriptures in himself.

Bibliography

Abelard. *Dialogue entre un philosophe, un juif, et un chrétien, Oeuvres choisis.* Translated by Maurice de Gandillac. Paris, 1945.

Adam of St. Victor. *Liturgical Poetry.* With translations by Digby S. Wrangham. 3 vols. London, 1881.

Adler, Michael. *The Jews of Mediaeval England.* London, 1939.

Adso. *Libellus de Antichristo. PL.* 101, cols. 1289–98.

Aelfric. *Lives of Saints.* Edited by W. W. Skeat. Vol. I, EETS 76, 82 (1881). Vol. II, EETS 92, 114 (1900).

————. *The Old English Version of the Heptateuch: Aelfric's Treatise on the Old and New Testament and his Preface to Genesis.* Edited by S. J. Crawford. EETS 160 (1922).

————. *The Sermones Catholici* or *Homilies.* With English version by Benjamin Thorpe. 2 vols. London, 1844, 1846.

Alcuin. *Opera Omnia. PL.* 100, 101.

Ambrose. *Select Works and Letters.* Nicene and Post-Nicene Fathers. 2d ser. Vol. X (1896).

Ancient Cornish Drama, The. Translated and edited by Edwin Norris. 2 vols. Oxford, 1859.

Anglo-Saxon Legends of St. Andrew and St. Veronica. Translated by Charles W. Goodwin. Cambridge, Eng., 1851.

Anglo-Saxon Minor Poems, The. Edited by Elliott Van Kirk Dobbie. *Anglo-Saxon Poetic Records.* Vol. VI. New York, 1942.

Anglo-Saxon Poetry. Translated and edited by R. K. Gordon. Everyman's Library. London, 1942.

Apocryphal Acts of the Apostles. Translated by W. Wright. Vol. II. London, 1871.

Apocryphal Gospels, Acts, and Revelations. Ante-Nicene Library. Vol. XVI (1870).

Athanasius. *On the Incarnation.* Translated by Archibald Robertson. London, 1891.

Auerbach, Erich. "Figura." Translated by Ralph Manheim. In *Scenes from the Drama of European Literature.* New York, 1959.

Augustine. *The City of God.* Translated by John Healey. London, 1940.

————. *Homilies on the Gospels.* Nicene and Post-Nicene Fathers. Vol. VI (1888).

————. *Opera Omnia. PL.* 33, 42.

————. *On the Spirit and the Letter.* Translated by W. J. Sparrow Simpson. London, 1925.

————. *Works.* Edited by Rev. Marcus Dods. Edinburgh, 1873. Vol. VII: *On the Trinity.* Vol. IX: *On Christian Doctrine, On Catechising, On*

Faith and the Creed. Vol. X: *Tracts on the Gospel according to St. John.*

Batiffol, Pierre. *History of the Roman Breviary.* Translated by Atwell M. Y. Bayley. London, 1898.

Bede. *Ecclesiastical History of the English Nation.* Translated by John Stevens. Revised by Lionel C. Jane. London, 1944.

————. *Opera Omnia. PL.* 90, 91, 92.

————. *Opera Omnia.* Edited by J. A. Giles. Vols. VIII, IX. London, 1844.

Bernard. *Life and Works.* Edited by Dom John Mabillon. Translated by Samuel J. Eales. Vols. III, IV. London, 1896.

Bethurum, D., ed. *Critical Approaches to Mediaeval Literature.* Selected Papers from the English Institute, 1958–59. New York, 1960.

Blickling Homilies. Translated by R. Morris. EETS 58, 63, 73 (1880).

Bloomfield, Morton W. *Piers Plowman as a Fourteenth-Century Apocalypse.* New Brunswick, N.J., 1961.

Blunt, John Elijah. *A History of the Jews in England.* London, 1830.

Book of Jubilees, The. Translated by R. H. Charles. London, 1902.

Breviarum ad Usum Insignis Ecclesiae Sarum. Edited by Francis Procter and Christopher Wordsworth. 3 vols. Cambridge, Eng., 1879–86. Vol. I: *Kalendarium et Temporale.*

Bright, James W. "The Relation of the Caedmonian Exodus to the Liturgy." *MLN,* XXVII (1912), 97–103.

Bromyard, John. *Summa Predicantium.* Basel, 1487.

Bruce, J. Douglas. "The Anglo-Saxon Version of the Book of Psalms Commonly Known as the *Paris Psalter,*" *PMLA,* IX (1894), 43–164.

————. "Immediate and Ultimate Source of the Rubrics and Introductions to the Psalms in the *Paris Psalter.*" *MLN,* VIII (1893), 72–82.

Butler, Alban. *Lives of the Saints.* Edited by Herbert Thurston and Norah Leeson. Vol. V. New York, 1936.

Caedmon Poems, The. Translated by Charles W. Kennedy. London, 1916. Reprint edition, Gloucester, Mass., 1965.

Cahier, Charles, and Martin, Arthur. *Monographie de la cathédrale de Bourges.* Paris, 1841–44. Part I: *Vitraux de XIII° siècle.*

Callus, D. A., ed. *Robert Grosseteste: Scholar and Bishop.* Essays in Commemoration of the Seventh Centenary of his Death. Oxford, 1955.

Campbell, Jackson J. *The Advent Lyrics of the Exeter Book.* Princeton, N.J., 1959.

Chaucer, Geoffrey. *Complete Works.* Edited by F. N. Robinson. Cambridge, Mass., 1933.

Chester Plays. Edited by Hermann Deimling. Vol. I, EETS (Extra Series) 62 (1893). Vol. II, EETS 115 (1916).

————. Edited by Thomas Wright. *Shakespeare Society.* Vol. XVII (1843).

Chronicon de Lanercost. Edited by Joseph Stevenson. Edinburgh, 1839.

Chrysostom. *Homilies on the Gospel of St. Matthew.* Nicene and Post-Nicene Fathers. Vol. X (1896).

Coghill, Nevill. *The Pardon of Piers Plowman.* Sir Israel Gollancz Memorial Lecture. British Academy. London, 1945.

Cursor Mundi. Edited by Richard Morris. Vol. I, EETS 57, 99, 101. Vol. II, EETS 59, 62. Vol. III, 66, 68 (1874–93).

Cynewulf. *The Christ of Cynewulf.* Edited by Albert S. Cook. Boston, 1900.

———. *Elene.* Edited, with Latin original, by Charles W. Kent. Boston, 1889.

———. *Poems of Cynewulf.* Translated by Charles W. Kennedy. London, 1910. Reprint edition, New York, 1949.

Cyprian. *Three Books of Testimonies against the Jews, Writings.* Ante-Nicene Library. Vol. XIII (1869).

Cyril of Jerusalem. *Catechetical Lectures.* Nicene and Post-Nicene Fathers. 2d ser. Vol. VII (1894).

"Dialogue of Athanasius and Zacchaeus." Translated by T. C. Conybeare. *Expositor,* V (1897), 300–20; 443–63.

Dialogus inter Christianum et Judaeum de Fide Catholica. PL. 163, cols. 1045–72. [Guillelmus de Campellis?]

Disputatio Ecclesiae et Synagogae. In Martène, Edmond, and Durand, Ursin, *Thesaurus Anecdotum.* Vol. V (1717), cols. 1497–1506.

Dudden, F. H. *The Life and Times of St. Ambrose.* Oxford, 1935.

Dunning, T. P. "The Structure of the B Text of *Piers Plowman.*" *RES,* VII (July, 1956), 225–37.

Epistle of Barnabas, The Apostolic Fathers. Ante-Nicene Library. Vol. I (1870).

Eusebius. *The Ecclesiastical History.* Translated by Hugh Lawlor and John Oulton. London, 1927.

———. *The Preparation for the Gospel.* Translated by Edwin H. Gifford. Oxford, 1903.

———. *The Proof of the Gospel.* Translated by W. J. Ferrar. London, 1920.

Evagrius. *Altercatio Legis inter Simoneum Iudaeum et Theophilum Christianum,* in *Corpus Scriptorum Ecclesiasticorum Latinorum.* Edited by E. Bratke. Vol. XXXV (1904).

Frank, R. W. "The Pardon Scene in Piers Plowman." *Speculum,* XXVII (1951), 323–24.

Friedman, Lee M. *Robert Grosseteste and the Jews.* Cambridge, Mass., 1934.

Gilbert Crispin. *Disputatio Judaei cum Christiano de Fide Christiana. PL.* 159, cols. 1005–36.

Gower, John. *Complete Works.* Edited by G. C. Macaulay. Oxford, 1902. Vol. IV: *Vox Clamantis.*

Gregory the Great. *Dialogues.* Edited by Edmond Gardner. London, 1911.

———. *Selected Epistles.* Nicene and Post-Nicene Fathers. 2d ser. Vol. XIII (1898).

Gregory Nazianzen. *Selected Works*. Nicene and Post-Nicene Fathers. 2d ser. Vol. VII (1894).

Gregory of Tours. *Les Livres des miracles* (Latin and French). Edited by H. L. Brodier. 4 vols. Paris, 1857–64.

Grosseteste, Robert. *De Cessatione Legalium. Parts I and II. A Critical Edition from the Extant MSS.* Edited by Arthur M. Lee. Ph.D. dissertation, University of Colorado, 1942. New York Public Library microfilm.

———. *Epistolae*. Edited by H. R. Luard. London, 1861. Vol. XXV: *Chronicles and Memorials of Great Britain and Ireland during the Middle Ages.*

Hammer on the Rock: A Short Midrash Reader. Edited by Nahum N. Glatzer. New York, 1962.

Harris, James Rendel. *Testimonies*. 2 vols. Cambridge, Eng., 1916–20.

Hegge Plays. Edited by K. J. Block (under title *Ludus Coventriae*). EETS (Extra Series) 120 (1922).

Herford, R. Travers. *Christianity in Talmud and Midrash*. London, 1903.

Hilary of Poitiers. *Select Works*. Nicene and Post-Nicene Fathers. 2d ser. Vol. IX (1899).

Hoffman, Richard L. " 'The Burning of Boke' in *Piers Plowman*." *MLQ*, XXV (March, 1964), 57–65.

Holmes, Urban T., and Klenke, Sister M. Amelia, *Chrétien, Troyes, and the Grail*. Chapel Hill, N.C., 1959.

Hunt, Richard William. "The Disputation of Peter of Cornwall against Symon the Jew." *Studies in Medieval History Presented to Frederick Maurice Powicke*. Oxford, 1948. Pp. 143–56.

Ignatius. *Epistles, The Apostolic Fathers*. Ante-Nicene Library. Vol. I (1870).

Irenaeus. *Against Heresies*. Ante-Nicene Library. Vol. IX (1871).

———. *The Demonstration of the Apostolic Preaching*. Translated by J. Armitage Robinson. London, 1920.

Isidore of Seville. *De Fide Catholica contra Judaeos*. PL. 83, cols. 449–538.

Jacobs, Joseph. *The Jews of Angevin England: Documents and Records*. London, 1893.

James, Montague Rhodes. *The Apocryphal New Testament*. Oxford, 1924.

Jerome. *Letters and Select Works*. Nicene and Post-Nicene Fathers. 2d ser. Vol. VI (1893).

Jewish Encyclopaedia, s.v. "Bible Exegesis," "Jesus of Nazareth," "Midrash."

Julian of Toledo. *De Comprobatione Aetatis Sextae*. PL. 96, cols. 537–86.

Junius Manuscript, The. Edited by G. P. Krapp. New York, 1931. Vol. I: *Anglo-Saxon Poetic Records*.

Justin Martyr. *Works*. A Library of Fathers of the Holy Catholic Church. Vol. XL. Oxford, 1861.

Kane, George. *Piers Plowman, The Evidence for Authorship*. London, 1965.

Krauss, S. "The Jews in the Works of the Church Fathers." *Jewish Quarterly Review*, V (1893), 112–57; VI (1894), 82–99, 225–61.

Lactantius. *The Divine Institutes.* Ante-Nicene Library. Vol. XXI (1870).

Langland, William. *Piers Plowman.* Edited by Elizabeth Salter and Derek Pearsall. Evanston, Ill., 1967.

————. *Piers Plowman: The A Version.* Edited by G. Kane. London, 1960.

————. *Piers the Ploughman.* Translated and edited by J. F. Goodridge. London, 1960.

————. *The Vision of Piers Plowman.* Translated by Henry W. Wells. New York, 1945.

————. *The Vision of William concerning Piers the Plowman, in Three Parallel Texts.* Edited by Walter W. Skeat. London, 1968.

Lawlor, John. *Piers Plowman: An Essay in Criticism.* London, 1962.

Legends of the Holy Rood. Edited by R. Morris. EETS 46 (1871).

Lévi, Israel. "Controverse entre un juif et un chrétien en XI° siècle." *Revue des études juives,* V (1882), 238–45.

Little, Andrew G. *The Grey Friars in Oxford.* Oxford, 1892.

Lovelich ["Lonelich"], Henry. *History of the Holy Grail.* Edited by F. J. Furnivall. EETS (Extra Series) 20, 24, 28, 30 (1877).

Lydgate, John. *The Pilgrimage of the Life of Man.* Edited by F. J. Furnivall and Katherine B. Locock. EETS (Extra Series) 77, 83, 92 (1899–1904).

Mâle, Emile. *Religious Art in France in the Thirteenth Century.* Translated by Dora Nussey. London, 1913.

Malory, Sir Thomas. *Works.* Edited by Eugène Vinaver. 3 vols. Oxford, 1947.

Middle English Harrowing of Hell and the Gospel of Nicodemus, The. Edited by W. H. Hulme. EETS (Extra Series) 100 (1907).

Middle English Sermons. Edited by Woodburn Ross. EETS 209 (1940).

Midrash Rabbah. Translated by H. Freedman and M. Simon. London, 1961.

Minor Poems of the Vernon MS. Part I, edited by Carl Horstmann. EETS 98 (1892). Part II. Edited by F. J. Furnivall. EETS 117 (1901).

Miroure of Mans Salvacionne, The. Edited by Alfred H. Huth. London, 1888.

Mystère d'Adam, Le. Translated by Edward Noble Stone. University of Washington Publications. Vol. IV, no. 2 (1926).

Nicolas de Lyra. *Biblia Sacra.* Vol. VI. Lyons, 1545.

Oesterley, W. O. E. *The Books of the Apocrypha.* London, 1916.

Old English Homilies. Edited by R. Morris. EETS 29, 34 (1868).

Origen. *Against Celsus.* Ante-Nicene Library. Vols. X (1869); XXIII (1872).

————. *Commentaries.* Ante-Nicene Library. Additional vol. (1896).

Orm. *Ormulum.* Edited by R. M. White and Robert Holt. 2 vols. Oxford, 1878.

Owst, G. R. *Literature and Pulpit in Medieval England.* Cambridge, 1933.

————. *Preaching in Medieval England.* Cambridge, Eng., 1936.

Paris, Matthew. *Chronica Majora.* Edited by H. R. Luard. London,

1872–73. *Chronicles and Memorials of Great Britain and Ireland during the Middle Ages.*

Pauphilet, Albert. *Etudes sur la queste del Saint Graal.* Paris, 1921.

Peter of Blois. *Contra Perfidiam Judaeorum. PL.* 207.

Pflaum, Hiram. *Der Allegorische Streit zwischen Synagoge und Kirche.* Geneva, 1935.

Philo Judaeus. *Works.* Translated by C. D. Yonge. London, 1854.

Physiologus. Translated by James Cargill. In William Rose, *The Epic of the Beast.* London, 1924.

Prymer, or Prayer Book of the Lay People in the Middle Ages, The. Edited by Henry Littlehales. London, 1891.

Pseudo-Augustine. *Adversus Quinque Haereses, PL.* 42, cols. 1099–1116; *Contra Judaeos, Paganos, et Arianos, Sermo de Symbolo. PL.* 42, cols. 1117–30. *De Altercatione Ecclesiae et Synagogae. PL.* 42, cols. 1131–40.

Pseudo-Cyprian. *De Montibus Sina et Sion. PL.* 4, cols. 989–1000.

Reidy, John. "Peris the Ploughman, Whiche a Pardoun He Hadde." *PMASAL,* L (1964), 535–44.

Richard of St. Victor. *A Treatise Named Benjamin,* in *The Cell of Self-Knowledge.* Edited by Edmond Gardner. London, 1910.

Robertson, D. W., Jr., and Huppé, Bernard F. *Piers Plowman and Scriptural Tradition.* Princeton, 1951.

Robinson, J. Armitage. *Gilbert Crispin, Abbot of Westminster.* Cambridge, Eng., 1911.

Roth, Cecil. *A History of the Jews in England.* Oxford, 1941.

Russell, D. S. *The Method & Message of Jewish Apocalyptic.* Philadelphia, 1964.

Salter, Elizabeth. *Piers Plowman: An Introduction.* Oxford, 1962.

Sarachek, Joseph. *The Doctrine of the Messiah in Mediaeval Jewish Literature.* New York, 1932.

Sarum Missal. Translated by Frederick E. Warren. 2 vols. London, 1911.

Schlauch, Margaret. "Allegory of Church and Synagogue." *Speculum,* XIV (1939), 448–64.

Sépét, Marius. "Les Prophètes du Christ." *Bibliothèque de l'école des Chartes,* XXVIII (1867), 1–27, 211–64; XXIX (1868), 105–39, 261–93; XXXVIII (1877), 397–443.

Smith, Ben H., Jr. *Traditional Imagery of Charity in Piers Plowman.* Studies in English Literature. Vol. XXI. The Hague, 1966.

Speculum Sacerdotale. Edited by Edward Weatherly. EETS 200 (1936).

A Stanzaic Life of Christ. Edited by Frances A. Foster. EETS 166 (1925).

Strack, Hermann L. *Introduction to the Talmud and Midrash.* New York, 1965.

Tertullian. *An Answer to the Jews.* Ante-Nicene Library. Vol. XXIII (1870).

Testaments of the Twelve Patriarchs, The. Translated and edited by R. H. Charles. in *Apocrypha and Pseudepigrapha of the Old Testament.* Vol. II. Oxford, 1913.

Thomas of Monmouth. *Life and Miracles of St. William of Norwich.* Translated and edited by Augustus Jessop and M. R. James. Cambridge, Eng., 1896.

Towneley Plays, The. Edited by Alfred W. Pollard. EETS (Extra Series), 71 (1897).

Turk, Milton Haight. *The Legal Code of Alfred the Great.* Halle, 1893.

Vasta, Edward. *The Spiritual Basis of Piers Plowman.* Studies in English Literature. Vol. XVIII. The Hague, 1965.

Vision of St. Paul, The. Ante-Nicene Library. Additional vol. (1896).

Walker, Marshall. "Piers Plowman's Pardon: A Note." *English Studies in Africa,* VIII (1965), 64–70.

Weavers' Pageant and the Shearmen and Taylors' Pageant, The. In *Two Coventry Corpus Christi Plays.* Edited by Hardin Craig. EETS 87 (1902).

Weber, Paul. *Geistliches Schauspiel und kirchliche Kunst.* Stuttgart, 1894.

Westcott, B. F. *Introduction to the Study of the Gospels.* London, 1895.

Williams, A. Lukyn. *Adversus Judaeos.* Cambridge, Eng., 1935.

Wilson, Edmund. *The Scrolls from the Dead Sea.* New York, 1960.

York Plays, The. Edited by Lucy Toulmin Smith. Oxford, 1885.

Young, Karl. *The Drama of the Mediaeval Church.* Oxford, 1933.

Index

Mass, 78, 143. *See also* Liturgy
Master of Divinity, 174–76
Matthew, Saint, 14, 49, 54, 57, 96, 123, 165
Meed, Lady, 48, 79, 120–21, 134–37
Melchizedek, 148–49, 151, 156–57, 178
Messia ben Joseph, 119
Messianic kingdom, 134–38
Messias (or Messiah). *See* Christ, Jesus
Michael, 59
Micheas (or Micah), 95, 100, 112, 145
Midrash, 14 ff. *See also* Exegesis
Minith, 56, 118
Miroure of Mans Salvacionne, 39, 70, 153, 182
Mohammed, 137
Moses, 4, 8–10, 16, 19–20, 22, 37, 38, 46, 51, 56, 57, 64, 72, 77–78, 102–3, 141 ff., 198, 199. *See also* Hope-Moses; The Law
Moslems, 73, 85, 116, 138. *See also* Gentiles

Nebuchadnezzar, 66
Neptune, 20
Nicolas de Lyra: *Biblia Sacra*, 187
Noe (or Noah), 57, 64, 65, 105, 141, 154–55, 160, 171, 182, 198
Numbers, 159

"O" antiphons, 64, 107, 151
Old and New Laws, 42, 141 ff., 162, 164, 167, 174–75, 182, 184 ff., 192. *See also* The Law
Old Testament. *See* Scriptures
Onkelos, 54
Origen, 55, 141, 187; *Against Celsus*, 187
Orm: *Ormulum*, 39, 156
Osee (or Hosea), 68
Oswy, King, 146

Pagans. *See* Gentiles
Palm Sunday, 124, 150–51
Pardon (of Piers), 48, 51, 166–69, 173, 176, 188 ff., 192
Paris Psalter, 26
Passion. *See* Christ, Jesus
Passover, 64, 145, 147, 150, 153, 155, 157, 175
Patience, 49, 173–76, 177, 191

Paul, Saint, 8, 16–18, 21, 29, 96, 98–100, 102–3, 113, 118, 143–46, 160, 180. *See also* Epistles of Saint Paul
Paul VI, Pope, 140
Pearsall, Derek, 11
Pentecost, 49, 90, 150
Perceval, 42, 115
Peter, Saint, 98, 99
Peter of Blois: *Contra Perfidiam Judaeorum*, 32, 111, 112, 115
Pharao (or Pharoah), 64, 70, 159
Pharisees, 17, 123
Phenenna, 148
Philo, 56
Physiologus, 104–5
Piers, 48–51, 81, 86, 89–92, 124, 164–69, 173–75, 177, 178, 190
Piers Plowman (Langland), 3, 4, 11, 24, 42–52; allegory of the Good Samaritan in, 180–84; Creation in, 77–79; dinner party in, 173–76; four daughters of God in, 184–85, 187–88; fulfillment of the law in, 161 ff.; harrowing of hell in, 185–88; Messias and the Jews in, 111 ff.; pagans and Jews in, 44–66, 84–85; pardon of Piers in, 166–69; plan of, 47–52, 163–66; relevance of, 193 ff.; Triune God in, 73 ff.; unity of the Testaments in, 46–47; A text: Passus VI, 47, 81; B text: Prologue, 48; Passus I, 3–4, 48, 75–79, 80, 162, 191–92; Passus II, 79; Passus III, 79, 134–38; Passus IV, 79, 137; Passus V, 79–81, 82, 163–65, 176; Passus VI, 164–65; Passus VII, 166–69, 176; Passus VIII, 48; Passus IX, 44, 75, 81–82, 169, 170; Passus X, 44, 73, 123, 170, 171; Passus XI, 44, 171, 172; Passus XII, 44–45, 83–84, 172–73; Passus XIII, 173, 177; Passus XV, 84–85, 121–22, 126, 138, 177; Passus XVI, 86–87, 123, 167, 178–79; Passus XVII, 73, 88, 164, 168, 179–80, 183–84; Passus XVIII, 89–90, 123–29, 164, 184–87; Passus XIX, 90, 91, 129–33, 187–90; Passus XX, 191; C text: Passus IV, 134; Passus VI, 163; Passus X, 165; Passus XIV, 172; Passus XVI, 174; Passus XIX, 88; Passus XXI, 125